**LIVING LANG**

# COMPLETE
# JAPANESE
## THE BASICS

Written by
Kumiko Ikeda Tsuji

ACKNOWLEDGMENTS

Thanks to the Living Language team: Tom Russell, Nicole Benhabib, Christopher Warnasch, Zvjezdana Vrzić, Suzanne McQuade, Shaina Malkin, Elham Shabahat, Sophie Chin, Denise DeGennaro, Linda Schmidt, Alison Skrabek, Lisbeth Dyer, and Tom Marshall. Special thanks to Mamori Sugita for reviewing the book.

Editor: Zvjezdana Vrzić, Ph.D.
Production Editor: Lisbeth Dyer
Production Manager: Thomas Marshall
Interior Design: Sophie Ye Chin

First Edition

ISBN: 978-1-4000-2417-9

I would like to express my gratitude to my editor Zvjezdana Vrzić for her useful comments. I also thank Suzanne McQuade and the other Living Language staff who were involved in this project. Finally, thanks go to my family and friends—especially my husband, Takanori—for their support and encouragement.

# COURSE OUTLINE

Welcome to *Complete Japanese: The Basics*! We know you're ready to jump right in and start learning Japanese, but before you do, you may want to spend some time familiarizing yourself with the structure of this course. It will make it easier for you to find your way around, and will really help you get the most out of this course.

## UNITS AND LESSONS

*Complete Japanese: The Basics* is made up of ten *Units*, each with its own topic, from talking about yourself and making introductions, to asking directions and going shopping. Each Unit is divided into four *Lessons*:

1. *Words*, featuring the essential vocabulary based on each Unit's topic;

2. *Phrases*, bringing words together into more complex structures and introducing a few idiomatic expressions;

3. *Sentences*, expanding on the vocabulary and phrases from previous lessons, using the grammar you've learned to form complete sentences; and,

4. *Conversation*, highlighting how everything works together in a realistic conversational dialogue.
The lessons are each comprised of the following sections:

### WORD LIST/PHRASE LIST/SENTENCE GROUP/CONVERSATION
Every lesson will begin with a list of words, phrases, or sentences, or a conversation. The grammar and exercises will be based on these lists or conversations, so it is important to spend as much time reading and rereading these as possible before getting into the heart of the lesson.

## NOTE

A brief section may appear after the list or dialogue to expand on any intricacies in the language or culture.

## NUTS & BOLTS

This is the nitty-gritty of each lesson, where we explain the grammar of the language, the Nuts & bolts that hold the pieces together. Pay close attention to these sections; this is where you'll get the most out of the language and learn what you need to learn to become truly proficient in Japanese.

## PRACTICE

It's important to practice what you've learned on a regular basis. You'll encounter practice sections throughout each lesson; take your time to complete these exercises before moving on to the next section. How well you do on each practice will determine whether or not you need to review a particular grammar point before you move on.

## TIP!

In order to enhance your experience, we'll offer you several tips for learning Japanese throughout the course. This could be a tip on a specific grammar point, additional vocabulary related to the lesson topic, or a tip on language learning in general. For more language learning tips, you can also refer to the Language Learning Tips section that follows this introduction.

## CULTURE NOTE AND LANGUAGE LINKS

Becoming familiar with the culture of Japan is nearly as essential to language learning as grammar. These sections allow you to get to know this culture better through facts about Japan and other bits of cultural information. We've also included the addresses for various websites you can visit on the internet to learn more about a particular country or custom.

## DISCOVERY ACTIVITIES

Discovery activities are another chance for you to put your new language to use. They will often require you to go out into the world and interact with other Japanese speakers, or simply to use the resources around your own home to practice your Japanese.

The coursebook also contains a Grammar Summary and Internet Resources to be used for further reference.

## LEARNER'S DICTIONARY

If you've purchased this book as a part of the complete audio package, you also received a Learner's dictionary with more than 20,000 of the most frequently used Japanese words, phrases, and idiomatic expressions. Use it as a reference any time you're stuck for words in the exercises and discovery activities, or as a supplemental study aid.

## AUDIO

This course works best when used along with its accompanying audio, which features key vocabulary, example sentences, and dialogues from the course. This audio can be used along with the book, or on the go for hands-free practice.

And that's it! The basics. To get even more out of this course, you may wish to read the Language Learning Tips section that follows this introduction. If you're confident that you know all you need to know to get started and wish to head straight for Unit 1, you can always come back to this section for tips on enhancing your learning experience.

Good luck!

If you're not sure about the best way to learn a new language, take a moment to read this section. It includes lots of helpful tips and practical advice on studying languages in general, improving vocabulary, mastering grammar, using audio, doing exercises, and expanding your learning experience. All of this will make learning more effective and more fun.

## GENERAL TIPS

Let's start with some general points to keep in mind about learning a new language.

### 1. FIND YOUR PACE

The most important thing to keep in mind is that you should always proceed at your own pace. Don't feel pressured into thinking that you only have one chance to digest information before moving on to new material. Read and listen to parts of lessons or entire lessons as many times as it takes to make you feel comfortable with the material. Regular repetition is the key to learning any new language, so don't be afraid to cover material again, and again, and again!

### 2. TAKE NOTES

Use a notebook or start a language journal so you can have something to take with you. Each lesson contains material that you'll learn much more quickly and effectively if you write it down, or rephrase it in your own words once you've understood it. That includes vocabulary, grammar points and examples, expressions from dialogues, and anything else that you find noteworthy. Take your notes with you to review wherever you have time to kill—on the bus or train, waiting at the airport, while dinner is cooking, or whenever you can find the time. Remember, practice (and lots of review!) makes perfect when it comes to learning languages.

## 3. Make a Regular Commitment

Make time for your new language. The concept of "hours of exposure" is key to learning a language. When you expose yourself to a new language frequently, you'll pick it up more easily. On the other hand, the longer the intervals between your exposure to a language, the more you'll forget. It's best to set time aside regularly for yourself. Imagine that you're enrolled in a class that takes place at certain regular times during the week, and set that time aside. Or use your lunch break. It's better to spend less time several days a week than a large chunk of time once or twice a week. In other words, spending thirty or forty minutes on Monday, Tuesday, Wednesday, Friday, and Sunday will be better than spending two and a half or three hours just on Saturday.

## 4. Don't Have Unrealistic Expectations

Don't expect to start speaking a new language as if it were your native language. It's certainly possible for adults to learn new languages with amazing fluency, but that's not a realistic immediate goal for most people. Instead, make a commitment to become "functional" in a new language, and start to set small goals: getting by in most daily activities, talking about yourself and asking about others, following TV and movies, reading a newspaper, expressing your ideas in basic language, and learning creative strategies for getting the most out of the language you know. Functional doesn't mean perfectly native fluent, but it's a great accomplishment!

## 5. Don't Get Hung Up on Pronunciation

"Losing the accent" is one of the most challenging parts of learning a language. If you think about celebrities, scientists, or political figures whose native language isn't English, they probably have a pretty recognizable accent. But that hasn't kept them from becoming celebrities, scientists, or political figures. Really young children are able to learn the sounds of any language in the world, and they can reproduce them perfectly. That's part of the process of learning a native language. As an adult, or even as an older child, this ability becomes reduced, so if you agonize over sounding like a native speaker in your new language, you're just setting yourself up for disappointment. That's not to say that you can't learn pronunciation well. Even adults can get pretty far through mimicking the sounds that they hear. So, listen carefully to the audio several times. Listening is a very important part of this process: you can't reproduce the sound until you learn to distinguish the sound. Then mimic what you hear. Don't be afraid of sounding strange. Just keep at it, and soon enough you'll develop good pronunciation.

### 6. Don't Be Shy
Learning a new language inevitably involves speaking out loud, and it involves making mistakes before you get better. Don't be afraid of sounding strange, or awkward, or silly. You won't: you'll impress people with your attempts. The more you speak, and the more you interact, the faster you'll learn to correct the mistakes you do make.

## TIPS ON LEARNING VOCABULARY
You obviously need to learn new words in order to speak a new language. Even though that may seem straightforward compared with learning how to actually put those words together in sentences, it's really not as simple as it appears. Memorizing words is difficult, even just memorizing words in the short term. But long term memorization takes a lot of practice and repetition. You won't learn vocabulary simply by reading through the vocabulary lists once or twice. You need to practice.

There are a few different ways to "lodge" a word in your memory, and some methods may work better for you than others. The best thing to do is to try a few different methods until you feel that one is right for you. Here are a few suggestions and pointers:

### 1. Audio Repetition
Fix your eye on the written form of a word, and listen to the audio several times. Remind yourself of the English translation as you do this.

## 2. SPOKEN REPETITION

Say a word several times aloud, keeping your eye on the written word as you hear yourself speak it. It's not a race—don't rush to blurt out the word over and over again so fast that you're distorting its pronunciation. Just repeat it, slowly and naturally, being careful to pronounce it as well as you can. And run your eye over the shape of the word each time you say it. You'll be stimulating two of your senses at once that way—hearing and sight—so you'll double the impact on your memory.

## 3. WRITTEN REPETITION

Write a word over and over again across a page, speaking it slowly and carefully each time you write it. Don't be afraid to fill up entire sheets of paper with your new vocabulary words.

## 4. FLASH CARDS

They may seem like child's play, but they're effective. Cut out small pieces of paper (no need to spend a lot of money on index cards) and write the English word on one side and the new word on the other. Just this act alone will put a few words in your mind. Then read through your "deck" of cards. First go from the target (new) language into English—that's easier. Turn the target language side face up, read each card, and guess at its meaning. Once you've guessed, turn the card over to see if you're right. If you are, set the card aside in your "learned" pile. If you're wrong, repeat the word and its meaning and then put it at the bottom of your "to learn" pile. Continue through until you've moved all of the cards into your "learned" pile.

Once you've completed the whole deck from your target language into English, turn the deck over and try to go from English into your target language. You'll see that this is harder, but also a better test of whether or not you've really mastered a word.

## 5. MNEMONICS

A mnemonic is a device or a trick to trigger your memory, like "King Phillip Came Over From Great Spain," which you may have learned in high school biology to remember that species are classified into kingdom, phylum, class, order, family, genus, and species. They work well for vocabulary, too. When you hear and read a new word, look to see if it sounds like anything—a place, a name, a nonsense phrase. Then form an image of that place or person or even nonsense scenario in your head. Imagine it as you say and read the new word. Remember that the more sense triggers you have—hearing, reading, writing, speaking, imagining a crazy image—the better you'll remember.

## 6. GROUPS

Vocabulary should be learned in small and logically connected groups whenever possible. Most of the vocabulary lists in this course are already organized this way. Don't try to tackle a whole list at once. Choose your method—repeating a word out loud, writing it across a page, etc., and practice with a small group.

## 7. PRACTICE

Don't just learn a word out of context and leave it hanging there. Go back and practice it in the context provided in this course. If the word appears in a dialogue, read it in the full sentence and call to mind an image of that sentence. If possible, substitute other vocabulary words into the same sentence structure ("John goes to the *library*" instead of "John goes to the *store*.") As you advance through the course, try writing your own simple examples of words in context.

## 8. COME BACK TO IT

This is the key to learning vocabulary—not just holding it temporarily in your short term memory, but making it stick in your long term memory. Go back over old lists, old decks of flashcards you made, or old example sentences. Listen to vocabulary audio from previous lessons. Pull up crazy mnemonic devices you created at some point earlier in your studies. And always be on the lookout for old words appearing again throughout the course.

## TIPS ON USING AUDIO

The audio in this course not only lets you hear how native speakers pronounce the words you're learning; it also serves as a second kind of "input" to your learning experience. The printed words serve as visual input, and the audio serves as *auditory* input. There are a few different strategies that you can use to get the most out of the audio. First, use the audio while you're looking at a word or sentence. Listen to it a few times along with the visual input of seeing the material. Then, look away and just listen to the audio on its own. You can also use the audio from previously studied lessons as a way to review. Put the audio on your computer or an MP3 player and take it along with you in your car, on the train, while you walk, while you jog, or anywhere you have free time. Remember that the more exposure you have to and contact you have with your target language, the better you'll learn.

## TIPS ON USING CONVERSATIONS

The conversations, or dialogues, in this course are a great way to see language in action, as it's really used by people in realistic situations. To get the most out of a dialogue as a language student, think of it as a cycle rather than a linear passage. First read through the dialogue once in the target language to get the gist. Don't agonize over the details just yet. Then, go back and read through a second time, but focus on individual sentences. Look for new words or new constructions. Challenge yourself to figure out what they mean by the context of the dialogue. After all, that's something you'll be doing a lot of in the real world, so it's a good skill to develop! Once you've worked out the details, read the dialogue again from start to finish. Now that you're very familiar with the dialogue, turn on the audio and listen to it as you read. Don't try to repeat yet; just listen and read along. This will build your listening comprehension. Then, go back and listen again, but this time pause to repeat the phrases or sentences that you're hearing and reading. This will build your spoken proficiency and pronunciation. Now listen again without the aid of the printed dialogue. By now you'll know many of the lines inside out, and any new vocabulary or constructions will be very familiar.

## TIPS ON DOING EXERCISES

The exercises are meant to give you a chance to practice the vocabulary and structures that you learn in each lesson, and of course to test yourself on retention. Take the time to write out the entire sentences to get the most out of the practice. Don't limit yourself to just reading and writing. Read the sentences and answer aloud, so you'll also be practicing pronunciation and spoken proficiency. As you gain more confidence, try to adapt the practice sentences by substituting different vocabulary or grammatical constructions, too. Be creative, and push the practices as far as you can to get the most out of them.

## TIPS ON LEARNING GRAMMAR

Each grammar point is designed to be as small and "digestible" as possible, while at the same time complete enough to teach you what you need to know. The explanations are intended to be simple and straightforward, but one of the best things you can do is to take notes on each grammar section, putting the explanations into your own words, and then copying the example sentences or tables slowly and carefully. This will do two things. It will give you a nice clear notebook that you can take with you so you can review and practice, and it will also force you to take enough time with each section so that it's really driven home. Of course, a lot of grammar is memorization—verb endings, irregular forms, pronouns, and so on. So a lot of the vocabulary learning tips will come in handy for learning grammar, too.

### 1. AUDIO REPETITION

Listen the audio several times while you're looking at the words or sentences. For example, for a verb conjugation, listen to all of the forms several times, reading along to activate your visual memory as well.

### 2. SPOKEN REPETITION

Listen to the audio and repeat several times for practice. For example, to learn the conjugation of an irregular verb, repeat all of the forms of the verb until you're able to produce them without looking at the screen. It's a little bit like memorizing lines for a play—practice until you can make it sound natural. Practice the example sentences that way as well, focusing of course on the grammar section at hand.

### 3. Written Repetition

Write the new forms again and again, saying them slowly and carefully as well. Do this until you're able to produce all of the forms without any help.

### 4. Flash Cards

Copy the grammar point, whether it's a list of pronouns, a conjugation, or a list of irregular forms, on a flashcard. Stick the cards in your pocket so you can practice them when you have time to kill. Glance over the cards, saying the forms to yourself several times, and when you're ready to test yourself, flip the card over and see if you can produce all of the information.

### 5. Grammar in the Wild

Do you want to see an amazing number of example sentences that use some particular grammatical form? Well, just type that form into a search engine. Pick a few of the examples you find at random, and copy them down into your notebook or language journal. Pick them apart, look up words you don't know, and try to figure out the other grammatical constructions. You may not get everything 100% correct, but you'll definitely learn and practice in the process.

### 6. Come Back to It

Just like vocabulary, grammar is best learned through repetition and review. Go back over your notes, go back to previous lessons and read over the grammar sections, listen to the audio, or check out the relevant section in the grammar summary. Even after you've completed lessons, it's never a bad idea to go back and keep the "old" grammar fresh.

# HOW TO EXPAND YOUR LEARNING EXPERIENCE

Your experience with your new language should not be limited to this course alone. Like anything, learning a language will be more enjoyable if you're able to make it a part of your life in some way. And you'd be surprised to know how easily you can do that these days!

## 1. USE THE INTERNET

The internet is an absolutely amazing resource for people learning new languages. You're never more than a few clicks away from online newspapers, magazines, reference material, cultural sites, travel and tourism sites, images, sounds, and so much more. Develop your own list of favorite sites that match your needs and interests, whether it's business, cooking, fashion, film, kayaking, rock climbing, or . . . well, you get the picture. Use search engines creatively to find examples of vocabulary or grammar "in the wild." Find a favorite blog or periodical and take the time to work your way through an article or entry. Think of what you use the internet for in English, and look for similar sites in your target language.

## 2. CHECK OUT COMMUNITY RESOURCES

Depending on where you live, there may be plenty of practice opportunities in your own community. There may be a cultural organization or social club where people meet. There may be a local college or university with a department that hosts cultural events such as films or discussion groups. There may be a restaurant where you can go for a good meal and a chance to practice a bit of your target language. Of course, you can find a lot of this information online, and there are sites that allow groups of people to get organized and meet to pursue their interests.

## 3. FOREIGN FILMS

Films are a wonderful way to practice hearing and understanding a new language. With English subtitles, pause, and rewind, they're practically really long dialogues with pictures! Not to mention the cultural insight and experience they provide. And nowadays it's simple to rent foreign DVDs online or even access films online. So, if you're starting to learn a new language today, go online and rent yourself some movies that you can watch over the next few weeks or months.

## 4. Music

Even if you have a horrible singing voice, music is a great way to learn new vocabulary. After hearing a song just a few times, the lyrics somehow manage to plant themselves in the mind. And with the internet, it's often very easy to find the entire lyric sheet for a song online, print it out, and have it ready for whenever you're alone and feel like singing.

## 5. Television

If you have access to television programming in the language you're studying, including of course anything you can find on the internet, take advantage of that! You'll most likely hear very natural and colloquial language, including idiomatic expressions and rapid speech, all of which will be a healthy challenge for your comprehension skills. But the visual cues, including body language and gestures, will help. Plus, you'll get to see how the language interacts with the culture, which is also a very important part of learning a language.

## 6. Food

A great way to learn a language is through the cuisine. What could be better than going out and trying new dishes at a restaurant with the intention of practicing your newly acquired language? Go to a restaurant, and if the names of the dishes are printed in the target language, try to decipher them. Then try to order in the target language, provided of course that your server speaks the language! At the very least you'll learn a few new vocabulary items, not to mention sample some wonderful new food.

## THE ROMANIZATION

The sounds of Japanese have been transcribed into the Roman alphabet, and all of the letters in the English language except **l**, **q**, and **x** are employed. Note that **c** is used only in the combination **ch**.

There are two major systems of romanization: the Hepburn System and the Japanese National System. The Hepburn System has a longer history and wider acceptance than does the Japanese National System. A slightly modified form of the Hepburn System is used here to present Japanese words and sentences. The system has been modified as follows:

a. So-called "long vowels" are written as double vowels instead of with a macron (ˉ) over the vowel symbol (i.e., **Tookyoo** instead of **Tōkyō**; **kuuki** instead of **kūki**).

b. The syllabic **n** is written as an **n** at all times (instead of as an **m** when it precedes **p**, **b**, or **m**).

## SIMPLE VOWELS

| a | like the **a** in *father*, but short and crisp: **kata** (*shoulder*) |
|---|---|
| i | like the **ee** in *keep*, but short and crisp: **ni** (*two*) |
| u | like the **u** in *put*, but without rounding the lips: **ushi** (*cow*) |
| e | like the **ay** in *may*, but without the final **y** sound: **te** (*hand*) |
| o | like the **o** in *go*, but without the final **u** sound: **son** (*loss*) |

The vowels **i** and **u** differ from the other vowels in that they tend to become "voiceless," or whispered, (1) when they are surrounded by the voiceless consonants **ch**, **f**, **h**, **k**, **p**, **s**, **sh**, **t**, and **ts**, or (2) when they are preceded by a voiceless consonant and followed by a silence or pause (as at the end of a sentence). This is especially true when the syllable in question is not accented. In the following examples, the underlined vowel is devoiced.

| | |
|---|---|
| arima**su** | *there is* |
| k**i**tte | *postage stamp* |

## DOUBLE VOWELS
All simple vowels can appear as double, or "long," vowels. A double vowel is always pronounced twice as long as a simple vowel.

| | |
|---|---|
| **aa** | pronounced twice as long as a single **a**: **haato** (*heart*) |
| **ii** | pronounced twice as long as a single **i**: **riiru** (*reel*) |
| **uu** | pronounced twice as long as a single **u**: **suugaku** (*math*) |
| **ee** | pronounced twice as long as a single **e**: **teeburu** (*table*) |
| **oo** | pronounced twice as long as a single **o**: **Tookyoo** (*Tokyo*) |

## OTHER COMPLEX VOWELS
All simple vowels can also appear in combination with one or more other simple vowels to form "complex vowels." In such combinations, each of the vowels has equal weight and is pronounced so that it retains the sound it has as a simple vowel.

| | |
|---|---|
| **au** | **a** and **u** are both pronounced and given equal clarity and length: **burausu** (*blouse*) |
| **ai** | **a** and **i** are both pronounced and given equal clarity and length: **hai** (*lung*) |

## CONSONANTS AND SEMI-VOWELS
The sounds **b, d, j, k, m, p, s, ts, v,** and **y** in Japanese sound almost like the same sounds in English. Pronounce the other sounds as follows.

| | |
|---|---|
| **ch** | as in *cheese*: **ocha** (*tea*) |
| **f** | by forcing the air out from between the lips; similar to English **wh**: **fune** (*ship*) |
| **g** | at the beginning of a word, somewhat like the **g** in the English word *go*; in the middle of a word, it resembles the **ng** in *singer*: **gin** (*silver*) |
| **h** | like the **h** in *hi* when it precedes **a**, **e**, or **o**; like the **h** in *hue* when it comes before **i** or **y**: **hidu** (*noon*) |
| **n** | as in *name* (but with the tip of the tongue touching the back of the teeth) when it precedes **a**, **e**, **o**, or **u**; like the first **n** in *onion* when it precedes **i** or **y**: **nashi** (*pear*) |
| **r** | by placing the tip of the tongue near the back of the upper teeth and quickly bringing it down; it sometimes sounds like the **r** in a British pronunciation of *very* ("veddy"): **roku** (*six*) |
| **sh** | somewhat like the English **sh** in *sheep*: **shichi** (*seven*) |
| **t** | as in the English *to*, but with the tip of the tongue touching the back of the upper teeth: **tamago** (*egg*) |
| **w** | like the **w** in *want*, but without rounding or protruding the lips; occurs only before **a**: **kawa** (*river*) |
| **z** | at the beginning of a word, like the **ds** in *beds*; in the middle of a word, like the **z** in *zero* (but some Japanese speakers do not make this distinction; they use the two sounds interchangeably): **zoo** (*elephant*) |

When a word begins with **ch**, **h**, **k**, **s**, **t**, or **ts**, and it joins with another word (which then precedes it) to make a new compound word, the initial letter or letters may undergo a change.

| | |
|---|---|
| ch | may become **j**, as it does in the change from **chie** (*wisdom*) to **warujie** (*guile, wiles*). |
| f and h | may become **p** or **b**, as **h** does in the change from **hanashi** (*story*) to **mukashibanashi** (*a story of the past*). |
| k | may become **g**, as it does in the change from **ken** (*a counter for houses*) to **sangen** (*three houses*). |
| s | may become **z**, as it does in the change from **sen** (*one thousand*) to **sanzen** (*three thousand*). |
| sh | may become **j**, as it does in the change from **shika** (*deer*) to **ojika** (*male deer*). |
| t | may become **d**, as it does in the change from **to** (*door, windows*) to **amado** (*storm window, Japanese rain window*). |
| ts | may become **z**, as it does in the change from **tsuki** (*month*) to **tsukizuki** (*monthly*). |

## DOUBLE CONSONANTS

When double **p, t, k,** or **s** (and **d, z,** or **g** in borrowed words) appear in words, as in **kippu** (*ticket*), the two consonants are pronounced separately, with a break in between them, so **kippu** is pronounced *kip-pu*. This same rule of pronunciation applies to consonant clusters **tch, tts,** and **ssh** (and **dj** in borrowed words), pronounced as *t-ch, t-ts,* and *s-sh.*

| | |
|---|---|
| **kippu** | *ticket* |
| **mattaku** | *indeed* |
| **nikki** | *diary* |
| **itchi** | *agreement* |

## THE SYLLABIC N

The syllabic **n** differs from the ordinary **n** in several ways.

a. It always forms a full syllable by itself (that is, it is always held as long as one full syllable). It never joins with a vowel or another consonant to form a syllable. If a vowel follows the syllabic **n**, there is always a syllable boundary between the **n** and the vowel.

For example, the following word has four syllables.

**gen'in** (*cause*)
**ge-n-i-n**

This is because each of the syllabic **n**'s has the value of a full syllable.

b. The syllabic **n** seldom appears at the beginning of a word.

c. Its sound changes depending on what follows it:

Before **n**, **ch**, **t**, and **d**, it is pronounced like the English n in *pen*, but the sound is held longer, as in the following examples.

| | |
|---|---|
| **konna** | *this sort of* |
| **hanchoo** | *group leader* |
| **chanto** | *properly* |
| **kondo** | *this time* |

Before **m**, **p**, or **b**, it is pronounced like the English **m**, but the sound is held longer.

| | |
|---|---|
| **sanmai** (*pronounced as* **sammai**) | *three sheets* |
| **shinpai** (*pronounced as* **shimpai**) | *worry, anxiety* |
| **kanban** (*pronounced as* **kamban**) | *signboard* |

Before a vowel or a semi-vowel (**w**, **y**), the syllabic **n** is pronounced somewhat like the English **ng** in *singer*, but without finishing the **g** sound, and the preceding vowel is often somewhat nasalized. Notice that an apostrophe is used when a vowel or **y** follows the syllabic **n**.

| | |
|---|---|
| gen'an | *original plan* |
| tan'i | *unit* |
| hon'ya | *bookstore* |
| shinwa | *mythology* |

When the syllabic **n** precedes **k, g,** or **s,** or when it appears at the end of a word (that is, when it is followed by a pause), it is pronounced as in (3) above.

| | |
|---|---|
| sonkei | *respect* |
| sangen | *three houses* |
| son | *loss* |
| kansei | *completion* |

CONTRACTIONS
The particle **de** (*at, by means of*) sometimes combines with the particle **wa** (*as for*) as follows: **de** plus **wa** = **ja**.

| | |
|---|---|
| **Nihon ja yasui desu.** | *It is cheap in Japan (but not here).* |

The **-te** form of the copula, **de** (from **desu**), can also combine with the particle **wa** as follows: **de** plus **wa** = **ja**.

| | |
|---|---|
| **Nihonjin ja arimasen.** | *She is not Japanese.* |

The **-te** form of a verb sometimes combines with the particle **wa** as follows: -**te** plus **wa** = **cha**, or -**de** plus **wa** = **ja**.

| | |
|---|---|
| **Itcha ikemasen.** | *You mustn't go.* |
| **Yonja ikemasen.** | *You mustn't read it.* |

## ACCENT

Word accent in Japanese is indicated by lowering the pitch of the voice after the accented syllable. Some words have an accent in Japanese; others do not. Accentless words are spoken with the voice pitch held even on all syllables of the word except the first, where the pitch is slightly lower. This is true regardless of the length of the word.

Certain words lose their accent when they are placed next to an accented word. The best way to learn about accent is by listening to the recordings that come with this course and native Japanese speakers.

## INTONATION

In a declarative sentence, there is a marked drop in the pitch of the voice on the last voiced syllable.

In a direct question, there may be a rising intonation on the last voiced syllable. This rise in pitch is optional when the sentence ends with the question particle **ka** or contains a question phrase, such as **doko e** (*where to*). When neither a question particle nor question word is used, the rising intonation is used.

## JAPANESE WRITING SYSTEM

You will learn more about the Japanese writing system in unit 1. In the following tables, the different characters used in Japanese are simply listed: first, the romanized transcription or romaji (R), then the hiragana (H), and finally, the katakana (K) characters.

| R | H | K | R | H | K | R | H | K | R | H | K | R | H | K |
|---|---|---|---|---|---|---|---|---|---|---|---|---|---|---|
| a | あ | ア | i | い | イ | u | う | ウ | e | え | エ | o | お | オ |
| ka | か | カ | ki | き | キ | ku | く | ク | ke | け | ケ | ko | こ | コ |
| sa | さ | サ | shi | し | シ | su | す | ス | se | せ | セ | so | そ | ソ |
| ta | た | タ | chi | ち | チ | tsu | つ | ツ | te | て | テ | to | と | ト |
| na | な | ナ | ni | に | ニ | nu | ぬ | ヌ | ne | ね | ネ | no | の | ノ |
| ha | は | ハ | hi | ひ | ヒ | fu | ふ | フ | he | へ | ヘ | ho | ほ | ホ |
| ma | ま | マ | mi | み | ミ | mu | む | ム | me | め | メ | mo | も | モ |
| ya | や | ヤ | | | | yu | ゆ | ユ | | | | yo | よ | ヨ |
| ra | ら | ラ | ri | り | リ | ru | る | ル | re | れ | レ | ro | ろ | ロ |
| wa | わ | ワ | | | | | | | | | | wo | を | ヲ |
| n' | ん | ン | | | | | | | | | | | | |

| R | H | K | R | H | K | R | H | K | R | H | K | R | H | K |
|---|---|---|---|---|---|---|---|---|---|---|---|---|---|---|
| ga | が | ガ | gi | ぎ | ギ | gu | く | グ | ge | げ | ゲ | go | ご | ゴ |
| za | ざ | ザ | ji | じ | ジ | zu | ず | ズ | ze | ぜ | ゼ | zo | ぞ | ゾ |
| da | だ | ダ | ji | ぢ | ヂ | zu | づ | ツ | de | で | デ | do | ど | ド |
| ba | ば | バ | bi | び | ビ | bu | ぶ | ブ | be | べ | ベ | bo | ぼ | ボ |
| pa | ぱ | パ | pi | ぴ | ピ | pu | ぷ | プ | pe | ぺ | ペ | po | ぽ | ポ |

| R | H | K | R | H | K | R | H | K |
|---|---|---|---|---|---|---|---|---|
| kya | きゃ | キャ | kyu | きゅ | キュ | kyo | きょ | キョ |
| sha | しゃ | シャ | shu | しゅ | シユ | sho | しょ | ショ |
| cha | ちゃ | チャ | chu | ちゅ | チユ | cho | ちょ | チョ |
| nya | にゃ | ニャ | nyu | にゅ | ニユ | nyo | にょ | ニョ |

*(continues)*

| R | H | K | R | H | K | R | H | K |
|---|---|---|---|---|---|---|---|---|
| hya | ひゃ | ヒャ | hyu | ひゅ | ヒュ | hyo | ひょ | ヒョ |
| mya | みゃ | ミャ | myu | みゅ | ミュ | myo | みょ | ミョ |
| rya | りゃ | リャ | ryu | りゅ | リュ | ryo | りょ | リョ |
| gya | ぎゃ | ギャ | gyu | ぎゅ | ギュ | gyo | ぎょ | ギョ |
| ja<br>(zya) | じゃ ジャ<br>ぢゃ ヂャ | | ju | じゅ ジュ<br>ぢゅ ヂュ | | jo | じょ ジョ<br>ぢょ ヂョ | |
| bya | びゃ | ビャ | byu | びゅ | ビュ | byo | びょ | ビョ |
| pya | ぴゃ | ピャ | pyu | ぴゅ | ピュ | pyo | ぴょ | ピョ |

# UNIT 1
## *Talking about yourself and making introductions*

**Konnichi wa!** (*Hello!*) In Unit 1, you will learn how to greet people, introduce yourself, and ask other people for their personal information, such as nationality, place of origin, special area of study or work, or languages they speak. You will also learn a few essential Japanese courtesy expressions.

——————————— Lesson 1 (words) ———————————

## WORD LIST 1

| | |
|---|---|
| **watashi** | *I* |
| **boku** (*used only by male speakers*) | *I* |
| **(o)namae** (*polite with* **o**) | *name* |
| **(go)juusho** (*polite with* **go**) | *address* |
| **denwa** | *telephone* |
| **keetai (denwa)** | *cellular phone* |
| **(o)denwa bangoo** (*polite with* **o**) | *telephone number* |
| **(go)shusshin** (*polite with* **go**) | *place of origin, hometown* |
| **dochira, doko** | *where* |
| **(go)senmon** (*polite with* **go**) | *specialization, special area of study or work* |
| **hooritsu** | *law* |
| **keezai** | *economy* |
| **keezaigaku** | *economics* |
| **daigaku** | *university* |
| **gakusee** | *student* |
| **daigakusee** | *college student* |
| **seminaa** | *seminar* |
| **bengoshi** | *lawyer* |
| **shigoto** | *job, work* |

| tomodachi | *friend* |
| sakubun | *composition* |
| kaiwa | *conversation* |
| shitsumon | *question* |
| kotae | *answer* |
| jikan | *time* |
| ima | *now* |
| kedo (*at the end of a sentence*) | *though, but* |
| demo (*at the beginning of a sentence*) | *however, but* |

NOTE 1

Generally, Japanese doesn't differentiate between the singular and plural forms of nouns. For instance, **tomodachi** can refer to either *friend* or *friends* depending on the context.

## NUTS & BOLTS 1
### JAPANESE MORAS

A mora is a unit of sound similar to a syllable and equivalent to a single beat in pronunciation. It can consist of a) a single vowel, such as /a/, /i/, /u/, /e/, or /o/, b) a combination of a consonant and a vowel, such as **/ha/, /so/, /ke/, /go/, /do/, /pa/**, or **/po/**, or c) a nasal consonant /n/, as in the word /se/n/mo/n/. In isolation, all moras have approximately the same length and loudness regardless of how many and which sounds they consist of. In Japanese writing, a single hiragana or katakana character corresponds to a mora, with some exceptions. The Japanese writing system will be discussed in more detail in the Nuts & bolts 2 section of this lesson.

Note that in Word list 1, Japanese words are written using Roman letters. In this course, we will use the standard Hepburn Romanization system with some variations to write Japanese, rather than actual Japanese characters.

In the standard Hepburn system, long vowels are represented by a single vowel or a combination of a vowel and **h**, as in **ah** and **oh**. In this text, as mentioned earlier, long vowels are represented by doubled vowels, like **aa** and **oo**, in order to remind students of their pronunciation. The following chart represents the different Japanese moras using Roman letters. Other mora types are used to write loanwords from other languages, such as /fi/ and /fe/, but those are not listed in this chart.

| a | i | u | e | o | | | | | |
|---|---|---|---|---|---|---|---|---|---|
| ka | ki | ku | ke | ko | ga | gi | gu | ge | go |
| sa | shi | su | se | so | za | ji | zu | ze | zo |
| ta | chi | tsu | te | to | da | ji | zu | de | do |
| na | ni | nu | ne | no | | | | | |
| ha | hi | fu | he | ho | ba | bi | bu | be | bo |
| ma | mi | mu | me | mo | | | | | |
| ya | | yu | | yo | | | | | |
| ra | ri | ru | re | ro | | | | | |
| wa | | | | wo | | | | | |
| n | | | | | | | | | |

| kya | kyu | kyo | gya | gyu | gyo | | | |
|-----|-----|-----|-----|-----|-----|---|---|---|
| sha | shu | sho | zya | ju | jo | | | |
| cha | chu | cho | | | | | | |
| nya | nyu | nyo | | | | | | |
| hya | hyu | hyo | bya | byu | byo | pya | pyu | pyo |
| mya | myu | myo | | | | | | |
| rya | ryu | ryo | | | | | | |

Note that, as mentioned earlier, each mora consists of either a single vowel or a combination of a consonant and a vowel, and that there is no mora that consists of only a consonant, with the exception of the nasal /n/ and double consonants like /ss/ in **shusshin** (*place of origin*), /kk/ in **gakkoo** (*school*), /tt/ in **chotto** (*a little*), and /pp/ in **roppyaku** (*six hundred*). Here are a few examples of Japanese words divided into moras:

keezai: /ke/e/za/i/
watashi: /wa/ta/shi/
senmon: /se/n/mo/n/
zyugyoo: /zyu/gyo/o/

## PRACTICE 1
Divide the following words into moras. Refer to tables above for help.

1. ima

2. boku

3. tomodachi

4. hooritsu

5. sakubun

6. demo

7. bengoshi

8. shusshin

9. dochira

10. seminaa

## WORD LIST 2

| | |
|---|---|
| Nihongo | *Japanese (language)* |
| Eego | *English (language)* |
| Chuugokugo | *Chinese (language)* |
| Supeingo | *Spanish (language)* |
| Furansugo | *French (language)* |
| Doitsugo | *German (language)* |
| Nihonjin | *Japanese (person, people)* |
| Amerikajin | *American (person, people)* |
| Chuugokujin | *Chinese (person, people)* |
| Supeinjin | *Spanish (person, people)* |

| | |
|---|---|
| Furansujin | *French (person, people)* |
| Doitsujin | *German (person, people)* |
| Mekishikojin | *Mexican (person, people)* |
| shoorai | *future* |
| hanashimasu | *speak* |
| sukoshi | *a little, a few* |
| sugoi | *wonderful, amazing, great* |
| (o)zyoozu (polite with o) | *skillful* |
| tabun | *perhaps* |

## NUTS & BOLTS 2
### THE BASICS OF THE JAPANESE WRITING SYSTEM

Three different types of characters are used to write Japanese: hiragana, katagana, and kanji characters. Hiragana and katakana are derived from simplified kanji, which derives from the Chinese script. In modern Japanese all three types of characters are used to write the language. The major difference between kanji and the other two scripts is that a kanji character is an ideographic symbol representing a concept or an idea rather than a single sound or a syllable. Each hiragana and katakana character, on the other hand, stands for a mora and is combined with other characters to form words.

Kanji is mainly used to write words of Chinese origin, but nouns, verb stems, and adjectives of Japanese origin are also written in kanji. Hiragana is used to write particles, postpositions, and endings of verbs and adjectives. Katakana is used to write foreign loanwords, such as **koohii** (*coffee*) and **terebi** (*television*). Hiragana and katakana characters together with their romanized transcriptions are listed in the *Japanese writing system* section at the beginning of the book.

Note that there are forty-six basic hiragana characters. Additional hiragana characters exist to represent moras consisting of voiced consonants /g/, /z/, /d/, /b/ and a vowel, such as /ga/, /zu/, /de/, and /bi/, and those consisting of /p/ and a vowel, like /pa/ and /po/. Note that there are also special hiragana characters for moras consisting of a consonant followed by /y/ and a vowel, such as /kya/, /chu/, /nyu/, and /hyo/. These characters are combinations of hiragana characters representing /ki/, /shi/, /chi/, /ni/, /hi/, /mi/, or /ri/ and small-size characters representing /ya/, /yu/, or /yo/.

**PRACTICE 2**
What kind of Japanese characters would you use to write the following words?

1. watashi                           a. hiragana

2. *particle* wa                     b. kanji

3. hanashimasu *(to speak)*          c. kanji and hiragana

4. Amerika                           d. katakana

5. Nihongo

**PRACTICE 3**
What language or languages are spoken in the following countries? Answer the questions in Japanese.

1. England

2. China

3. Mexico

4. Belgium

5. Switzerland

# Culture note

Particles attaching to the end of names are used in Japanese as forms of address equivalent to English titles. These particles are called honorifics, and they are used to indicate the level of formality or informality of a relationship. A very commonly used particle is **san,** which usually follows the last name, as in **Suzuki-san** and **Mori-san.** This honorific is roughly equivalent to the use of *Mr., Mrs.,* or *Ms.* in English. In formal situations, including the workplace, first names are not used in Japan. Titles, such as **sensee** (*teacher*) or **buchoo** (*division manager*) are commonly used instead of **san,** as in **Suzuki sensee** (*teacher Suzuki*) and **Mori buchoo** (*division manager Mori*).

The way of addressing friends is more flexible. It is common for female speakers to address their female friends by their first name followed by **san,** like **Mariko-san** and **Sayuri-san,** but they may address each other by their first name without **san,** like **Mariko** and **Sayuri.** When they address their male friends, they often attach either **san** or **kun** to the last or the first name, like **Tanaka-san/Tanaka-kun** and **Kenji-san/Kenji-kun.** Male friends often address each other by their last name without **san** or **kun,** like **Suzuki** and **Mori.**

When male speakers address their female friends, they often attach **san** to the last or the first name, like **Yamada-san** and **Junko-san,** but they may address their female friends by their last or first name without **san,** like **Yamada** and **Junko.** Thus, there are many variations, and the form of address mainly depends on how the relationship was first established. Among teenagers the way of addressing friends is more flexible. It is also common to use nicknames among friends and family members.

## ANSWERS
**PRACTICE 1: 1.** /i/ma/; **2.** /bo/ku/; **3.** /to/mo/da/chi/;
**4.** /ho/o/ri/tsu/; **5.** /sa/ku/bu/n/; **6.** /de/mo/; **7.** /be/n/go/shi/;
**8.** /shu/s/shi/n/; **9.** /do/chi/ra/; **10.** /se/mi/na/a/

**PRACTICE 2: 1.** b; **2.** a; **3.** c; **4.** d; **5.** b

**PRACTICE 3: 1.** eego; **2.** chuugokugo; **3.** supeingo;
**4.** furansugo; **5.** doitsugo, furansugo, itariago

## PHRASE LIST 1

| | |
|---|---|
| **Ohayoo (gozaimasu).** | *Good morning.* |
| (*polite with* **gozaimasu**) | |
| **Konnichi wa.** | *Good afternoon./Hello.* |
| **Konban wa.** | *Good evening.* |
| **Oyasuminasai.** | *Good night.* |
| **Sayoonara.** | *Good-bye.* |
| **Hajimemashite.** | *How do you do.* |
| **Doozo yoroshiku (onegaishimasu).** | *Nice to meet you.* |
| **Kochira koso doozo yoroshiku** | *Nice to meet you, too.* |
| **(onegaishimasu).** | |
| **Tanaka-san** | *Mr. Tanaka, Mrs. Tanaka,* |
| | *Ms. Tanaka* |
| **sore kara** | *and then* |
| **Sore zya mata.** | *See you then.* |
| **mada mada** | *not yet* |
| **Soo desu ka?** | *Is that so?* |
| **Soo desu ka.** | *I see.* |
| **Soo desu ne.** | *Yes, it is./Let me see.* |

NOTE 1

**Yoroshiku** can have different meanings depending on the context. For instance, when it is used in a situation where a person is meeting someone for the first time, it is equivalent to *Nice to meet you*. It can also be used when asking someone to do something, but there is no exact English equivalent of this usage. It can be roughly translated as *Please do it properly* or *I leave it entirely to you*. If the words **doozo** and **onegaishimasu** are added to **yoroshiku**, as in **Doozo yoroshiku onegaishimasu** (*Nice to meet you*), the expression is more polite.

## NUTS & BOLTS 1
### THE POSSESSIVE CONSTRUCTION

Before getting into the structure of Japanese sentences, let's learn about how Japanese nouns can be combined to form the possessive construction. This construction is used to say that something or someone belongs to someone. For instance, the phrase *John's DVD* expresses a possessive relationship between the nouns *John* and *DVD*. In Japanese, the possessive marker **no** is used, roughly equivalent to the English *'s* or preposition *of*.

**John no DVD**
*John's DVD*

**Mariko-san no tomodachi**
*Mariko's friend(s)*

**Suzuki-san no senmon**
*Mr./Mrs./Ms. Suzuki's specialialization*

The Japanese possessive construction can also indicate a location. In this case, the possessor (the location) consists of a noun and a postposition. A postposition is similar to a preposition, such as *at, to,* or *with*, but it follows the noun rather than preceding it, as in English. The Japanese postpositions **kara** (*from*) and **e** (*to*) are used in the following examples.

**Amerika kara no tomodachi**
*a friend/friends from the U.S.A.*

**Nihon e no hikooki**
*an airplane/airplanes to Japan*

**No** can also connect more than two nouns, as in the structure X **no** Y **no** Z, to indicate possession.

**watashi no tomodachi no DVD**
*my friend's/friends' DVD*

**Supeingo no kaiwa no kurasu**
*Spanish conversation class*

**Lisa no Nihongo no kurasu no sensee**
*the teacher of Lisa's Japanese class*

The Japanese possessive construction appears very simple, but be careful to keep straight the order of the different nouns, as word order indicates the relationship among them. Note that the noun denoting the possessed always comes last in a sequence.

## PRACTICE 1
Translate the following English phrases into Japanese using the possessive marker **no**.

1. *Lisa's DVD*

2. *French class (lit., class of French)*

3. *John's friend*

4. *Mr. Smith's lawyer*

5. *economics seminar (lit., seminar of economics)*

6. *Bill's specialization*

## PHRASE LIST 2

| | |
|---|---|
| **Nyuu Yooku no shusshin** | *native of New York, from New York* |
| **sakubun no kurasu** | *composition class* |
| **Nihongo no kaiwa no kurasu** | *Japanese conversation class* |
| **Eekaiwa no kurasu** | *English conversation class* |
| **Eego to Supeingo to Furansugo** | *English, Spanish, and French* |
| **tokorode** | *by the way* |
| **korekara** | *from now* |
| **Shitsuree desu ga . . .** | *Excuse me, but . . .* |
| **nizyuugo sai** | *twenty-five years old* |

| Ohisashiburi desu./ | *Long time, no see.* |
| Shibaraku desu./ | |
| Gobusatashite orimasu. | |
| Ogenki desu ka?/Ogenki?/Genki? | *How are you?* |
| Okagesama de. (*formal*)/ | *I'm fine, thank you.* |
| Genki desu. (*informal*) | |
| Doomo arigatoo (gozaimasu). | *Thank you (very much).* |

NOTE 1
Note the contracted form **Eekaiwa** (**Eego + kaiwa**), meaning *English conversation.* In contrast, the expressions meaning *Japanese conversation, Spanish conversation, German conversation,* and *French conversation* are not contracted, but the possessive particle **no** is optional: **Nihongo (no) kaiwa, Supeingo (no) kaiwa, Doitsugo (no) kaiwa, Furansugo (no) kaiwa.**

NOTE 2
**Ogenki?** is less formal than **Ogenki desu ka?**; **Genki?** is an informal question used in informal situations and among friends.

## NUTS & BOLTS 2
### JAPANESE SENTENCE STRUCTURE: X WA Y DESU
Now, let's talk about the following basic sentence construction.

> **X wa Y desu.**

This construction corresponds to the English *X am/is/are Y* construction. In Japanese, X is a topic of a sentence (similar to the subject of a sentence in English), Y provides some information about X, and **desu** is a copula corresponding to the English *am/is/are.* The topic of the sentence is always followed by the particle **wa.** A direct English translation of this construction is *As for X, I/he/she/it/you/we/they am/is/are Y.*

**John-san wa Amerikajin desu.**

*John is American.*

**Brown-san wa bengoshi desu.**

*Mr./Ms. Brown is a lawyer.*

**Mariko-san wa Ichiroo-san no tomodachi desu.**

*Mariko is Ichiro's friend.*

In the above examples, Y is a noun. In the last example, Y, **Ichiroo-san no tomodachi**, is a possessive phrase. Y can also be an adjective, such as *interesting* or *expensive*; a numeral, such as *twenty-five years old* or *five hundred yen*; a demonstrative, such as *this* or *there*; or a time-adverb, such as *today*. Look at the following examples.

**Hooritsu no seminaa wa omoshiroi desu.**

*Law seminars are interesting.* (**omoshiroi** means *interesting*)

**Tomoko-san wa juukyuu sai desu.**

*Tomoko is nineteen years old.* (**juukyuu sai** means *nineteen years old*)

**Watashi no daigaku wa are desu.**

*My university is that one (over there).* (**are** means *that one*)

**Keezaigaku no seminaa wa kyoo desu.**

*The economics seminar is today.* (**kyoo** means *today*)

One of the characteristics of Japanese is that the topic of a sentence, or **X wa,** can be dropped if it can be understood from the context. For instance, if Mr. Tanaka is introducing himself to his new colleagues, he can just say **Tanaka desu,** instead of **Watashi wa Tanaka desu,** because his colleagues know that he is talking about himself. So, even though the basic sentence structure is **X wa Y desu**, you will often hear only **Y desu** without **X wa.**

## PRACTICE 2

Choose the appropriate phrases to complete the sentences below. Each phrase can be used only once.

1. John-san wa nyuuyooku no _____.
2. Lopez-san wa _____.
3. Sayuri-san wa Mika-san no _____.
4. Mariko-san no senmon wa _____.
5. Shusshin wa _____.

a. Pari *(Paris)* desu
b. tomodachi desu
c. Mekishikojin desu
d. bengoshi desu
e. hooritsu desu

## PRACTICE 3

Choose the appropriate expression on the right side in response to those on the left side.

1. Ogenki desu ka?
2. Doozo yoroshiku.
3. Oikutsu desu ka?
4. Sayoonara.
5. Ohisashiburi desu.

a. Kochira koso doozo yoroshiku.
b. Sanzyuuni sai desu.
c. Ee, okagesama de.
d. Soo desu ne. Ogenki desu ka?
e. Zya mata.

### Tip!

If you'd like to practice reading the Japanese writing, do what Japanese children do and start practicing the hiragana and katakana first. Once you are able to recognize the hiragana and katakana, you can start learning kanji. A good way to practice the hiragana and katakana characters is to use flash cards, with words in Roman letters on one side and words in hiragana or katakana on the other. Of course, flash cards are also useful for practicing kanji. You can also browse Japanese websites, such as those of Japanese newspapers, in order to get an opportunity to practice the Japanese scripts. The URLs of two major newspapers are www.asahi.com and www.yomiuri.co.jp. Your persistence and practice will pay off soon.

## ANSWERS

**PRACTICE 1: 1.** Lisa no DVD; **2.** Furansugo no kurasu; **3.** John no tomodachi; **4.** Smith-san no bengoshi; **5.** keezaigaku no seminaa; **6.** Bill no senmon

**PRACTICE 2: 1.** d; **2.** c; **3.** b; **4.** e; **5.** a

**PRACTICE 3: 1.** c; **2.** a; **3.** b; **4.** e; **5.** d

────────── Lesson 3 (sentences) ──────────

## SENTENCE GROUP 1

| | |
|---|---|
| **Onamae wa?** | *What's your name?* |
| **John Clark desu.** | *My name is John Clark. (lit., It's John Clark.)* |
| **Watashi wa Amerikajin desu.** | *I'm American.* |
| **Goshusshin wa dochira desu ka?** | *Where are you from?* |
| **Shusshin wa Honkon desu.** | *I'm from Hong Kong. (lit., As for my place of origin, it is Hong Kong.)* |
| **Nyuu Yooku no shusshin desu.** | *I'm from New York. (lit., New York is my place of origin.)* |
| **Gosenmon wa (nan desu ka)?** | *What's your specialization?* |
| **Watashi no senmon wa keezai desu.** | *My specialization is economics.* |
| **Gakusee desu ka?** | *Are you a student?* |
| **Hai, gakusee desu.** | *Yes, I'm a student.* |
| **Oshigoto wa nan desu ka?** | *What's your occupation?* |
| **Bengoshi desu.** | *I'm a lawyer.* |

## NUTS & BOLTS 1

### JAPANESE SENTENCE STRUCTURE: WORD ORDER AND PHRASAL PARTICLES

Japanese word order is quite different from word order in English. Basic word order in English is Subject-Verb-Object (SVO), as in *Rebecca speaks Japanese*. In Japanese, on the other hand, it is Subject-Object-Verb (SOV).

**Rebecca ga Nihongo o hanashimasu.**
*Rebecca speaks Japanese.*

**Kenta ga hon o yomimasu.**
*Kenta reads a book.*

While the order of other sentence elements is relatively flexible in Japanese, the verb is always at the end of the sentence. Compare the English sentence

*Ichiro <u>speaks</u> English.*

with its Japanese translation,

**Ichiroo-san ga Eego o <u>hanashimasu</u>.**

Literally, the sentence can be translated as: *Ichiro (subject particle) English (object particle) speaks.* So, the verb *speaks* precedes the direct object in English, but its equivalent, **hanashimasu,** follows the direct object in Japanese.

While the basic word order in Japanese is SOV, the Object-Subject-Verb (OSV) word order is also possible. The OSV word order is used especially when the object needs to be emphasized.

In addition, the position of adverbs in the sentence is quite flexible. The following examples show different word orders that the same sentence can take.

**Ichiroo-san wa mainichi Eego o hanashimasu.**
*Ichiroo speaks English every day. (lit., Ichiroo every day English speaks.)*

**Mainichi Ichiroo-san wa Eego o hanashimasu.**
*Every day, Ichiroo speaks English. (lit., Every day Ichiroo English speaks.)*

**Ichiroo-san wa Eego o mainichi hanashimasu.**
*Ichiroo speaks English every day. (lit., Ichiroo English every day speaks.)*

**Eego o ichiroo-san wa mainichi hanashimasu.**
*It is English that Ichiroo speaks every day. (lit., English, Ichiroo every day speaks.)*

**Eego o mainichi ichiroo-san wa hanashimasu.**
*It is English that Ichiroo speaks every day. (lit., English, every day Ichiroo speaks.)*

In the last two sentences, the direct object **Eego** (*English*) is emphasized and therefore placed at the beginning of the sentence. As pointed out in Lesson 2, the topic of a sentence is often dropped when it can be understood from the context. If the situation or context allows, an object can be dropped, too.

Because the word order in Japanese is so free, phrasal particles are used to indicate the function of nouns in a sentence as either topic, subject, or object: **wa, ga,** or **o**. (Remember that we discussed the possessive particle **no** earlier.) **Ga** marks a subject noun, and a direct object noun is marked by the particle **o**. If a noun is familiar from the situational context or previous speech, it is followed by the topic marker **wa**. Like **no**, these particles always follow the noun.

**John-san ga Nihongo o hanashimasu.**
*John speaks Japanese. (lit., John Japanese speaks.)*

**John-san wa Nihongo o hanashimasu.**
*As for John, he speaks Japanese. (lit., As for John, Japanese speaks.)*

Note that in the second example above, **John** is the topic of the sentence, and **Nihongo o hanashimasu** (*speaks Japanese*) is the new information provided about it. As mentioned earlier, whenever a subject of a sentence has been introduced in previous speech and hence, is known to both the speaker and the listener, it has to be followed by the topic marker **wa**. Here are two more examples.

**Kyoo John-san ga kimasu.**
*Today, John will come.*

**John-san wa Supeingo o hanashimasu.**
*As for John, he speaks Spanish.*

The noun **John-san** cannot be marked by **ga** in the second example because it was already introduced in the first sentence.

### PRACTICE 1
Fill in the blanks with the particles **wa, ga, o,** or **no.**

1. Suzuki-san _____ nihonjin desu.

2. Mariko-san _____ senmon _____ keezai desu.

3. Ichiroo-san _____ Yukari-san _____ tomodachi desu.

4. Lisa-san _____ sakubun o kakimasu *(write)*.

5. John-san _____ doitsugo _____ hanashimasu.

### PRACTICE 2
Pick the correct word order by choosing either *a* or *b*.

1. a. John-san wa Amerikajin desu.

   b. John-san wa desu Amerikajin.

2. a. Ichiroo-san wa hanashimasu Eego to Supeingo o.

   b. Ichiroo-san wa Eego to Supeingo o hanashimasu.

3. a. Lisa-san no Honkon desu shusshin wa.

   b. Lisa-san no shusshin wa Honkon desu.

4. a. Suzuki-san ga Nihonjin desu.

   b. Suzuki-san Nihonjin ga desu.

5. a. Ryooshin wa ima Itaria ni imasu.

   b. Imasu ryooshin ima Itaria ni.

## SENTENCE GROUP 2

| | |
|---|---|
| Nanigo o hanashimasu ka? | *What language(s) do you speak?* |
| John-san wa Eego to Supeingo o hanashimasu. | *John speaks English and Spanish.* |
| John-san wa Furansugo mo hanashimasu. | *John also speaks French.* |
| Nihongo wa mada mada desu yo. | *As for Japanese, I'm not good at it yet. (lit., As for Japanese, not yet, not yet.)* |
| Oikutsu desu ka?/Nansai desu ka? | *How old are you?* |
| Nijuugo sai desu. | *I'm twenty-five years old.* |
| Korekara zyugyoo desu ka? | *Are you going to the class now? (lit., From now is [it] a class?)* |
| Nihongo no kaiwa no kurasu desu. | *It's a Japanese conversation class.* |

## NUTS & BOLTS 2
### PHRASAL PARTICLE MO

The particle **mo** corresponds to the English *too, also,* or *both . . . and*. It is used in the following constructions:

> **X mo**
> (*X too, also X*)

and

> **X mo Y mo**
> (*both X and Y*)

**Mo** can follow a noun, a time adverb, a demonstrative, or a numeral, but it cannot follow a verb or an adjective. Take a look at some examples.

**John-san wa Amerikajin desu.**
*John is American.*

**Mary-san mo Amerikajin desu.**
*Mary is American, too. (lit., Mary too is American.)*

**Ichiroo-san no senmon wa hooritsu desu.**
*Ichiro's special area of study is law.*

**Mariko-san no senmon mo hooritsu desu.**
*Mariko's specialization is also law.*

**Tsuyoshi-san wa Supeingo o hanashimasu.**
*Tsuyoshi speaks Spanish.*

**Tsuyoshi-san wa Furansugo mo hanashimasu.**
*Tsuyoshi speaks French, too.*

**Kore** (*this*) **wa DVD desu.**
*This is a DVD.*

**Sore** (*that*) **mo DVD desu.**
*That is a DVD, too.*

**Kyoo** (*today*) **wa samui** (*cold*) **desu.**
*It's cold today.*

**Ashita** (*tomorrow*) **mo samui desu.**
*It will be cold tomorrow, too. (lit., It is cold tomorrow, too.)*

Note that **mo** can also follow a postposition.

**Amerika kara gakusee ga kimasu** (*come*)**.**
*Students will come from the U.S.A.*

**Mekishiko kara mo gakuscc ga kimasu.**
*Students will also come from Mexico.*

Note that in the above examples, **mo** replaces phrasal particles **wa, ga,** and **o**, but co-occurs with postpositions, such as **kara** (*from*) and others. Now let's look at examples where **mo** is used in the structure **X mo Y mo.**

**John-san mo Mary-san mo Amerikajin desu.**
*Both John and Mary are American.*

**Ichiroo-san no senmon mo Mariko-san no senmon mo hooritsu desu.**
*Both Ichiroo's specialization and Mariko's specialization are law.*

**Tsuyoshi-san wa Supeingo mo Furansugo mo hanashimasu.**
*Tsuyoshi speaks both Spanish and French.*

## PRACTICE 3
Combine sentences in *a* and *b* using the construction **X mo Y mo** by filling in the blanks in *c* with appropriate words and placing the appropriate particles in parentheses.

1. a. Suzuki-san wa Nihonjin desu.

   b. Mori-san mo Nihonjin desu.

   c. _____ ( ) _____ ( ) Nihonjin desu.

2. a. Ichiroo-san wa bengoshi desu.

   b. Mariko-san mo bengoshi desu.

   c. _____ ( ) _____ ( ) bengoshi desu.

3. a. Jiroo-san no senmon wa keezai desu.

   b. Yukari-san no senmon mo keezai desu.

   c. Jiroo-san ( ) _____ ( ) Yukari-san ( ) _____ ( ) keezai desu.

4. a. John-san wa Nyuu Yooku no shusshin desu.

   b. Mary-san mo Nyuu Yooku no shusshin desu.

   c. _____ ( ) _____ ( ) Nyuu Yooku no shusshin desu.

5. a. Lopez-san wa Supeingo o hanashimasu.

   b. Lopez-san wa Eego mo hanashimasu.

   c. Lopez-san wa _____ ( ) _____ ( ) hanashimasu.

## Culture note

There are subtle differences in how everyday greetings are used in the United States and in Japan. For example, in the U.S., people may repeatedly say *hello* or *hi* to greet again someone they have already seen on the same day. The Japanese **konnichi wa** corresponds to *good afternoon* or *hello*, but it cannot be used for such repeated greetings. Instead, people usually just bow by moving their heads slightly downward to acknowledge the person; sometimes, the greeting **doomo** may also be used. This type of bow is called **eshaku**. Similarly, while the Japanese phrase **Ogenki desu ka?** can be translated as *How are you?*, it is actually not used in the same way as the English phrase. **Ogenki desu ka?** is used only with someone you have not seen in a while, and unlike the English phrase, it is meant as a real question demanding an answer.

## ANSWERS

**PRACTICE 1: 1.** ga/wa (*depending on the context*); **2.** no, ga/wa (*depending on the context*); **3.** ga/wa (*depending on the context*), no; **4.** ga/wa (*depending on the context*), o; **5.** ga/wa (*depending on the context*), o

**PRACTICE 2: 1.** a; **2.** b; **3.** b; **4.** a; **5.** a

**PRACTICE 3: 1.** <u>Suzuki-san</u> (mo) <u>Mori-san</u> (mo) Nihonjin desu. **2.** <u>Ichiroo-san</u> (mo) <u>Mariko-san</u> (mo) bengoshi desu. **3.** Jiroo-san (no) <u>senmon</u> (mo) Yukari-san (no) <u>senmon</u> (mo) keezai desu. **4.** <u>John-san</u> (mo) <u>Mary-san</u> (mo) Nyuu Yooku (no) shusshin desu. **5.** Lopez-san wa <u>Supeingo</u> (mo) <u>Eego</u> (mo) hanashimasu.

--- Lesson 4 (conversations) ---

## CONVERSATION 1

Lisa and John came to Japan to study Japanese. They meet before their Japanese class.

> Lisa:  Ohayoo gozaimasu. Lisa Chen desu.
> John:  Ah, hajimemashite. John Clark desu. Doozo
>  yoroshiku.

Lisa: Kochira koso doozo yoroshiku.
John: Lisa-san wa Chuugokujin desu ka?
Lisa: Ee. Shusshin wa Honkon desu. John-san wa?
John: Boku wa Amerikajin desu.
Lisa: Soo desu ka. Goshusshin wa dochira desu ka?
John: Nyuu Yooku desu.
Lisa: Hee, Nyuu Yooku desu ka! Ii desu ne. John-san wa nanigo o hanashimasu ka?
John: Eego to sukoshi Doitsugo to Nihongo o hanashimasu. Lisa-san wa?
Lisa: Etto, watashi wa Chuugokugo to Eego to Furansugo o hanashimasu.
John: Hee, sugoi desu ne. Sore kara Lisa-san wa Nihongo mo hanashimasu ne?
Lisa: Ee, demo Nihongo wa mada mada desu yo.

Lisa: *Good morning. I'm Lisa Chen.*
John: *Ah, how do you do. I'm John Clark. Nice to meet you.*
Lisa: *Nice to meet you, too.*
John: *Are you Chinese, Lisa?*
Lisa: *Yes, I'm from Hong Kong. What about you, John?*
John: *I'm American.*
Lisa: *I see. Where are you from?*
John: *I'm from New York.*
Lisa: *Oh, New York! That's nice. What languages do you speak, John?*
John: *I speak English and a little German and Japanese. What about you, Lisa?*
Lisa: *I speak Chinese, English, and French.*
John: *Wow, that's great. In addition, you also speak Japanese, right, Lisa?*
Lisa: *Yes, but my Japanese is not good yet.*

NOTE 1
The hesitation markers **ano** and **etto** correspond to English *ah* and *uh* and can be used when a speaker needs time to produce the

next sentence, but they are often used even when a speaker knows exactly what he or she is going to say. This use of **ano** and **etto** is similar to *you know* in English. The exclamation **hee** corresponds to the English *wow* and is used when the speaker is impressed by what the addressee said. Your Japanese will sound much more natural if you use these discourse markers appropriately.

## NUTS & BOLTS 1
### QUESTIONS

There are two types of questions: *yes-no* questions, such as *Are you okay?*, and questions with question words, such as *Who is there?* It is very easy to make a *yes-no* question in Japanese. All you have to do is add a question marker, **ka,** to the end of a sentence, without changing the word order. Here are the schematic forms of the two most common types of yes-no questions in Japanese.

> **X wa Y desu ka?**
> **X wa Y o (verb) ka?**

**Lopez-san wa Mekishikojin desu ka?**
*Is Mr./Ms. Lopez Mexican?*

**Ichiroo-san wa bengoshi desu ka?**
*Is Ichiro a lawyer?*

**Mariko-san wa Furansugo o hanashimasu ka?**
*Does Mariko speak French?*

Notice that only the subject marker **wa** is used in questions. Now let's look at questions with question words. The following are common Japanese question words.

## QUESTION WORDS

| nan(i) | *what* |
| --- | --- |
| dare | *who* |
| dochira, doko | *where* |
| itsu | *when* |
| ikura | *how much* |
| ikutsu | *how many, how old* |
| nande, naze, dooshite | *why* |

To make a question with a question word, you just need to re-place the word that the question is about with the right question word, without any change in word order, and add **ka** at the end.

**Shusshin wa <u>Tookyoo</u> desu.**
*I'm from Tokyo.*

**(Go)shusshin wa <u>dochira/doko</u> desu ka?**
*Where are you from?*

**Mariko-san no senmon wa <u>keezai</u> desu.**
*Mariko's specialization is economics.*

**Mariko-san no senmon wa <u>nan</u> desu ka?**
*What's Mariko's specialization?*

**John-san wa <u>Eego to Doitsugo</u> o hanashimasu.**
*John speaks English and German.*

**John-san wa <u>nanigo</u> o hanashimasu ka?**
*What language(s) does John speak?*

**Lopez-san wa <u>Mekishikojin</u> desu.**
*Mr./Ms. Lopez is Mexican.*

**Lopez-san wa <u>nanijin</u> desu ka?**
*What nationality is Mr./Ms. Lopez?*

The question word **nan(i)** (*what*) has two forms: **nan** and **nani**. Before **desu ka, nan** is always used, as in **Senmon wa nan desu ka?** (*What is your specialization?*). **Nani,** unlike **nan,** replaces the core part of a word—for example, **Doitsu** in **Doitsugo** (*German language*)—while the remaining **-go** is added to **nani,** which becomes **nanigo** (*what language*). Likewise, the **jin** in **Mekishikojin** (*Mexican [nationality]*) is added to **nani,** and it becomes **nanijin** (*what nationality*). Questions with question words will be further discussed in Lesson 7.

## PRACTICE 1
Make questions for the given answers by filling in the blanks with appropriate question words.

nanigo, nanijin, doko, nansai, nan

1. Q. Ichiroo-san wa _____ desu ka?

   A. Sanjuugo-sai desu.

2. Q. Shusshin wa _____ desu ka?

   A. Koobe desu.

3. Q. Tanaka-san wa _____ o hanashimasu ka?

   A. Nihongo to Eego o hanashimasu.

4. Q. Senmon wa _____ desu ka?

   A. Hooritsu desu.

5. Q. John-san wa _____ desu ka?

   A. Amerikajin desu.

## CONVERSATION 2

Peter runs into Kenji at the university cafeteria.

Peter: Konnichi wa, Kenji-san.
Kenji: Ah, Peter-san. Konnichi wa. Korekara zyugyoo desu ka?
Peter: Ee, Nihongo no sakubun no kurasu desu. Sorekara keezaigaku no seminaa.
Kenji: Keezaigaku no seminaa? Sugoi desu ne.
Peter: Demo, seminaa wa Eego desu yo.
Kenji: Soo desu ka. Zyaa, Peter-san no senmon wa keezaigaku desu ka?
Peter: Ee. Kenji-san wa?
Kenji: Boku no senmon wa hooritsu desu.
Peter: Jaa, shoorai wa bengoshi desu ka?
Kenji: Uun, tabun ne.
Peter: Kenji-san mo korekara zyugyoo desu ka?
Kenji: Un. Boku wa Supeingo no kaiwa no kurasu desu.
Peter: Soo desu ka. Sorezya mata.


Peter: *Hello, Kenji.*
Kenji: *Oh, Peter. Hello. Are you going to a class now?*
Peter: *Yes. It's a Japanese composition class. And then a seminar in economics.*
Kenji: *A seminar in economics? That's great.*
Peter: *But the seminar is in English.*
Kenji: *I see. Then, is economics your specialization, Peter?*
Peter: *Yes. What about you, Kenji?*
Kenji: *My specialization is law.*
Peter: *So, will you be a lawyer in the future?*
Kenji: *Well, perhaps.*
Peter: *Are you also going to a class now, Kenji?*
Kenji: *Yes. I have a Spanish conversation class.*
Peter: *I see. See you later.*

## NOTE 2

There are a few different words you can use when you want to say *yes* in Japanese. The most formal word is **hai**, but **ee** is also used frequently in daily conversations. **Un** is used to say *yes* when talking to friends and family. **Iie** and **ie** are formal ways of saying *no*, but among friends and family, **uun**—which can also mean *well*, according to the context—is more commonly used.

## NOTE 3

We said earlier that a subject or an object can be omitted from a sentence if it is understood from the context. For instance, when asking for someone's personal information, it is common to say **Onamae wa?** (*[What's] your name?*), **Gojuusho wa?** (*[What's] your address?*), **Gosenmon wa?** (*[What's] your specialization?*), etc., without expressing **nan desu ka** (*what is it*) or **doko desu ka** (*where is it*). To ask *What about you?* use **X-san wa?**

## NUTS & BOLTS 2
### SENTENTIAL PARTICLES KA, YO, AND NE

The sentential particle **ka** is used when making questions, but it can also be used to express mild surprise. In this case, **ka** is often pronounced as **kaa**.

**Akira-san wa nijuugo-sai desu yo.**

*Akira is twenty-five years old.*

**Nijuugo-sai desu kaa.**

*Twenty-five years old, right?*

**Nijuugo-sai desu ka?**

*Twenty-five years old? Really?*

**Nijuugo-sai desu kaa**, with a falling intonation, expresses a speaker's mild surprise. **Nijuugo-sai desu ka?** with a rising intonation can either be used as an echo-question, confirming what a speaker heard, or as an expression of the speaker's surprise. Note that only the part of the sentence that a speaker wants to confirm, such as **nijuugo-sai desu kaa** (*twenty-five years old*), is repeated. The difference between **ka** with a falling intonation and **ka** with a rising intonation is also demonstrated in the following examples.

**Akira-san wa nijuugo-sai desu yo.**
*Akira is twenty-five years old.*

**Soo desu ka.**
*I see . . . / Really . . .*

**Soo desu ka?**
*Is that so?/Really?*

When used with a falling intonation, **soo desu ka** indicates that a speaker is accepting the information he or she received with mild surprise. When **Soo desu ka?** is pronounced with a rising intonation, it indicates that a speaker does not fully accept the information he or she received.

In addition to **ka**, the sentential particles **ne** and **yo** are often added to sentences in daily conversations. **Ne** is used when seeking or expressing agreement.

**Sugoi desu ne?**
*That's great, isn't it?*

**Soo desu ne.**
*Yes, it is.*

**Ne** is also used when confirming a piece of information.

**Sore kara Nihongo mo hanashimasu ne?**
*And you also speak Japanese, right?*

**Soo desu ne?**
*Right?*

Note that, depending on the intonation, **soo desu ne** can be used to express (falling intonation) as well as seek (rising intonation) agreement. **Soo desu ne** can also mean *Let me see*, but in this case, **ne** is often lengthtened to **nee**.

**Paatii** (*party*) **wa itsu ga ii desu ka?**
*When shall we have a party? (lit., As for a party, when is good?)*

**Soo desu nee . . . Ashita** (*tomorrow*) **ga ii desu.**
*Let me see . . . Tomorrow is good.*

The particle **yo** is used when making assertions.

**Nihongo wa mada mada desu yo.**
*As for Japanese, I'm not good at it yet. (I assure you.)*

**Lopez-san wa Mekishikojin desu yo.**
*As for Mr./Ms. Lopez, he/she is a Mexican. (I assure you.)*

Note that **yo** is usually not translated into English. The particles **ne** and **yo** are frequently used in everyday conversation, but they are not used in formal writing.

### PRACTICE 2
Use the right particle: **ka, ne,** or **yo.** (Take a clue from the given answer or the definition.)

1. A: Nanijin desu ( )?

   B: Supeinjin desu.

2. A: Ojoozu desu ( ).

   B: Iie, mada mada desu ( ).

3. A: Karin-san wa Doitsujin desu.

   B: Hee, soo desu ( ).

4. John-san wa bengoshi desu ( ). (*assertion*)

5. Mariko-san no senmon wa keezai desu ( )?
   (*confirming the information*)

## *Cool links*

Japanese culture is fascinating, so getting involved in Japanese cultural events in your area will make for an enriching experience. The homepage of the National Association of Japan-America Societies provides the links to the societies and centers in different states in the U.S. Go to www.us-japan.org, click on Societies/Centers, and then select your area to check out what's happening near you. This may also be an opportunity for you to meet Japanese people and practice your Japanese.

## ANSWERS

**PRACTICE 1:** 1. nansai; 2. doko; 3. nanigo; 4. nan; 5. nanijin

**PRACTICE 2:** 1. ka; 2. ne, yo; 3. ka; 4. yo; 5. ka

# UNIT 2
## *Talking about family*

In Unit 2, you will learn how to talk about your and other people's families, occupations, and work. You will also learn how to count from one to twenty in Japanese.

──────────── Lesson 5 (words) ────────────

## WORD LIST 1

| | |
|---|---|
| **(go)kazoku** (*polite with* **go**) | *family* |
| **(go)ryooshin** (*polite with* **go**) | *parents* |
| **(go)kyoodai** (*polite with* **go**) | *siblings* |
| **(go)fuufu** (*polite with* **go**) | *married couple* |
| **(go)shinseki** (*polite with* **go**) | *relatives* |
| **chichi** | *one's own father* |
| **haha** | *one's own mother* |
| **ani** | *one's own older brother* |
| **ane** | *one's own older sister* |
| **imooto** | *one's own younger sister* |
| **otooto** | *one's own younger brother* |
| **sofu** | *one's own grandfather* |
| **sobo** | *one's own grandmother* |
| **otto, shujin** | *one's own husband* |
| **tsuma, kanai** | *one's own wife* |
| **kodomo** | *child* |
| **musuko** | *one's own son* |
| **musume** | *one's own daughter* |
| **itoko** | *cousin* |
| **uchi** | *house, one's home, one's family* |
| **minasan** | *everyone* |
| **imasu** | *to be, to exist (for animate subjects)* |

## NUTS & BOLTS 1
### Static verb IMASU and the nominative marker GA

The verb **imasu** (*to be*) is used to describe the existence of animate subjects, such as people and animals. It is used in the following construction:

> **X ga imasu.**
> *There is/are X.*

As you learned in Lesson 3, the phrasal particle **ga** marks the subject of a sentence. It is very important to remember that the subject of **imasu** has to be animate. In Lesson 10, you will learn another static verb, **arimasu**, which is used to describe the location of inanimate subjects. Note that the English *there is/there are* construction requires a mention of a location, but in Japanese, the location does not have to be explicit. If a location is mentioned, the location noun is followed by the postposition **ni** (*at, in*), as in **Nyuu Yooku ni** (*in New York*). The following sentences show how this structure is used.

**Chichi ga Nyuu Yooku ni imasu.**
*My father is in New York.*

**Nihonjin ga imasu.**
*A Japanese person is there./Japanese people are there.*

**Amerikajin ga imasu.**
*An American person is there./American people are there.*

**Imasu** can also be used to express possession with animate subjects. When used in the meaning of possession, the possessor noun is expressed as the topic of the sentence followed by the topic particle **wa**; the possessed noun is the subject of the verb **imasu**.

**Watashi wa kazoku ga imasu.**
*I have a family. (lit., As for me, there is a family.)*

**Hiroshi-san wa Amerikajin no tomodachi ga imasu.**

*Hiroshi has (an) American friend(s). (lit., As for Hiroshi, there is/are [an] American friend[s].)*

Note that since Japanese, unlike English, doesn't distinguish between the singular and plural forms of nouns, as pointed out in Lesson 1, there are two possible translations for most of the sentences above. In actual use, the context indicates which meaning is intended.

## PRACTICE 1
Translate the following Japanese sentences into English.

1. Tanaka-san ga imasu.

2. Watashi wa ane ga imasu.

3. Yukari-san wa Chuugokujin no tomodachi ga imasu.

4. Itariajin ga imasu.

5. Peter-san wa Nihonjin no tomodachi ga imasu.

6. Gokyoodai ga imasu ka?

## PRACTICE 2
Translate the following English sentences into Japanese.

1. *Mr. Smith is there.*

2. *Children are there.*

3. *I have an older brother.*

4. *I have a younger sister.*

5. *Is a French person there?*

## WORD LIST 2

| | |
|---|---|
| otoosan | *someone's father* |
| okaasan | *someone's mother* |
| oniisan | *someone's older brother* |
| oneesan | *someone's older sister* |
| ojiisan | *someone's grandfather* |
| obaasan | *someone's grandmother* |
| goshujin | *someone's husband* |
| okusan | *someone's wife* |
| okosan, kodomosan | *someone's child* |
| musukosan | *someone's son* |
| musumesan, ojoosan | *someone's daughter* |
| kaishain | *company employee* |
| chuugakkoo | *junior high school* |
| kookoo | *high school* |
| suugaku | *mathematics* |
| ongaku | *music* |
| sensee, kyooshi | *teacher* |
| isha | *medical doctor* |
| shufu | *housewife* |
| ginkooin | *bank clerk* |
| kangofu, kangoshi | *female nurse, nurse* |
| webudezainaa | *web designer* |
| mainichi | *every day* |
| enjinia, gishi | *engineer* |
| denki gishi | *electrical engineer* |
| keeri | *accounting* |
| tantoo | *being in charge* |
| (o)kyuuryoo (*polite with* o) | *salary* |

## NUTS & BOLTS 2
### Two different groups of family terms

As you can see in the Word lists 1 and 2, two different terms are used to refer to the same family members, depending on whether you're talking about your own or someone else's family members. The following chart summarizes this terminology.

| | ONE'S OWN FAMILY MEMBER | SOMEONE ELSE'S FAMILY MEMBER |
|---|---|---|
| *father* | chichi | otoosan |
| *mother* | haha | okaasan |
| *older brother* | ani | oniisan |
| *older sister* | ane | oneesan |
| *younger brother* | otooto | otootosan |
| *younger sister* | imooto | imootosan |
| *grandfather* | sofu | ojiisan |
| *grandmother* | sobo | obaasan |
| *husband* | otto, shujin | goshujin |
| *wife* | tsuma, kanai | okusan |
| *child* | kodomo | kodomosan |
| *son* | musuko | musukosan |
| *daughter* | musume | musumesan, ojoosan |

In informal situations, such as when talking to family members or close friends, people often employ terms used to refer to someone else's family to talk about their own family members. This is not the case when talking about a younger brother, younger sister, husband, wife, child, son, or daughter. You can never use **otootosan, imootosan, goshujin, okusan, kodomosan, musukosan,** or **musumesan** to refer to your own family members.

## PRACTICE 3
You are introducing your family members to others. Fill in the blanks with the appropriate family terms.

1. _____ desu.    *(This) is my father.*

2. _____ desu.    *(This) is my mother.*

3. _____ desu.    *(This) is my grandmother.*

4. _____ desu.    *(This) is my older brother.*

5. _____ desu.    *(This) is my older sister.*

6. _____ desu.    *(This) is my younger brother.*

## PRACTICE 4
Imagine you are showing your friend a picture of Ms. Yamada's family. Fill in the blanks with the appropriate family terms.

1. Yamada-san no _____ desu.    *(This) is Ms. Yamada's father.*

2. Yamada-san no _____ desu.    *(This) is Ms. Yamada's mother.*

3. Yamada-san no _____ desu.    *(This) is Ms. Yamada's grandfather.*

4. Yamada-san no _____ desu.    *(This) is Ms. Yamada's older sister.*

5. Yamada-san no _____ desu.    *(This) is Ms. Yamada's older brother.*

6. Yamada-san no _____ desu.    *(This) is Ms. Yamada's younger sister.*

### *Culture note*
There are different ways of addressing one's own parents in Japanese. The most common way is to address your father as **otoosan** and your mother as **okaasan**. In the western part of Japan, such as

Kyoto and Osaka, one's father is often addressed as **otoochan** and one's mother as **okaachan,** especially by children and teenagers. Children often address their father as **papa** and their mother as **mama,** but some people continue to use these words even after they have grown up. It is just a matter of preference. To some people, it sounds awkward if people in their thirties or forties use **papa** and **mama** when addressing their own parents, but to others, the use of these loanwords is fine and even fashionable.

## ANSWERS
**PRACTICE 1: 1.** Mr./Ms. Tanaka is there. **2.** I have (an) older sister(s). **3.** Yukari has (a) Chinese friend(s). **4.** (An) Italian person/people is/are there. **5.** Peter has (a) Japanese friend(s). **6.** Do you have any siblings?

**PRACTICE 2: 1.** Smith-san ga imasu. **2.** Kodomo ga imasu. **3.** (Watashi wa) ani ga imasu. **4.** (Watashi wa) imooto ga imasu. **5.** Furansujin ga imasu ka?

**PRACTICE 3: 1.** Chichi; **2.** Haha; **3.** Sobo; **4.** Ani; **5.** Ane; **6.** Otooto

**PRACTICE 4: 1.** otoosan; **2.** okaasan; **3.** ojiisan; **4.** oneesan; **5.** oniisan; **6.** imootosan

──────────── Lesson 6 (phrases) ────────────

## PHRASE LIST 1
| | |
|---|---|
| **gonin kazoku** | *five people in a family* |
| **sannin kyoodai** | *three children in a family* |
| **hitorikko** | *only child* |
| **ryooshin to issho ni** | *together with parents* |

NOTE I
Note that the postposition **to** is used in the last phrase in the meaning of *with*. Remember that we encountered it used with the meaning of *and* earlier.

## NUTS & BOLTS 1
### Counting from 1–20: Numbers and People

Japanese has a complex counting system. It will be discussed in more detail in Lesson 9; in this lesson, let's learn how to count from one to twenty and how to count people.

| | | | |
|---|---|---|---|
| *one* | ichi | *one person* | hitori |
| *two* | ni | *two people* | futari |
| *three* | san | *three people* | sannin |
| *four* | shi, yon | *four people* | yonin |
| *five* | go | *five people* | gonin |
| *six* | roku | *six people* | rokunin |
| *seven* | shichi, nana | *seven people* | shichinin, nananin |
| *eight* | hachi | *eight people* | hachinin |
| *nine* | kyuu, ku | *nine people* | kyuunin, kunin |
| *ten* | juu | *ten people* | juunin |
| *eleven* | juuichi | *eleven people* | juuichinin |
| *twelve* | juuni | *twelve people* | juuninin |
| *thirteen* | juusan | *thirteen people* | juusannin |
| *fourteen* | juushi | *fourteen people* | juuyonin |
| *fifteen* | juugo | *fifteen people* | juugonin |
| *sixteen* | juuroku | *sixteen people* | juurokunin |
| *seventeen* | juushichi, juunana | *seventeen people* | juushichinin, juunananin |
| *eighteen* | juuhachi | *eighteen people* | juuhachinin |
| *nineteen* | juukyuu, juuku | *nineteen people* | juukyuunin, juukunin |
| *twenty* | nijuu | *twenty people* | nijuunin |

If you know how to count from one to ten, you can automatically form numbers from eleven to twenty. For instance, **juuichi** (*eleven*) is a combination of ten and one, and **juugo** (*fifteen*) is a combination of ten and five. **Nijuu** (*twenty*) is a combination of two and ten.

The ending **nin** has to be attached to numbers when counting people. Note that the expressions **hitori** (*one person*) and **futari** (*two people*) are irregular and don't have this ending.

## PRACTICE 1
How do you say these numbers in Japanese?

1. fifteen

2. three

3. sixteen

4. ten

5. seven

6. eighteen

7. four

8. eleven

9. nine

10. twenty

## PRACTICE 2
Give the Japanese equivalent.

1. seven people

2. one person

3. four people

4. ten people

5. two people

6. sixteen people
7. twenty people
8. three people
9. nine people
10. eleven people

### PHRASE LIST 2

| | |
|---|---|
| chichi mo haha mo | *both my father and mother* |
| kookoo no suugaku no sensee | *high school mathematics teacher* |
| chuugaku no Eego no sensee | *junior high school English teacher* |
| daigaku no keezai no sensee | *university economics teacher* |
| keeri no tantoo | *being in charge of accounting* |
| Andy-san no okyuuryoo no tantoo | *being in charge of Andy's salary* |
| donna shigoto | *what kind of work* |
| Amerika ni imasu | *to be in the U.S.A.* |
| soshite | *and, and then* |
| shigoto no ato de | *after work* |

### NUTS & BOLTS 2
#### WORD ORDER IN JAPANESE NOUN PHRASES

In Lesson 2 you learned about the Japanese possessive construction. Now, let's look at the word order within all kinds of noun phrases. As pointed out in Lesson 2, the possessor marker **no** can connect two or more nouns, as in:

**John no otoosan no kaisha**
*John's father's company*

In some cases the order of words within noun phrases is the same as that in corresponding English noun phrases.

**Amerika no eega**
*an American movie*

**Mary-san no daigaku**

*Mary's university*

**kookoo no suugaku no sensee**

*high school mathematics teacher*

**chuugaku no ongaku no sensee**

*junior high school music teacher*

In other cases the order of nouns within Japanese and English noun phrases differs.

**Ken-san no daigaku no sensee**

*a professor at Ken's university (lit., Ken's university's professor)*

**Andy-san no okyuuryoo no tantoo**

*being in charge of Andy's salary (lit., Andy's salary's being in charge)*

In either case in Japanese, the base noun that is modified by other parts of a noun phrase appears at the end of the phrase. For instance, in the case of **kookoo no suugaku no sensee** and **Ken-san no daigaku no sensee, sensee** is modified by **kookoo no suugaku no** and **Ken-san no daigaku no**. Likewise, in the case of **Andy-san no okyuuryoo no tantoo, tantoo** is modified by **Andy-san no okyuuryoo**. Because in these cases a modifying phrase contains more than one noun, like **kookoo no suugaku, Ken-san no daigaku,** and **Andy-san no okyuuryoo,** their relationship needs to be determined next, and again, it is determined based on word order. In the case of **kookoo no suugaku** and **Ken-san no daigaku, suugaku** and **daigaku** are modified by **kookoo no** and **Ken-san no,** respectively. In the case of **Andy-san no okyuuryoo, okyuuryoo** is modified by **Andy-san.**

## PRACTICE 3
Choose the right translation for the following noun phrases.

1. *Sam's mother's older sister*

   a. okaasan no Sam no oneesan

   b. Sam no okaasan no oneesan

   c. oneesan no okaasan no Sam

2. *Yumiko's French teacher*

   a. Yumiko-san no Furansugo no sensee

   b. Furansugo no sensee no Yumiko-san

   c. sensee no Yumiko-san no Furansugo

3. *employees at a Japanese company*

   a. kaisha no shain no Nihon

   b. Nihon no kaisha no shain

   c. kaisha no Nihon no shain

4. *economics class at a university*

   a. daigaku no kurasu no keezaigaku

   b. kurasu no keezaigaku no daigaku

   c. daigaku no keezaigaku no kurasu

5. *my Spanish friend Carlos*

   a. Supeinjin no Carlos no tomodachi

   b. Supeinjin no tomodachi no Carlos

   c. Carlos no Supeinjin no tomodachi

## ANSWERS

**PRACTICE 1: 1.** juugo; **2.** san; **3.** juuroku; **4.** juu; **5.** nana, shichi; **6.** juuhachi; **7.** yon, shi; **8.** juuichi; **9.** kyuu, ku; **10.** nijuu

**PRACTICE 2: 1.** nananin, shichinin; **2.** hitori; **3.** yonin; **4.** juunin; **5.** futari; **6.** juurokunin **7.** nijuunin; **8.** sannin; **9.** kyuunin, kunin; **10.** juuichinin

**PRACTICE 3: 1.** b; **2.** a; **3.** b; **4.** c; **5.** b

—————————— Lesson 7 (sentences) ——————————

## SENTENCE GROUP 1

| | |
|---|---|
| **Nannin kazoku desu ka?** | *How many people are there in your family?* |
| **Gonin kazoku desu.** | *There are five people in my family.* |
| **Nannin kyoodai desu ka?** | *How many children do your parents have?* |
| **Sannin kyoodai desu.** | *My parents have three children.* |
| **Kyoodai ga nannin imasu ka?** | *How many siblings do you have?* |
| **Kyoodai ga futari imasu.** | *I have two siblings.* |
| **Gokazoku wa minasan Amerika ni imasu ka?** | *Is your family all in the U.S.A.?* |
| **Ane to otooto wa ryooshin to issho ni ima Tookyoo ni imasu.** | *My older sister and younger brother are now in Tokyo with my parents.* |
| **Sore zya mata shigoto no ato de.** | *See you after work, then.* |

## NUTS & BOLTS 1
### QUESTIONS WITH QUESTION WORDS

As discussed in Lesson 4, the formation of simple yes-no questions and questions with question words is very simple in Japanese. Questions with question words were briefly introduced in Lesson 4, but let's look at them more closely here. First look at the following examples where questions with **nan(i)** (*what*) and its variants are listed.

**Nan desu ka?**
*What is it/he/she?/What are they?*

**Nansai desu ka?**
*How old are you?*

**Nannin desu ka?**
*How many people?*

**Nanigo o hanashimasu ka?**
*What language(s) do you speak?*

**Nanijin desu ka?**
*What nationality are you?*

Remember that only **nan** can appear before the copula **desu**. Also, some counters are combined with **nan**, like **nannin** and **nansai**, but others take **nani**, like **nanigo** and **nanijin**. Now, let's look at questions with other question words.

**Doko/Dochira desu ka?** (more polite with **dochira**)
*Where is it?*

**(O)ikutsu desu ka?** (more polite with **o**)
*How old are you?/How many?* (without **o**)

**Dare/Donata desu ka?** (more polite with **donata**)
*Who is/are he/she/it/they?*

**Itsu desu ka?**
*When is it?*

**(O)ikura desu ka?** (polite with **o**)
*How much is/are it/they?*

**Donna oshigoto desu ka?**
*What kind of job is it?*

**Dooshite/Naze/Nande desu ka?**
*Why is it?*

Note that **dochira** and **donata** are polite forms of **doko** and **dare,** respectively. As discussed earlier, when forming questions with question words, you replace a word in question with a question word. Look at the following examples and compare the position of the question words in the questions with the position of the words being questioned in the answers.

Q. **Goshusshin wa dochira desu ka?**
*Where are you from? (lit., Where is your place of origin?)*

A. **(Shusshin wa) oosaka desu.**
*I'm from Osaka. (lit., [My place of origin] is Osaka.)*

Q. **Shitsuree desu ga, oikutsu/nansai desu ka?**
*Excuse me, but how old are you?*

A. **Sanjuugo-sai desu.**
*I'm thirty-five years old.*

Q. **Hai, donata desu ka?** (A doorbell rings.)
*Yes, who is it?*

A. **Koyama desu.**
*It's Koyama.*

Q. Seminaa wa itsu desu ka?

*When is the seminar?*

A. (Seminaa wa) ashita desu.

*(The seminar) is tomorrow.*

Q. Osushi wa ikura desu ka?

*How much is sushi?*

A. (Sushi wa) sanzen-en (*three thousand yen*) desu.

*(Sushi) is three thousand yen.*

Q. John-san wa donna hito desu ka?

*What kind of person is John?*

A. John-san wa ii hito desu.

*John is a good person.*

Q. Dooshite/Naze/Nande desu ka? (Your question to a friend who cannot come to the party.)

*Why is it?*

A. Byooki desu kara (*because*).

*That's because I'm sick.*

## PRACTICE 1
Fill in the blanks with appropriate question words.

dare, itsu, nannin, nansai, dochira

1. A: Goshusshin wa _____ desu ka?

   B: Sapporo desu.

2. A: Gokazoku wa _____ desu ka?

   B: Gonin desu.

3. A: Shitsuree desu ga, _____ desu ka?

   B: Nijuusan-sai desu.

4. A: Paatii *(party)* wa _____ desu ka?

   B: Ashita desu.

5. A: _____ desu ka? (You are pointing to a woman in a photograph.)

   B: John-san no oneesan desu.

## SENTENCE GROUP 2

| | |
|---|---|
| Otootosan wa kaishain desu ka? | *Is your younger brother a company employee?* |
| Chichi mo haha mo kyooshi desu. | *Both my father and my mother are teachers.* |
| Chichi wa kookoo no suugaku no sensee de, haha wa chuugaku no Eego no sensee desu. | *My father is a high school mathematics teacher, and my mother is a junior high school English teacher.* |
| Oneesan mo sensee desu ka? | *Is your older sister also a teacher?* |
| Andy-san no gokazoku wa? | *What about your family, Andy?* |
| Uchi wa chichi wa isha de, haha wa shufu desu. | *As for my family, my father is a doctor, and my mother is a housewife.* |
| Andy-san no oshigoto wa? | *What's your occupation, Andy?* |
| Watashi wa denkigishi desu. | *I'm an electrical engineer.* |
| Ono-san wa keeri no tantoo desu ne? | *Mr. Ono, you are in charge of accounting, right?* |
| Shain no okyuuryoo no tantoo desu. | *I'm in charge of employees' salaries.* |

## NUTS & BOLTS 2
### TE-FORM OF THE COPULA DESU

When one or more nouns are connected, the postposition **to** *(and, with)* is used in Japanese.

**sensee to seeto**

*a teacher and a student*

Unlike in English, the same word cannot be used to connect verbs, adjectives, and a copula **desu**. To connect two or more actions, events, or descriptions, a so-called **te**-form of verbs, adjectives, and copula **desu** is used. The following English sentences show the contexts where **te**-forms would need to be used in Japanese.

*I got up at 6, had breakfast, and left home at 7:00.*
*This apartment is clean, spacious, and inexpensive.*
*Mariko is nineteen years old and a college student.*

We will discuss the **te**-form of verbs and adjectives in Lesson 16 and Lesson 38; here we're focusing on **de**, the **te**-form of copula **desu**. See how the first two sentences in the following example are combined into one sentence in the third example.

**Chris-san wa Amerikajin desu.**
*Chris is American.*

**Chris-san wa bengoshi desu.**
*Chris is a lawyer.*

**Chris-san wa Amerikajin de, bengoshi desu.**
*Chris is American and a lawyer.*

Here are some more examples.

**Kyoko-san wa daigakusee desu.**
*Kyoko is a college student.*

**Kyoko-san no senmon wa keezai desu.**
*Kyoko's specialty is economics.*

**Kyoko-san wa daigakusee de, senmon wa keezai desu.**
*Kyoko is a college student, and her specialty is economics.*

**Chichi wa isha desu.**
*My father is a doctor.*

**Haha wa shufu desu.**
*My mother is a housewife.*

**Chichi wa isha de, haha wa shufu desu.**
*My father is a doctor, and my mother is a housewife.*

Note that the **te**-form does not express tense, which is expressed by the last copula, verb, or adjective in a sentence. The copula **desu**—and its plain form counterpart **da**—expresses present or future tense, and its **te**-form **de** makes no reference to tense.

## PRACTICE 2
Connect sentences using **de,** the **te**-form of the copula **desu.**

1. Watashi wa Amerikajin desu. Shusshin wa Nyuu Yooku desu.

2. Ani wa suugaku no kyooshi desu. Ane wa ginkooin desu.

3. Lopez-san wa Mekishikojin desu. Lopez-san wa Supeingo to Eego o hanashimasu.

4. Lisa-san wa daigakusee desu. Lisa-san no senmon wa keezai desu.

5. Chichi mo haha mo kyooshi desu. Chichi mo haha mo Tookyoo ni imasu.

*Tip!*

Describe your family using **te**-form of the copula **desu** as much as possible. You can talk about their occupations, ages, places of origin, languages they speak, etc. Next describe someone else's family—for instance, your friend's family—again using **te**-form of the copula **desu**. In this way you can practice two different forms of family terms, and at the same time, practice connecting two or more sentences together.

## ANSWERS

**PRACTICE 1: 1.** dochira; **2.** nannin; **3.** nansai; **4.** itsu; **5.** dare

**PRACTICE 2: 1.** Watashi wa Amerikajin de, shusshin wa Nyuu Yooku desu. **2.** Ani wa suugaku no kyooshi de, ane wa ginkooin desu. **3.** Lopez-san wa Mekishikojin de, Supeingo to Eego o hanashimasu. **4.** Lisa-san wa daigakusee de, senmon wa keezai desu. **5.** Chichi mo haha mo kyooshi de, Tookyoo ni imasu.

——————— Lesson 8 (conversations) ———————

## CONVERSATION 1

Andy and his Japanese colleague Mr. Ono are talking about their family on their way to their company.

Ono: Andy-san wa nannin kazoku desu ka?

Andy: Gonin kazoku desu. Chichi to haha to ani to imooto to watashi desu.

Ono: Soo desu ka. Gokazoku wa minasan Amerika ni imasu ka?

Andy: Ryooshin to imooto wa Amerika ni imasu. Demo, ani wa ima Mekishiko ni imasu.

Ono: Hee. Mekishiko desu ka.

Andy: Ono-san wa gokyoodai ga imasu ka?

Ono: Ee, sannin imasu. Ane to imooto to otooto desu.

Andy: Zyaa, yonin kyoodai desu ne. Ono-san no gokazoku wa minasan Tookyoo ni imasu ka?

Ono: Iie. Ane wa ima Oosaka ni imasu. Sore kara imooto to otooto wa ryooshin to issho ni Nagano ni imasu.

Andy: Soo desu ka. Jaa, goshusshin wa Nagano desu ka?

Ono: Ee, soo desu yo. Ah, kaisha desu ne. Jaa, mata shigoto no ato de.

Andy: Sore zya, mata.

Ono: Andy, how many people are in your family?

Andy: There are five people in my family: my father, mother, older brother, younger sister, and me.

Ono: I see. Are they all in the U.S.A.?

Andy: My parents and younger sister are in the U.S.A. But my older brother is currently in Mexico.

Ono: Oh, Mexico.

Andy: Do you have any siblings, Mr. Ono?

Ono: Yes, I have three siblings. An older sister, a younger sister, and a younger brother.

Andy: Then, there are four children in your family, right? Is your whole family in Tokyo, Mr. Ono?

Ono: No. My older sister is now in Osaka. And, my younger sister and younger brother are in Nagano with my parents.

Andy: I see. Then, are you from Nagano?

Ono: Yes, that's right. Oh, we have arrived at the company. So, see you again after work.

Andy: See you then.

NOTE I

Note that there is an important distinction between the sentences **Kyoodai ga sannin imasu** and **Sannin kyoodai desu**. The first sentence means the subject has three siblings, and the second sentence means there is a total of three children in a family.

**(Watashi wa) kyoodai ga sannin imasu** is easier to understand because its English translation is *I have three siblings*, and it indicates that there are three siblings besides the speaker. However, **(Watashi wa) sannin kyoodai desu** may be a little confusing. In this case, **sannin kyoodai** is treated as a unit, and the direct translation of the sentence is *(As for me,) there are three siblings*, indicating that the speaker is counted in the group of three siblings.

# NUTS & BOLTS 1
## Describing the location of subjects

You learned how to describe the existence of animate subjects, such as people and animals in Lesson 5. Now let's learn how to express the location of such subjects. As mentioned in Lesson 5, the location is marked by the postposition **ni** in the following structure.

> **Y ni X ga imasu.**
> *There is/are X in Y.*

**Oosaka ni sofu to sobo ga imasu.**
*I have a grandfather and grandmother in Osaka.*

**Honkon ni tomodachi ga imasu.**
*I have (a) friend(s) in Hong Kong.*

**Okinawa ni shinseki ga imasu.**
*I have relatives in Okinawa.*

Note that these sentences in general describe who is at a certain location. So, the first sentence above can be the answer to the following question.

**A: Oosaka ni dare ga imasu ka?**
*Who do you have in Osaka?*

**B: (Oosaka ni) sofu to sobo ga imasu.**
*I have a grandfather and grandmother (in Osaka).*

When answering the question, it is therefore not necessary to express **Oosaka ni** (*in Osaka*) because it is understood from the context. To describe where someone is, the following structure is used, with the location phrase following a topic.

> **X wa Y ni imasu.**
> *X is in/at Y. (lit., As for X, it/he/she is in Y.)*

**Ani wa Doitsu ni imasu.**
*My older brother is in Germany.*

**Ane wa Kanada ni imasu.**
*My older sister is in Canada.*

**Chichi to haha wa Tookyoo ni imasu.**
*The father and mother are in Tokyo.*

Since these sentences are describing where the subject is, the first sentence above can be the answer to the following question.

**Q. Oniisan wa doko ni imasu ka?**
*Where is your older brother?*

**A. (Ani wa) Nyuu Yooku ni imasu.**
*My older brother is in New York. (lit., As for my older brother, he is in New York.)*

In this case, **ani wa** can be dropped in the answer because it is understood from the context.

## PRACTICE 1
Answer the following questions with sentences using the structure **Y ni X ga imasu.** X is provided in parentheses.

1. Tookyoo ni dare ga imasu ka? (tomodachi)

2. Daidokoro *(kitchen)* ni dare ga imasu ka? (haha)

3. Ima *(living room)* ni dare ga imasu ka? (chichi)

4. Niwa *(garden)* ni dare ga imasu ka? (otooto to imooto)

5. Senmenjo ni dare ga imasu ka? (ani)

## PRACTICE 2

Answer the following questions with sentences using the structure X **wa** Y-location **ni imasu**. The location is provided in parentheses.

1. Goryooshin wa doko desu ka? (Amerika)

2. Imootosan wa doko desu ka? (gakkoo)

3. Oniisan wa doko desu ka? (kaisha)

4. Suzuki-san wa doko desu ka? (daigaku)

5. Oneesan wa doko desu ka? (Furansu)

## CONVERSATION 2

Andy and Mr. Ono are walking to the train station after the work.

Andy: Ono-san no otoosan wa kaishain desu ka?

Ono: Iie, chichi mo haha mo kyooshi desu. Chichi wa kookoo no suugaku no sensee de, haha wa chuugaku no Eego no sensee desu.

Andy: Zyaa, oneesan to imootosan mo sensee desu ka?

Ono: Ane wa ongaku no sensee desu ga, imooto wa webudezainaa desu. Andy-san no gokazoku wa?

Andy: Uchi wa chichi wa isha de, haha wa shufu desu. Ani wa ginkooin de, imooto wa kangofu desu.

Ono: Soo desu ka. Soshite, Andy-san wa enjinia desu ne?

Andy: Ee, denki gishi desu. Ono-san wa keeri no tantoo desu ne?

Ono: Un, Andy-san no okyuuryoo no tantoo desu yo.

Andy: Soo desu kaa. Hahahahaha. (laughing)

*Andy: Mr. Ono, is your father a company employee?*

*Ono: No. Both my father and mother are school teachers. My father is a high school math teacher, and my mother is a junior high school English teacher.*

*Andy:* Then, your older sister and younger sister are also teachers?

*Ono:* My older sister is a music teacher, but my younger sister is a web designer. What about your family, Andy?

*Andy:* As for my family, my father is a doctor, and my mother is a homemaker. My older brother is a bank clerk, and my younger sister is a nurse.

*Ono:* I see. And, Andy, you are an engineer, right?

*Andy:* Yes, I'm an electrical engineer. Mr. Ono, you are in charge of the accounting, right?

*Ono:* Yes, I'm in charge of your salary, Andy.

*Andy:* I see. (laughing)

## NUTS & BOLTS 2
### HONORIFIC PREFIXES O- AND GO-

An honorific is a word or a word prefix or suffix that conveys respect towards other people. Honorifics are similar to titles like *Mr., Ms., Sir,* or *Dr.* You learned earlier the honorific suffix -**san**, which was introduced in Lesson 1. The system of Japanese honorifics is complex. For instance, verbs too can have honorifics attached to them and have two different forms: the honorific form and the humble form.

In this lesson, we look at honorific prefixes **o-** and **go-**, which usually attach to nouns to make them sound more polite. Some nouns take **o** and others take **go**, but it is not the case that every noun can take either **o** or **go**. At this level, it is not necessary to worry about which nouns take **o** or **go** and which nouns do not. As you are exposed to the language, you will naturally learn it. Here are some examples of words with the honorific prefix.

| kazoku *(family)* | gokazoku |
|---|---|
| kyoodai *(siblings)* | gokyoodai |
| kodomo *(child)* | okosan |

| | |
|---|---|
| namae *(name)* | onamae |
| denwa *(telephone)* | odenwa |
| shigoto *(job, work)* | oshigoto |
| ryooshin *(parents)* | goryooshin |
| fuufu *(married couple)* | gofuufu |
| shinseki *(relatives)* | goshinseki |
| juusho *(address)* | gojuusho |
| ikutsu *(how old)* | oikutsu |
| kyuuryoo *(salary)* | okyuuryoo |

If you add honorific prefixes to words when talking to someone, your language will be more polite and hence, will show respect toward the addressee. For instance, when you are telling your own name and address, you will say **Namae wa X desu** (*My name is X*) and **Juusho wa X desu** (*My address is X*), whereas when asking someone's name and address, it is more polite if you say **Onamae wa nan desu ka?** (*What is your name?*) and **Gojuusho wa dochira desu ka?** (*What is your address?*). By adding honorific prefixes, the language becomes more formal, and hence, you can show respect toward the addressee.

It is important to remember that honorific prefixes cannot be added to words when talking about oneself. In some cases, even when talking about oneself, an honorific prefix cannot be avoided, because with time it got inseparable from a word. For instance, very common words **okane** (*money*) and **ocha** (*tea*) are usually used in the formal form in all occasions; **kane** and **cha** are infrequent. Finally, note that female speakers tend to add honorific prefixes more often when they talk about others to be more polite and often, to sound more sophisticated.

## PRACTICE 3
Pick the right form of the word according to the context.

1. _____ wa nannin desu ka?

   a. kyoodai

   b. gokyoodai

2. Watashi wa _____ ga futari imasu.

   a. kyoodai

   b. gokyoodai

3. Watashi no _____ wa ima Tookyoo ni imasu.

   a. ryooshin

   b. goryooshin

4. _____ wa ogenki desu ka?

   a. ryooshin

   b. goryooshin

5. _____ desu yo. (You are talking to a division manager at your company.)

   a. Denwa

   b. Odenwa

## PRACTICE 4
Fill in the blanks with the appropriate words. You are allowed use the same word more than once.

desu, de, imasu, hanashimasu

1. Ani wa ima kyooto ni _____.

2. Takashi-san wa nanigo o _____ ka?

3. Lisa-san wa chuugokujin _____, shusshin wa honkon desu.

4. Chichi mo haha mo ginkooin _____.

5. Gokyoodai wa _____ ka?

---

## *Cool links*

You can browse more than 1,800 books and videos about Japanese culture and life on the O-Hayo Sensei's Japan Bookstore webpage at www.ohayosensei.com/books/Welcome.html. Books on various subjects, such as travel and exploration, living, the traditional world, and contemporary and pop culture, can be found on the site, and they are all written in English. O-Hayo Sensei is a free electronic newsletter listing English teaching jobs in Japan, which you can view at www. ohayosensei.com/current.html.

---

## ANSWERS
**PRACTICE 1: 1.** Tookyoo ni tomodachi ga imasu. **2.** Daidokoro ni haha ga imasu. **3.** Ima ni chichi ga imasu. **4.** Niwa ni otooto to imooto ga imasu. **5.** Senmenjo ni ani ga imasu.

**PRACTICE 2: 1.** (Ryooshin wa) Amerika ni imasu. **2.** (Imooto wa) gakkoo ni imasu. **3.** (Ani wa) kaisha ni imasu. **4.** (Suzuki-san wa) daigaku ni imasu. **5.** (Ane wa) Furansu ni imasu.

**PRACTICE 3: 1.** b; **2.** a; **3.** a; **4.** b; **5.** b

**PRACTICE 4: 1.** imasu; **2.** hanshimasu; **3.** de; **4.** desu; **5.** imasu

# UNIT 3
## *Everyday life*

Welcome to Unit 3! Here you will learn how to talk about your daily life. You will also learn how to express your likes and dislikes.

────────────── Lesson 9 (words) ──────────────

## WORD LIST 1

| | |
|---|---|
| Nichiyoobi | *Sunday* |
| Getsuyoobi | *Monday* |
| Kayoobi | *Tuesday* |
| Suiyoobi | *Wednesday* |
| Mokuyoobi | *Thursday* |
| Kin'yoobi | *Friday* |
| Doyoobi | *Saturday* |
| mainichi | *every day* |
| kyoo | *today* |
| ashita | *tomorrow* |
| kinoo | *yesterday* |
| asatte | *the day after tomorrow* |
| ototoi | *the day before yesterday* |
| heejitsu | *weekday* |
| shuumatsu | *weekend* |
| konshuu | *this week* |
| raishuu | *next week* |
| senshuu | *last week* |
| asa | *morning* |
| hiru | *noon* |
| yuugata | *early evening* |
| yoru, ban | *evening, night* |

| | |
|---|---|
| gogo | *afternoon, p.m.* |
| gozen | *morning, a.m.* |
| asagohan | *breakfast* |
| hirugohan | *lunch* |
| bangohan, yuuhan | *dinner* |
| yoku | *often* |
| tokidoki | *sometimes* |
| tamani | *once in a while* |
| a(n)mari (+ negative) | *not so often, not so much* |

## NUTS & BOLTS 1
### COUNTERS

As pointed out in Lesson 6, counters are terms similar to English expressions like *a piece of, a loaf of, a glass of,* and *a cup of.* They stand between the number and the noun that the number modifies. The difference is that Japanese must use counters in combination with numbers regardless of the type of noun that follows; in English, the quantity expressions above are only used with so-called mass nouns, e.g., *a cup of tea,* or nouns denoting objects that cannot be counted.

Japanese has many different types of counters, and they are classified according to the physical properties of the object a noun represents. One of the counters, **nin**, used when counting people, was already introduced in Lesson 6, but there are some other counters you should become familiar with at this level. For instance, **mai** is used when thin flat objects, such as *paper, handkerchiefs, T-shirts,* and *blankets,* are counted; **hon** is used when long cylindrical objects, such as *pens, pencils,* and *umbrellas,* are counted.

**kami** (*paper*) **juu-mai**

*ten pieces of paper*

**hankachi** (*handkerchief*) **sanmai**

*three handkerchiefs*

**enpitsu** (*pencil*) **ni-hon**
*two pencils*

**pen gohon**
*five pens*

Note that a counter usually follows a noun. The position of a counter will be discussed more in Lesson 10. The following chart gives counters for several different types of objects in combination with numbers from one to ten. A counter attaches to the end of a number. Since you already learned how to count people in Lesson 6, this will be a review for you.

| | -nin | -hiki | -mai | -hon | -satsu |
|---|---|---|---|---|---|
| | *people* | *animals* | *thin flat objects* | *long cylindrical objects* | *bound objects (e.g., books)* |
| 1 | hitori | ippiki | ichimai | ippon | issatsu |
| 2 | futari | nihiki | nimai | nihon | nisatsu |
| 3 | sannin | sanbiki | sanmai | sanbon | sansatsu |
| 4 | yonin | yonhiki | yonmai | yonhon | yonsatsu |
| 5 | gonin | gohiki | gomai | gohon | gosatsu |
| 6 | rokunin | roppiki | rokumai | roppon | rokusatsu |
| 7 | nananin, shichinin | nanahiki | nanamai | nanahon | nanasatsu |
| 8 | hachinin | happiki | hachimai | happon | hassatsu |
| 9 | kyuunin | kyuuhiki | kyuumai | kyuuhon | kyuusatsu |
| 10 | juunin | juppiki | juumai | juppon | jussatsu |

Notice that there are some irregularities and variations in the form of numbers and counters. For instance, *one person* and *two people* are not **ichinin** and **ninin**, but instead, **hitori** and **futari**, as pointed out in Lesson 6; *one (long cylindrical object)* and *three (long cylindrical objects)* are not **ichihon** and **sanhon**, but **ippon** and **sanbon**.

In Lesson 6, you also learned how to count from one to ten using numbers of Chinese origin, such as **ichi, ni, san,** etc. Now, let's learn how to count some objects using native Japanese numbers.

| 1 | hitotsu | 6 | muttsu |
|---|---------|---|--------|
| 2 | futatsu | 7 | nanatsu |
| 3 | mittsu | 8 | yattsu |
| 4 | yottsu | 9 | kokonotsu |
| 5 | itsutsu | 10 | too |

Native Japanese numbers only exist to count from one to ten, so you have to use numbers of Chinese origin from eleven on. These numbers are often used to count round objects such as balls, apples, oranges, and eggs, as well as objects that are not clearly categorized, such as furniture pieces, boxes, mountains, or stars. Also, when counting abstract things, such as ideas, questions, and problems, the native Japanese numbers are used.

**Ringo (*apple*) o hitotsu tabemasu.**
*I eat one apple.*

**Orenji (*orange*) mo mittsu tabemasu.**
*I eat three oranges, too.*

**Sofaa (*sofa*) o hitotsu kaimasu (*to buy*).**
*I will buy one sofa.*

**Shitsumon ga futatsu arimasu (*to exist*).**
*I have two questions.*

**Mondai** (*problem*) **ga hitotsu arimasu.**
*There's one problem.*

## PRACTICE 1
Which counter should you use when counting the following items? Match the right counter with the noun.

1. gakusee          a. mai

2. zasshi           b. hon

3. inu *(dog)*      c. nin

4. T-shatsu *(T-shirt)*   d. hiki

5. boorupen *(ballpoint pen)*   e. satsu

## PRACTICE 2
Fill in the blanks with the appropriate number and a counter combination.

Ex. Kodomo ga <u>sannin</u> imasu. (*three*)

1. Hon *(book)* ga _____ arimasu. *(six)*

2. Enpitsu *(pencil)* ga _____ arimasu. *(three)*

3. Kami ga _____ arimasu. *(twenty)*

4. Gakusee ga _____ imasu. *(fifteen)*

5. Inu ga _____ imasu. *(one)*

6. Ringo ga _____ arimasu. *(ten)*

## PRACTICE 3
Provide the Japanese equivalent for the following English words.

1. *Friday*

2. *Sunday*

3. *Tuesday*

4. *Monday*

5. *Wednesday*

6. *Saturday*

7. *Thursday*

## WORD LIST 2

| | |
|---|---|
| seekatsu | *life* |
| jugyoo | *class* |
| ryoori | *cooking, cuisine* |
| hon | *book* |
| shoosetsu | *novel* |
| shinbun | *newspaper* |
| zasshi | *magazine* |
| apaato | *apartment* |
| heya | *room* |
| ima | *living room* |
| shinshitsu | *bedroom* |
| daidokoro | *kitchen* |
| senmenjo | *area with a wash stand* |
| yokushitsu | *bathroom* |
| otearai, toire | *toilet* |
| genkan | *entrance hall* |
| kaidan | *stairs* |
| niwa | *garden, yard* |
| sofaa | *sofa* |
| teeburu | *table* |
| tsukue | *desk* |
| isu | *chair* |
| beddo | *bed* |
| tansu | *chest of drawers* |
| reezooko | *refrigerator* |
| denshirenji | *microwave oven* |

| sentakuki | *washing machine* |
| terebi | *television* |
| taihen | *hard* |
| totemo | *very* |
| isogashii | *busy* |
| tanoshii | *enjoyable* |
| semai | *narrow* |
| hiroi | *spacious* |
| arimasu | *to exist* |
| shimasu | *to do* |
| rirakkusushimasu | *to relax* |
| nemasu | *to sleep, to go to bed* |
| araimasu | *to wash* |
| hairimasu | *to enter* |
| migakimasu | *to brush, to polish* |
| yomimasu | *to read* |
| suki | *to like* |
| kirai | *to dislike* |

NOTE

Even though **suki** and **kirai** correspond to the English verbs *to like* and *to dislike*, they are not verbs but **na**-adjectives, one of the groups of adjectives that will be discussed in Lessons 21, 25, and 30. Because they are adjectives, **suki** and **kirai** have to be used with the verb **desu**.

## NUTS & BOLTS 2
### CONJUGATION OF THE COPULA DESU
You learned about the copula **desu** and its **te**-form **de** in Lessons 3 and 7. Now let's look at the different tense forms of **desu**. Note that the copula **desu**, its plain-form counterpart **da**, to be discussed in Lesson 11, and all other verbs do not change their form with respect to person and number (e.g., *I walk* vs. *he walks* vs. *they walk* in English); they do change their forms to denote the difference in tense (e.g., *I walk* vs. *I walked*) and the affirmative vs. negative distinction

(e.g., *I walk* vs. *I don't walk*). Since Japanese does not distinguish between the present tense and the future tense, the term "non-past" is used in the following chart to refer to both concepts together.

| NON-PAST | | PAST | | |
| --- | --- | --- | --- | --- |
| AFFIRMATIVE | NEGATIVE | AFFIRMATIVE | NEGATIVE | TE-FORM |
| desu | ja arimasen/ de wa arimasen, ja nai desu/ de wa nai desu | deshita | ja arimasen deshita/de wa arimasen deshita, ja nakatta desu/ de wa nakatta desu | de |

Note that there are two different forms for the negative **desu**. Negative expressions with **ja** are more colloquial than those with **de wa** and are therefore heard more often in everyday conversation. The following sentences are affirmative and negative pairs.

**Watashi wa Nihonjin desu.**
*I am Japanese.*

**Watashi wa Nihonjin ja arimasen/ja nai desu.**
*I am not Japanese.*

**Ryoori ga suki desu.**
*I like cooking.*

**Ryoori ga suki ja arimasen/ja nai desu.**
*I don't like cooking.*

**Watashi wa gakusee deshita.**
*I was a student.*

**Watashi wa gakusee ja arimasen deshita/ja nakatta desu.**
*I was not a student.*

## PRACTICE 4

Turn the following sentences into a negative form.

1. Watashi wa Amerikajin desu.

2. John-san wa daigakusee deshita.

3. Lisa-san wa bengoshi desu.

4. Imooto wa tenisu ga suki desu.

5. Ani wa Eego no jugyoo ga suki deshita.

### Discovery activities

Practice counters by counting things around your house. Open the refrigerator and check how many oranges, apples, cucumbers, or other fruits or vegetables you have in it. Make a list in Japanese using appropriate counters. Next, go to the bookshelf and count in Japanese how many books are there. Because you can count only up to twenty at this moment, you can stop counting at that number. After that, check the pen and pencil holder and count how many ballpoint pens, pencils, etc., you have there. Also, check the computer printer and see how many sheets of papers are left in the paper feeder. Feel free to continue with other objects around the house in a similar way.

## ANSWERS

PRACTICE 1: 1. c; 2. e; 3. d; 4. a; 5. b

PRACTICE 2: 1. rokusatsu; 2. sanbon; 3. nijuumai; 4. juugonin; 5. ippiki; 6. too

PRACTICE 3: 1. Kin'yoobi; 2. Nichiyoobi; 3. Kayoobi; 4. Getsuyoobi; 5. Suiyoobi; 6. Doyoobi; 7. Mokuyoobi

PRACTICE 4: 1. Watashi wa Amerikajin ja arimasen/nai desu. 2. John-san wa daigakusee ja arimasen deshita/nakatta desu. 3. Lisa-san wa bengoshi ja arimasen/nai desu. 4. Imooto wa tenisu ga suki ja arimasen/nai desu. 5. Ani wa Eego no jugyoo ga suki ja arimasen deshita/nakatta desu.

## PHRASE LIST 1

| | |
|---|---|
| **Doo desu ka?** | *How is it?* |
| **Tookyoo no seekatsu** | *life in Tokyo* |
| **Nihongo no jugyoo** | *Japanese class* |
| **shoosetsu ya zasshi** | *(a) novel, (a) magazine, and so on* |
| **chotto taihen** | *a little hard* |
| **totemo isogashii** | *very busy* |
| **Getsuyoobi kara** | *from Monday* |
| **Kin'yoobi made** | *until Friday* |
| **ohiru made** | *until noon* |
| **seminaa ni demasu** | *attend the seminar* |
| **senshuu no Nichiyoobi** | *last Sunday* |
| **sorekara** | *and then* |
| **kao o araimasu** | *to wash (one's) face* |
| **ha o migakimasu** | *to brush (one's) teeth* |
| **shawaa o abimasu** | *to take a shower* |
| **ofuro ni hairimasu** | *to take a bath* |

NOTE 1

There is a distinction between the postpositions **to** and **ya**, which in English are both translated as *and*. **A to B** means *A and B*, but **A ya B** means *A and B, among other things*. So, for instance, if you are asked what is on the desk, you can just mention a couple of things on the desk, among others, by using **ya**, whereas you have to enumerate everything on the desk when using **to**.

## NUTS & BOLTS 1

STATIC VERB ARIMASU *(to be/to exist)*

The static verb **imasu** *(to be, to exist)* was introduced in Lesson 5. Now let's learn another static verb, **arimasu** *(to be, to exist)*. As discussed in Lesson 5, the subject of **imasu** has to be animate, such as a person or an animal. In case of **arimasu**, the subject has to be an inanimate object, such as a book, a room or a table. **Arimasu** is used in the following structure.

> **X ga arimasu.**
> *There is X./These are X.*

**Hon ga arimasu.**
*There is a book./There are books. (lit., Books exist./[A] book exists.)*

**Tsukue ga arimasu.**
*There is a desk./There are desks.*

**Sofaa ga arimasu.**
*There is a sofa./There are sofas.*

**Ima ga arimasu.**
*There is a living room./There are living rooms.*

Just like **imasu**, **arimasu** can express the notion of possession.

**Jugyoo ga arimasu.**
*I have a class./I have classes.*

**Eego no kyookasho** (*textbook*) **ga arimasu ka?**
*Do you have an English textbook?*

**Hai, arimasu.**
*Yes, we have.*

The location of inanimate subjects can be specified in the same way as the location of animate subjects discussed in Lesson 8.

**Ima ni sofaa ga arimasu.**
*There's a sofa in the living room.*

**Daidokoro ni reezooko ga arimasu.**
*There's a refrigerator in the kitchen.*

As pointed out in Lesson 8, these sentences are describing what exists at a certain location. So, for instance, the first sentence above can be the answer to the following question.

Q. Ima ni nani ga arimasu ka?

*What's in the living room?*

A. (Ima ni) sofaa ga arimasu.

*There's a sofa in the living room.*

As pointed out in Lesson 8, in the answer, **ima ni** (*in the living room*) can be dropped because it is understood from the context. Just like with **imasu**, if you want to describe where something is, use the structure **X wa Y**-location **ni arimasu**.

**Shinbun wa ima ni arimasu.**

*The newspaper is in the living room. (lit., As for the newspaper, it is in the living room.)*

**Denshirenji wa daidokoro ni arimasu.**

*The microwave oven is in the kitchen. (lit., As for the microwave oven, it is in the kitchen.)*

For instance, the first sentence above can be the answer to the following question.

Q. Shinbun wa doko ni arimasu ka?

*Where is the newspaper?*

A. (Sinbun wa) ima ni arimasu.

*The newspaper is in the living room.*

Here, **shinbun wa** can be dropped from the answer because it is understood from the context.

## PRACTICE 1

Answer the following questions with sentences using the structures **Y ni X ga arimasu** and **Y ni X ga imasu** as appropriate. Remember that Y marks location. X is provided in parentheses.

1. Senmenjo ni nani ga arimasu ka? (sentakuki)
2. Ima ni nani ga arimasu ka? (sofaa ya teeburu)
3. Daidokoro ni nani ga arimasu ka? (reezooko ya denshirenji)
4. Genkan ni dare ga imasu ka? (chichi)
5. Heya ni nani ga arimasu ka? (tansu ya tsukue ya isu)

## PRACTICE 2

Answer the following questions with sentences using the structures **X wa Y ni arimasu** and **X wa Y ni imasu** as appropriate. The location noun is provided in parentheses.

1. Beddo wa doko desu ka? (shinshitsu)
2. Terebi wa doko desu ka? (ima)
3. Denshirenji wa doko desu ka? (daidokoro)
4. Nihongo no hon wa doko desu ka? (daigaku)
5. Suzuki-san no oniisan wa doko desu ka? (apaato)

## PHRASE LIST 2

| | |
|---|---|
| Lisa-san no apaato | *Lisa's apartment* |
| maa maa | *so-so* |
| Ryoori ga suki desu. | *I like cooking. (lit., Cooking is liked.)* |
| Ryoori ga kirai desu. | *I dislike cooking. (lit., Cooking is disliked.)* |
| heya ga futatsu to daidokoro | *two rooms and a kitchen* |
| ima to shinshitsu | *a living room and a bedroom* |
| ima ni | *in the living room* |
| shinshitsu ni | *in the bedroom* |

| | |
|---|---|
| sofaa to teeburu to terebi | *a sofa, a table, and a television* |
| beddo to tsukue | *a bed and a desk* |
| chotto semai | *a little small (lit., narrow)* |

## NUTS & BOLTS 2
### EXPRESSING QUANTITY OF EXISTING ITEMS

To specify the number of items that exist, the number accompanied by an appropriate counter is placed just before the verb:

> **X ga** + numeral + counter + **arimasu/imasu**.

The following sentences illustrate how this structure is used.

**Heya ga mittsu arimasu.**
*There are three rooms.*

**Sofaa ga hitotsu arimasu.**
*There is one sofa.*

**Hon ga gosatsu arimasu.**
*There are five books.*

**Enpitsu ga roppon arimasu.**
*There are six pencils.*

**Inu ga sanbiki imasu.**
*There are three dogs./I have three dogs.*

**Kodomo ga sannin imasu.**
*There are three children./I have three children.*

It is important to know that the numeral + counter phrase in this structure doesn't need to be followed by any particle. The location of items can be expressed in the same way as illustrated in Lesson 8 and Nuts & bolts 1 section of this lesson.

**Ima ni isu ga itsutsu arimasu.**
*There are five chairs in the living room.*

**Shinshitsu ni tansu ga hitotsu arimasu.**
*There's one chest of drawers in the bedroom.*

**Niwa ni kodomo ga sannin imasu.**
*There are three children in the garden.*

## PRACTICE 3
Translate into English.

1. Pen ga ippon arimasu.

2. T-shatsu ga gomai arimasu.

3. Ane ga futari imasu.

4. Nooto (*notebook*) ga jussatsu arimasu.

5. Heya ga itsutsu arimasu.

## PRACTICE 4
Match each sentence with the right translation.

1. *I have one younger brother.*      a. Pen ga sanbon arimasu.

2. *There are two rooms.*      b. Kami ga gomai arimasu.

3. *There are three pens.*      c. Otooto ga hitori imasu.

4. *There are eight books.*      d. Heya ga futatsu arimasu.

5. *There are six sheets of paper.*      e. Hon ga hassatsu arimasu.

## *Cool links*

Because you are learning Japanese, you probably want to know what is happening in Japan, right? Of course, it is possible to obtain up-to-date Japanese news online. The URLs of some of the websites are listed here.

www.asahi.com/english

www.yomiuri.co.jp/dy/

www.nni.nikkei.co.jp

## ANSWERS

**PRACTICE 1: 1.** Senmenjo ni sentakuki ga arimasu. **2.** Ima ni sofaa ya teeburu ga arimasu. **3.** Daidokoro ni reezooko ya denshirenji ga arimasu. **4.** Genkan ni chichi ga imasu. **5.** Heya ni tansu ya tsukue ya isu ga arimasu.

**PRACTICE 2: 1.** Beddo wa shinshitsu ni arimasu. **2.** Terebi wa ima ni arimasu. **3.** Denshirenji wa daidokoro ni arimasu. **4.** Nihongo no hon wa daigaku ni arimasu. **5.** Suzuki-san no oniisan wa apaato ni imasu.

**PRACTICE 3: 1.** *There's one pen.* **2.** *There are five T-shirts.* **3.** *I have two older sisters.* **4.** *A microwave oven is in the kitchen.* **4.** *There are ten notebooks.* **5.** *There are five rooms.*

**PRACTICE 4: 1.** c; **2.** d; **3.** a; **4.** e; **5.** b

─────── Lesson 11 (sentences) ───────

## SENTENCE GROUP 1

| | |
|---|---|
| **Tookyoo no seekatsu wa doo desu ka?** | *How's your life in Tokyo?* |
| **Chotto taihen desu.** | *It's a bit hard.* |
| **Tanoshii desu.** | *It's fun.* |
| **Heejitsu wa mainichi totemo isogashii desu.** | *On weekdays, I am very busy every day.* |
| **Shuumatsu wa nani o shimasu ka?** | *What do you do on weekends?* |

| Hooritsu no seminaa ni demasu. | *I attend a law seminar.* |
| Nichiyoobi wa rirakkusushimasu. | *I relax on Sunday.* |
| Jugyoo ga Getsuyoobi kara Kin'yoobi made arimasu. | *I have classes from Monday to Friday.* |
| Tamani ohiru made nemasu. | *Once in a while, I sleep until noon.* |
| Gogo wa tokidoki shoosetsu ya zasshi o yomimasu. | *I sometimes read a novel, magazines, and so on, in the afternoon.* |

## NUTS & BOLTS 1
### GA AS OBJECT MARKER

You learned earlier that direct objects are marked by the particle **o** in Japanese, while subjects are followed by the particle **ga**. When expressing likes or dislikes in Japanese, **na**-adjectives **suki** (*like*) and **kirai** (*dislike*) are used and their logical objects are marked by **ga** as well.

> X wa Y ga suki/kirai desu.

**Watashi wa tenisu ga suki desu.**
*I like tennis.*

Note that the English subject *I* corresponds to the Japanese topic noun **watashi wa**, and the English direct object *tennis* corresponds to the Japanese subject noun **tenisu ga**. So, you can think of the Japanese structure as similar to the English passive construction, as in *Tennis is liked by me.* Here are more examples.

**Chichi wa gorufu ga suki desu.**
*My father likes golf.*

**Imooto wa keeki ga suki desu.**
*My younger sister likes cake.*

A similar construction is used to express understanding using the verb **wakarimasu** (*to understand*).

| X wa Y ga wakarimasu. |
| --- |

The following sentences illustrate this structure.

**Ichiroo-san wa Eego ga wakarimasu.**
*Ichiro understands English.*

**Nihongo ga wakarimasu ka?**
*Do you understand Japanese?*

## PRACTICE 1
The following people like the item expressed by the noun inside the parentheses. Make sentences using **suki desu** to express that.

1. John (piza [*pizza*])

2. Lisa (ryoori)

3. Ichiroo (tenisu)

4. Mariko (shoosetsu)

5. Judy (Furansugo no jugyoo)

## SENTENCE GROUP 2

| | |
| --- | --- |
| **Apaato wa doo desu ka?** | *How's your apartment?/What's your apartment like?* |
| **Apaato ga suki desu.** | *I like my apartment.* |
| **Apaato ga daisuki desu.** | *I like my apartment very much./I love my apartment.* |
| **Apaato ga kirai desu.** | *I don't like my apartment. (lit., I dislike my apartment.)* |
| **Heya ga futatsu to daidokoro ga arimasu.** | *There are two rooms and a kitchen.* |

| Heya wa ima to shinshitsu desu. | *The rooms are a living room and a bedroom.* |
| Takusan kagu ga arimasu ka? | *Is there a lot of furniture?* |
| Ima ni sofaa to teeburu to terebi ga arimasu. | *There are a sofa, a table, and a television in the living room.* |
| Heya wa chotto semai desu kedo, daidokoro wa hiroi desu yo. | *The rooms are a bit small (lit., narrow) but the kitchen is spacious.* |
| Ryoori ga suki desu ka? | *Do you like cooking?* |
| Maa maa desu. | *So-so.* |

## NUTS & BOLTS 2

### DA: THE PLAIN FORM OF COPULA DESU

You are already familiar with the conjugation of the copula **desu** and its **te**-form **de**. Now, let's look at the conjugation of **da**, the plain form of **desu**.

| NON-PAST | | PAST | |
|---|---|---|---|
| AFFIRMATIVE | NEGATIVE | AFFIRMATIVE | NEGATIVE |
| da | ja nai/de wa nai | datta | ja nakatta/de wa nakatta |

As pointed out in Lesson 9, **ja** is the contracted form of **de wa** and more colloquial than **de wa**. While **ja** is more often used in everyday conversation, **de wa** is used in formal writting. Similarly, the polite form of the copula, **desu**, is used in formal settings, and its plain form, **da**, is used in casual settings. The following sentences would be more likely to be used among friends and family members.

**Lopez-san wa Mekishikojin da yo.**
*Mr./Mrs./Ms. Lopez is Mexican (I assure you).*

**John-san wa bengoshi da yo.**
*John is a lawyer (I assure you).*

**Kyoo wa Nichiyoobi ja nai yo.**
*Today is not Sunday (I assure you.)*

**Lisa-san wa sensee ja nakatta ne.**
*Lisa was not a teacher, right?*

**Kinoo wa Doyoobi datta ne.**
*Yesterday was Saturday, wasn't it?*

In daily conversations, **da** is usually accompanied by sentential particles **ne** or **yo**. Without them, the expression sounds bookish. Also, note that in questions, **da**, as well as the question particle **ka**, is dropped.

**John-san wa bengoshi?** (with rising intonation)
*Is John a lawyer?*

**Kyoo wa Nichiyoobi?** (with rising intonation)
*Is it Sunday today?*

**Lopez-san wa Mekishikojin?** (with rising intonation)
*Is Mr./Mrs./Ms. Lopez Mexican?*

## PRACTICE 2
Change the sentences using **da**, the plain form of copula **desu**.

Ex. Kyoo wa Getsuyoobi desu yo.–Kyoo wa Getsuyoobi <u>da</u> yo.
Ashita wa Doyoobi ja arimasen yo.–Ashita wa Doyoobi <u>ja nai</u> yo.

1. John-san wa Igirisujin ja arimasen ne.

   John-san wa Igirisujin _____ ne.

2. Ototoi wa Mokuyoobi deshita ne.

   Ototoi wa Mokuyoobi _____ ne.

3. Mariko-san wa daigakusee desu yo.

Mariko-san wa daigakusee _____ yo.

4. Nihongo no hon ja arimasen ne.

Nihongo no hon _____ ne.

5. Seminaa wa kinoo ja arimasen deshita yo.

Seminaa wa kinoo _____ yo.

## Culture note

The Japanese word **kirai** corresponds to English *to dislike*. However, the expression **a(n)mari suki ja arimasen/nai desu** (*don't like so much*) is more often used to express dislike. This is because indirectness is expected given the importance placed on politeness in Japanese society. Using **a(n)mari suki ja arimasen**, instead of **kirai desu**, helps avoid sounding abrupt or impolite. Also, Japanese speakers can just simply say **a(n)mari** without even uttering the rest of the sentence. The addressee will understand what the speaker is trying to say from the context.

## ANSWERS
PRACTICE 1: 1. John-san wa piza ga suki desu. 2. Lisa-san wa ryoori ga suki desu. 3. Ichiroo-san wa tenisu ga suki desu. 4. Mariko-san wa shoosetsu ga suki desu. 5. Judy-san wa Furansugo no jugyoo ga suki desu.

PRACTICE 2: 1. John-san wa Igirisujin ja nai ne. 2. Ototoi wa Mokuyoobi datta ne. 3. Mariko-san wa daigakusee da yo. 4. Nihongo no hon ja nai ne. 5. Seminaa wa kinoo ja nakatta yo.

## CONVERSATION 1

Daisuke and Ellie are talking about their daily life at a university cafeteria.

Daisuke: Ellie-san, Tookyoo no seekatsu wa doo desu ka?

Ellie: Nihongo no jugyoo ga Getsuyoobi kara Kin'yoobi made arimasu kara, chotto taihen desu. Demo, tanoshii desu yo.

Daisuke: Boku mo heejitsu wa mainichi totemo isogashii desu.

Ellie: Daisuke-san wa shuumatsu wa nani o shimasu ka?

Daisuke: Doyoobi wa yoku keezaigaku no seminaa ni demasu ga, Nichiyoobi wa rirakkusu shimasu.

Ellie: Rirakkusu?

Daisuke: Un. Takusan nemasu yo. Tamani ohiru made nemasu. Sore kara gogo wa tokidoki shoosetsu ya zaashi o yomimasu.

Ellie: Hee. Ii desu ne.


Daisuke: *Ellie, how's your life in Tokyo?*

Ellie: *I have Japanese classes from Monday to Friday, so it's a bit hard. But I enjoy it.*

Daisuke: *I am also very busy every day on weekdays.*

Ellie: *What do you do on weekends, Daisuke?*

Daisuke: *I often attend a seminar in economics on Saturdays, but I just relax on Sundays.*

Ellie: *Relax?*

Daisuke: *Yes. I sleep a lot. I sometimes sleep until noon. And then from time to time, I read a novel, magazines, and so on, in the afternoon.*

Ellie: *Oh, that's nice, isn't it?*

NOTE 1

You have already learned several Japanese postpositions, such as **ni,** **kara,** and **made.** Remember that postpositions always follow nouns.

## NUTS & BOLTS 1
### THE BASICS OF JAPANESE VERBS: VERB FORMS, CLASSES, AND TENSE

There are two basic verb forms in Japanese: the **masu**-form and the plain form. The **masu**-form is a polite form of verbs, and the plain form is an informal form of verbs, normally used when talking to family members and friends. The plain form is also used in newspaper writing. The plain form of verbs will be discussed in Lesson 13, so let's learn the **masu**-form of verbs in this lesson. The **masu**-form is obtained by adding **masu** to the verb stem in the case of a non-past affirmative verb forms like **hanashimasu,** **arimasu,** and **imasu.** Remember that the term "non-past" is used because the present tense and the future tense are not distinguished in Japanese.

Japanese verbs can be divided into three different classes. As pointed out in Lesson 9, Japanese verbs, as well as the copula **desu** (and its plain-form counterpart **da**), only conjugate with respect to tense and to the affirmative and negative distinction. The following table represents the non-past tense affirmative form.

| Non-past tense affirmative form | | |
| --- | --- | --- |
| Class I (**u**-verbs) | Class II (**ru**-verbs) | Class III (irregular verbs) |
| **hanashimasu** (*speak/speaks*) | **demasu** (*attend/attends, leave/leaves*) | **kimasu** (*come/comes*) |
| **yomimasu** (*read/reads*) | **nemasu** (*sleep/sleeps, go/goes to bed*) | **shimasu** (*do/does*) |

There are only two verbs in Class III, and they are the irregular verbs **kimasu** (*come/comes*) and **shimasu** (*do/does*). The conjugation of the **masu**-form of verbs is very simple because it is the same for all three verb classes. For the non-past tense negative form, **masen** is attached instead of **masu**.

| Non-past negative form | | |
|---|---|---|
| Class I (**u**-verbs) | Class II (**ru**-verbs) | Class III (irregular verbs) |
| **hanashimasen** (*do/does not speak*) | **demasen** (*do/does not attend, do/does not leave*) | **kimasen** (*do/does not come*) |
| **yomimasen** (*do/does not read*) | **nemasen** (*do/does not sleep, do/does not go to bed*) | **shimasen** (*do/does not do*) |

For the past tense affirmative form, change **masu** to **mashita**.

| Past affirmative form | | |
|---|---|---|
| Class I (**u**-verbs) | Class II (**ru**-verbs) | Class III (irregular verbs) |
| **hanashimashita** (*spoke*) | **demashita** (*attended, left*) | **kimashita** (*came*) |
| **yomimashita** (*read*) | **nemashita** (*slept, went to bed*) | **shimashita** (*did*) |

For the past tense negative form, just add **deshita** to the non-past tense negative form.

| Past negative form | | |
|---|---|---|
| Class I (**u**-verbs) | Class II (**ru**-verbs) | Class III (irregular verbs) |
| **hanashimasen deshita** (*did not come*) | **demasen deshita** (*did not attend, did not leave*) | **kimasen deshita** (*did not speak*) |
| **yomimasen deshita** (*did not do*) | **nemasen deshita** (*did not sleep, did not go to bed*) | **shimasen deshita** (*did not read*) |

## PRACTICE 1

Fill in the blanks with the appropriate form of the verbs in parentheses.

1. Kinoo jugyoo ni _____ ka? (demasu)

   *Did you attend the class yesterday?*

2. Ashita tomodachi ga _____. (kimasu)

   *A friend/Friends of mine is/are coming tomorrow.*

3. Senshuu hon o _____. (yomimasu)

   *I did not read a book/books last week.*

4. John-san wa Supeingo o _____. (hanashimasu)

   *John does not speak Spanish.*

5. Shuumatsu seminaa ga _____ ka? (arimasu)

   *Was there a seminar on the weekend?*


## CONVERSATION 2

Jessica is talking with her Japanese friend Ryoko in a university cafeteria.

Ryoko: Jessica-san no apaato wa doo desu ka?

Jessica: Ii desu yo. Heya ga futatsu to daidokoro ga arimasu. Heya wa ima to shinshitsu desu.

Ryoko: Soo desu ka. Takusan kagu ga arimasu ka?

Jessica: Iie. Ima ni sofaa to teeburu to terebi ga arimasu. Soshite shinshitsu ni beddo to tansu to tsukue ga arimasu. Chotto semai desu kedo, daidokoro wa hiroi desu yo.

Ryoko: Jessica-san wa ryoori ga suki desu ka?

Jessica: Ee, suki desu yo. Ryoko-san no apaato wa doo desu ka?

Ryoko: Etto, maa maa desu.

Ryoko: How's your apartment, Jessica?

Jessica: It's nice. There are two rooms and a kitchen. The rooms are a living room and a bedroom.

Ryoko: I see. Is there a lot of furniture?

Jessica: No. There is a sofa, a table and a television in the living room. And there is a bed, a chest of drawers, and a desk in the bedroom. The rooms are a bit small, but the kitchen is big.

Ryoko: Do you like cooking, Jessica?

Jessica: Yes, I like it. How's your apartment, Ryoko?

Ryoko: Well, so-so.

NOTE 1

The expression **maa maa desu** (*so-so*) is often used in everyday conversation. You can avoid saying either *good* or *bad* by using this expression. It is a convenient expression to remember.

## NUTS & BOLTS 2

### CONJUNCTIONS KARA, NODE, KEDO, AND GA

Conjunctions **kara** (*so*) and **node** (*because, since*) are used to express the reason or cause. **Kara** and **node** appear at the end of a sentence where the reason is stated; this sentence is followed by a second sentence where the conclusion or the result is stated. **Kara** can follow either the polite or the plain form of a verb, copula, or adjective, but **node** usually follows only the plain form. The following sentences show how **kara** and **node** are used. Note that **da**, the plain form of the copula **desu**, becomes **na** before **node**.

**Daidokoro ga ookii desu kara/ookii kara, ii desu.**

**Daidokoro ga ookii node, ii desu.**

*The kitchen is big, so it is good.*

**Ashita tomodachi ga kimasu kara/kuru kara, seminaa ni demasen.**

**Ashita tomodachi ga kuru node, seminaa ni demasen.**

*I will not attend the seminar because friends/a friend of mine will come tomorrow.*

Gakusee desu kara/gakusee da kara, benkyooshimasu.

Gakusee na node, benkyooshimasu.

*I study because I'm a student.*


Kyoo wa Nichiyoobi desu kara/Nichiyoobi da kara, ohiru made nemashita.

Kyoo wa Nichiyoobi na node, ohiru made nemashita.

*Since it is Sunday today, I slept until noon.*


Now, let's look at conjunctions **kedo** (*but*) and **ga** (*but*). **Kedo** and **ga** appear at the end of the first sentence just like **kara** and **node**. The following sentences show them used in example sentences. **Kedo** and **ga** can be used interchangeably.

Ashita wa Nichiyoobi desu kedo/ga, seminaa ga arimasu.

*It's Sunday tomorrow, but there is a seminar.*

John-san wa Amerikajin desu kedo/ga, Nihongo o hanashimasu.

*John is American but speaks Japanese.*


Now, let's compare **kedo** and **ga** with **demo** (*but*) which was introduced in Lesson 1. Note that **demo** appears at the beginning of an independent sentence, whereas **kedo** and **ga** appear at the end of a subordinate sentence.

Ashita wa Doyoobi desu kedo/ga, jugyoo ga arimasu.

*It is Saturday tomorrow, but there is a class/there are classes.*

Ashita wa Doyoobi desu. Demo, jugyoo ga arimasu.

*It is Saturday tomorrow. But, there is a class/there are classes.*

## PRACTICE 2

Connect the two sentences using the conjunctions given in parentheses.

1. a. Kyoo wa Nichiyoobi desu.

   b. Rirakkusu shimasu. (kara)

2. a. Heya wa semai desu.

   b. Kagu ga takusan arimasu.(kedo)

3. a. Ashita wa Doyoobi desu.

   b. Jugyoo ga arimasu. (ga)

4. a. Hon ga suki desu.

   b. Yoku hon o yomimasu. (node)

5. a. Haha wa Tookyoo ni imasu.

   b. Chichi wa ima Nyuu Yooku ni imasu. (demo)

---

### Tip!

It is very important to practice the key structures in as many ways as possible. For instance, you can say **X ga arimasu/imasu** by substituting **X** with whatever you see in your surroundings. If you are at home, **X** can be your family members, furniture, electric appliances, books, food, etc. If you are at your school, **X** can be your classmates, teachers, desks, textbooks, etc. If you are at your office, **X** can be your boss, colleagues, office supplies, computers, copy machines, etc. If you don't know the Japanese word for **X** or for a location, you can even say it in your own language. The most important thing is to keep repeating the key structures until you stop thinking about how they are put together.

---

## ANSWERS

**PRACTICE 1: 1.** demashita; **2.** kimasu; **3.** yomimasen deshita; **4.** hanashimasen; **5.** arimashita

**PRACTICE 2: 1.** Kyoo wa Nichiyoobi desu kara, rirakkusushimasu. **2.** Heya wa semai desu kedo, kagu ga takusan arimasu. **3.** Ashita wa Doyoobi desu ga, jugyoo ga arimasu. **4.** Hon ga suki na node, yoku hon o yomimasu. **5.** Haha wa Tookyoo ni imasu. Demo, chichi wa ima Nyuu Yooku ni imasu.

# UNIT 4
## *Work and school*

Welcome to Unit 4! You've done a great job so far and learned a lot of Japanese words and structures. In Unit 4, you will learn how to talk about such important things such as your school or your work.

———————— Lesson 13 (words) ————————

### WORD LIST 1

| | |
|---|---|
| yoochien | *kindergarten* |
| shoogakkoo | *elementary school* |
| daigakuin | *graduate school* |
| daigakuinsee | *graduate student* |
| toshokan | *library* |
| shinrigaku | *psychology* |
| keieigaku | *business management* |
| repooto | *report* |
| happyoo | *presentation* |
| gruupu happyoo | *group presentation* |
| miitingu | *meeting* |
| densha | *train* |
| chikatetsu | *subway* |
| basu | *bus* |
| kuruma | *car* |
| shinkansen | *Japanese bullet train* |
| hikooki | *airplane* |
| kami | *paper* |
| enpitsu | *pencil* |
| pen | *pen* |

| boorupen | *ballpoint pen* |
|---|---|
| mannenhitsu | *fountain pen* |
| benkyooshimasu/benkyoosuru | *to study* |
| nyuugakushimasu/nyuugakusuru | *to enter school* |
| sotsugyooshimasu/sotsugyoosuru | *to graduate* |
| ikimasu/iku | *to go* |
| kimasu/kuru | *to come* |
| kaerimasu/kaeru | *to go back, to return* |
| modorimasu/modoru | *to return* |
| norimasu/noru | *to ride, to get on* |
| orimasu/oriru | *to get off* |
| karimasu/kariru | *to borrow* |
| kashimasu/kasu | *to lend* |
| ichinenkan | *for a year* |
| hantoshikan | *for half a year* |

NOTE 1

From this point on, both the **masu**-form and the dictionary form (plain non-past affirmative form) of verbs will be listed in all word lists.

## NUTS & BOLTS 1
### THE PLAIN NON-PAST TENSE FORM OF VERBS

In Lesson 12, it was pointed out that there are two basic verb forms in Japanese—the **masu**-form and the plain form. The plain form is mostly used in more casual settings, whereas the **masu**-form is more formal. Let's look at the plain form of verbs now. Remember that, as discussed in Lesson 12, Japanese verbs can be divided into three different classes. The following chart lists some of the verbs in each group.

| Class I | Class II | Class III |
|---|---|---|
| hanashimasu (*to speak*) | tabemasu (*to eat*) | shimasu (*to do*) |
| yomimasu (*to read*) | nemasu (*to sleep, to go to bed*) | kimasu (*to come*) |
| ikimasu (*to go*) | mimasu (*to see, to watch*) | |
| kaimasu (*to buy*) | oshiemasu (*to teach*) | |
| arimasu (*to exist*) | imasu (*to exist*) | |

Remember that only **shimasu** and **kimasu** make up the Class III verbs. Now, let's look at the plain non-past forms of the above verbs.

| Class I | | Class II | | Class III | |
|---|---|---|---|---|---|
| Non-past affirmative | Non-past negative | Non-past affirmative | Non-past negative | Non-past Affirmative | Non-past negative |
| hanasu | hanasanai | taberu | tabenai | suru | shinai |
| yomu | yomanai | neru | nenai | kuru | konai |
| iku | ikanai | miru | minai | | |
| kau | kawanai | oshieru | oshienai | | |
| aru | nai | iru | inai | | |

The plain non-past affirmative form is called the dictionary form because verbs are listed in this form in dictionaries. When you compare a **masu**-form and a dictionary form of a Class I verb, you will notice that if you drop -**imasu** from the **masu**-form and then attach -**u**, you will get the dictionary form of the verb. Likewise, if you drop the final -**u** from the dictionary form and attach -**imasu**, you will get the verb's **masu**-form counterpart. Note that in the case of **hanashimasu** (*to speak*), you need to drop -**himasu** in order to get the dictionary form. This rule applies to the verbs whose **masu**-form ends with -**shimasu**, like **hanashimasu** (*to speak*), **sagashimasu** (*to look for*), and **hikkoshimasu** (*to move [to a* *new location]*). Next, in order to get the plain non-past negative form of Class I verbs, you drop -u from the dictionary form and attach -**anai**. Note that in case of **kau** (*to buy*) you need to attach -**wanai** instead of -**anai** in order to get the plain non-past negative form. This rule applies to the verbs whose dictionary forms end with -au, such as **kau** (*to buy*), **au** (*to meet*), **tsukau** (*to use*), and **arau** (*to wash*). Also, it is important to remember that the plain non-past negative form of **aru** (*to exist*) is **nai**.

Now, let's look at the conjugation of Class II verbs. The conjugation of Class II verbs is much simpler. If you drop -**masu** from the **masu**-form of verbs and attach -**ru**, you will get the dictionary form counterparts of the verbs, and if you attach -**nai**, you will get the plain non-past negative form. It is also useful to remember that the dictionary forms of Class II verbs end with either -**iru** or -**eru**, e.g., **taberu** (*to eat*) and **miru** (*to see*), with some exceptions. Some of the exceptions are **kaeru** (*to return*), **hairu** (*to enter*), **kiru** (*to cut*), and **hashiru** (*to run*). These end with -**eru** or -**iru**, but they are Class I verbs. It is clear by now that Class I and Class II verbs are also called **u**-verbs and **ru**-verbs because their dictionary forms end with -**u** and -**ru** respectively. As for the conjugation of Class III verbs, you just have to memorize them. It should not be so difficult because there are only two verbs in this class.

## PRACTICE 1
Are the following verbs Class I, Class II or Class III?

1. taberu (*to eat*)

2. yomu (*to read*)

3. suru (*to do*)

4. miru (*to see*)

5. kuru (*to come*)

6. iku (*to go*)

7. neru (*to sleep, to go to bed*)

8. kaku (*to write*)

9. aru (*to exist*, for inanimate subjects)

10. iru (*to exist*, for animate subjects)

## PRACTICE 2
Give the plain non-past negative form of the following verbs.

1. taberu (*to eat*)

2. yomu (*to read*)

3. suru (*to do*)

4. miru (*to see*)

5. kuru (*to come*)

6. iku (*to go*)

7. neru (*to sleep, to go to bed*)

8. kau (*to buy*)

9. aru (*to exist*, for inanimate subjects)

10. iru (*to exist*, for animate subjects)

## WORD LIST 2

| | |
|---|---|
| kaisha | *company* |
| booekigaisha | *trading company* |
| jimusho | *office* |
| hooritsu jimusho | *law firm* |
| maaketingu | *marketing* |
| rirekisho | *resume* |
| fakkusu | *fax* |
| kopii | *copy* |
| konpyuuta/konpyuutaa | *computer* |
| waapuro | *word processor* |

| | |
|---|---|
| shimasu/suru | *to do* |
| tsukaimasu/tsukau | *to use* |
| wakarimasu/wakaru | *to understand* |
| hatarakimasu/hataraku | *to work* |
| sagashimasu/sagasu | *to look for* |
| tabun | *perhaps* |
| takusan | *many, much* |

## PRACTICE 3

Give the dictionary forms of the following verbs.

1. shimasu (*to do*)

2. ikimasu (*to go*)

3. mimasu (*to see*)

4. yomimasu (*to read*)

5. nemasu (*to sleep, to go to bed*)

6. kimasu (*to come*)

7. arimasu (*to exist*)

8. tabemasu (*to eat*)

9. sagashimasu (*to look for*)

10. imasu (*to exist*, for animate subjects)

### *Tips!*

Mastering the conjugation of the plain form of verbs is the key to improving your Japanese. The best way to become comfortable with these forms is to keep reviewing them every day. Even though there are rules you can apply when conjugating verbs, the best way is to repeat the different forms many times until you can produce them without thinking. For instance, pick five verbs every morning and conjugate them as many times as possible throughout the day. You will be able to conjugate them easily by the evening.

## ANSWERS

**PRACTICE 1: 1.** Class II; **2.** Class I; **3.** Class III; **4.** Class II; **5.** Class III; **6.** Class I; **7.** Class II; **8.** Class I; **9.** Class I; **10.** Class II

**PRACTICE 2: 1.** tabenai; **2.** yomanai; **3.** shinai; **4.** minai; **5.** konai; **6.** ikanai; **7.** nenai; **8.** kawanai; **9.** nai; **10.** inai

**PRACTICE 3: 1.** suru; **2.** iku; **3.** miru; **4.** yomu; **5.** neru; **6.** kuru; **7.** aru; **8.** taberu; **9.** sagasu; **10.** iru

―――――――――― Lesson 14 (phrases) ――――――――――

## PHRASE LIST 1

| | |
|---|---|
| **daigaku de benkyooshimasu** | *study/studies at a university* |
| **daigaku ni/e ikimasu** | *go/goes to a university* |
| **daigaku ni nyuugakushimasu** | *enter a university* |
| **daigaku o sotsugyooshimasu** | *graduate/graduates from a university* |
| **daigakuin ni/e modorimasu** | *return/returns to graduate school* |
| **miitingu ni demasu** | *attend/attends a meeting* |
| **Nihon ni/e ryuugakushimasu** | *study/studies abroad in Japan* |
| **Nihongo o benkyooshi ni** **Nihon ni/e kimashita** | *came to Japan to study Japanese* |
| **densha ni norimasu** | *get/gets on a train* |
| **densha o orimasu** | *get/gets off a train* |
| **hon o karimasu** | *borrow/borrows a book/books* |
| **hon o kashimasu** | *lend/lends a book/books* |
| **benkyooshite imasu** | *am/is/are studying* |
| **shoogakkoo kara kookoo made** | *from elementary school to high school* |
| **repooto ya happyoo** | *report and presentation, among other things* |

NOTE I
Note that in the expression **daigaku o sotsugyooshimasu** (*to graduate from a university*), **daigaku o** (*university*) is followed by the

object marker **o**. This is because in Japanese, unlike in English, the word has a role of a direct object.

## NUTS & BOLTS 1
### POSTPOSITIONS E, NI, AND DE

The postposition **ni**, marking a location of an item that exists, used in the structure **X wa Y ni arimasu/imasu** was introduced in Lesson 10. Now, let's look at other Japanese postpositions **e** and **de**, as well as **ni**.

| e ni | PLACE e/ni ikimasu, kimasu, kaerimasu, modorimasu, etc. | *to go, to come, to go back, to return,* etc., *to* PLACE |
|---|---|---|
| de | PLACE de + action verb | action verb + *at/in* PLACE |

As shown in the chart above, **e** and **ni** correspond to English *to* and express the direction of the motion. Note that the translation of **ni** in English is not always *to*, even though the direction of the motion meaning is there, e.g., **densha ni noru** (*to get on a train*) and **miitingu ni deru** (*to attend a meeting*). The following sentences illustrate how **e** and **ni** are used.

**Mainichi gakkoo e/ni ikimasu.**
*I go to school every day.*

**Lisa-san wa daigaku e/ni kimasen deshita.**
*Lisa didn't come to the university.*

**Raishuu Nihon e/ni kaerimasu.**
*I will go back to Japan next week.*

**Itsu Amerika e/ni modorimasu ka?**
*When are you returning to the U.S.A.?*

As you can see from the examples, **e** and **ni** can be used interchangeably when a motion verb follows them. Now, let's look at **de**. As indicated in the chart above, **de** marks a place where some action takes place. The following sentences illustrate its use.

**Daigaku de tenisu o shimasu.**
*I play tennis at the university.*

**Uchi de hon o yomimasu.**
*I read a book at home.*

**Masao-san wa kaisha de hatarakimasu.**
*Masao works at a company.*

**John-san wa Nihon de Nihongo o benkyooshimasu.**
*John studies Japanese in Japan.*

**De** is also used when referring to means and instruments, similar to *by* and *with* in English.

**Basu de gakkoo e/ni ikimasu.**
*I go to school by bus.*

**Pen de tegami o kakimasu.**
*I write a letter with a pen.*

**Nihongo de hanashimasu.**
*I speak in Japanese. (lit., using Japanese)*

## PRACTICE 1
Fill in the blanks with the postpositions **e, ni,** or **de**.

1. John-san wa ashita Nyuu Yooku _____ kaerimasu.

   *John will return to New York tomorrow.*

2. Ima _____ konpyuuta o tsukaimashita.

   *I used a computer in the living room.*

3. Mainichi chikatetsu _____ daigaku _____ ikimasu.

*I go to the university by subway every day.*

4. Mannenhitsu _____ namae o kakimashita.

*I wrote my name with a fountain pen.*

5. Shuumatsu uchi _____ shoosetsu o yomimashita.

*I read a novel at home on the weekend.*

## PHRASE LIST 2

| | |
|---|---|
| bengoshi no shigoto | *lawyer's work* |
| maaketingu no shigoto | *marketing job* |
| Amerika no hooritsu jimusho | *law firm in the U.S.A.* |
| nihon no kaisha | *Japanese company* |
| nihongo o tsukaimasu | *use/uses Japanese* |
| shigoto de tsukaimasu | *use/uses at work* |
| shigoto o sagashimasu | *look/looks for a job* |
| Tookyoo de shigoto o sagashimasu | *look/looks for a job in Tokyo* |
| kaisha de hatarakimasu | *work/works at a company* |
| amari tsukaimasen | *don't/doesn't use so often/much* |
| yoku wakarimasen | *don't/doesn't understand well* |
| Nyuu Yooku ni wa | *in New York* |
| mada wakarimasen | *don't/doesn't know yet* |
| mada daigakusee desu | *still a college student* |

NOTE I

**Mada** can combine with both the negative and the affirmative form of verbs, copula, and adjectives. When associating with the affirmative form, it means *still*. For example, **Mada daigakusee desu** and **Mada isogashii desu** mean *I'm still a college student* and *I'm still busy* respectively. When combined with the negative form, **mada** means *not yet*. For example, **Mada wakarimasen** and **Mada uchi ni kaerimasen** mean *I don't know yet* and *I don't go home yet* respectively.

## NUTS & BOLTS 2
### EXPRESSING A PURPOSE USING NI

Purpose, as in English *I went home to eat*, is expressed in Japanese by adding the postposition **ni** to the conjunctive form of a verb. The conjunctive form of a verb is obtained by taking off **masu** from the **masu**-form of the verb.

| Masu-form of the verb | Conjunctive form of the verb |
| --- | --- |
| **benkyooshimasu** (*to study*) | **benkyooshi** |
| **tabemasu** (*to eat*) | **tabe** |
| **kaimasu** (*to buy*) | **kai** |
| **hanashimasu** (*to speak*) | **hanashi** |

Take a look at the following examples.

**Nihongo o <u>benkyooshi ni</u> Nihon e/ni kimashita.**
*I came to Japan to study Japanese.*

**Hirugohan o <u>tabe ni</u> uchi e/ni kaerimasu.**
*I go home to eat lunch.*

**Tenisu o <u>shi ni</u> daigaku e/ni ikimasu.**
*I go to the university to play tennis.*

**Eega o <u>mi ni</u> Ginza e/ni ikimashita.**
*I went to Ginza to see a movie.*

The phrase expressing a destination can also precede the phrase expressing a purpose. So, for instance, the following word order is possible for the first and the second sentences above.

**<u>Nihon e/ni</u> Nihongo o benkyooshi ni kimashita.**
*I came to Japan to study Japanese.*

<u>Uchi e/ni</u> hirugohan o tabe ni kaerimasu.

*I go home to eat lunch.*

## PRACTICE 2
Translate into English.

1. Suzuki-san wa eego o benkyooshi ni Amerika e/ni kimashita.

2. Tookyoo e/ni shigoto o sagashi ni ikimasu.

3. Otooto wa konpyuutaa o kai ni Akihabara *(name of a town in Tokyo)* e/ni ikimashita.

4. Terebi o mi ni uchi e/ni kaerimasu.

5. Ane wa toshokan e/ni hon o kari ni ikimashita.

---

### *Cool links*

You can get interesting information about the Japanese educational system on the following website:

http://web-japan.org/kidsweb/japan/schools.html.

Even though this page is designed for children, it offers good information about the Japanese school system that can be shared by adults as well.

---

## ANSWERS
PRACTICE 1: **1.** e/ni; **2.** de; **3.** de, e/ni; **4.** de; **5.** de

PRACTICE 2: **1.** *Mr./Ms. Suzuki came to the U.S.A. to study English.* **2.** *I will go to Tokyo to look for a job.* **3.** *My younger brother went to Akihabara to buy a computer.* **4.** *I will go home to watch T.V.* **5.** *My older sister went to the library to borrow books.*

## SENTENCE GROUP 1

| | |
|---|---|
| Nihon no daigaku de benkyooshimashita ka? | *Did you study at a university in Japan?* |
| Nihon no daigaku o sotsugyooshimashita. | *I graduated from university in Japan.* |
| Sorekara daigakuin e/ni ikimashita. | *After that, I went to graduate school.* |
| Amerika no daigaku o sotsugyooshimashita ka? | *Did you graduate from a university in the U.S.A.?* |
| Shoogakkoo kara kookoo made wa Amerika deshita. | *As for elementary school to high school, they were in the U.S.A.* |
| Sore kara Igirisu no daigaku ni nyuugakushimashita. | *After that, I started college (lit., entered the university) in England.* |
| Daigakuin de keieigaku o benkyooshite imasu. | *I am studying business management in graduate school.* |
| Ichinenkan Nihongo o benkyooshi ni Nihon e/ni kimashita ga, mata Amerika no daigakuin e/ni modorimasu. | *I came to Japan to study Japanese for a year but will return to graduate school in the U.S.A. again.* |
| MBA no kurasu wa doo desu ka? | *How are MBA classes?* |
| Repooto ya happyoo ga takusan arimasu kara, totemo taihen desu. | *There are a lot of reports, presentations, and so on, so it is very hard.* |
| Guruupu happyoo mo arimasu kara, yoku miitingu ni demasu. | *There are also group presentations, so I often attend meetings.* |

## NUTS & BOLTS 1

### THE TE-FORM OF VERBS

Every verb has a te-form, used when connecting two or more verbs, as in the English *I came home, ate dinner, took a shower, and went to bed.* The **te**-form of a verb is also used when making a request, as in *Please tell me*, and in forming the progressive form, as in *I am studying now.* Since the **te**-form of verbs is used frequently in everyday conversation, it is very important to remember it. The following chart represents the **te**-form of verbs in the three different verb classes.

| Class I | | Class II | | Class III | |
|---|---|---|---|---|---|
| Dictionary form | Te-form | Dictionary form | Te-form | Dictionary form | Te-form |
| **hanasu** | **hanashite** | **taberu** | **tabete** | **suru** | **shite** |
| **yomu** | **yonde** | **neru** | **nete** | **kuru** | **kite** |
| **iku** | **itte** | **miru** | **mite** | | |
| **aru** | **atte** | **Iru** | **ite** | | |

First, let's look at the **te**-form of Class I verbs. Class I verbs can be divided into four categories based on the formation of their **te**-form.

1. If the dictionary form of the verbs ends in **-ku**, like **kaku** (*to write*) or **-gu**, like **nugu** (*to take off [shoes, clothes]*), you drop **-ku** and **-gu** and attach **-ite** and **-ide** instead. So, you get **kaite** and **nuide**. Please note that **iku** (*to go*) is an exception, and its **te**-form is **itte**.

2. If the dictionary form of the verbs ends with **-u**, **-tsu**, or **-ru**, like **tsukau** (*to use*), **tatsu** (*to stand up*) and **modoru** (*to return*), you drop **-u**, **-tsu**, or **-ru** and attach **-tte**. So, you get **tsukatte**, **tatte**, and **modotte** respectively.

3. If the dictionary form of the verbs ends with **-mu**, **-nu**, or **-bu**, like **yomu** (*to read*), **shinu** (*to die*) and **asobu** (*to play [a game]*), you drop **-mu**, **-nu**, or **-bu** and attach **-nde**. So, you get **yonde**, **shinde**, and **asonde**.

4. If the dictionary form of verbs ends with -su, like **hanasu** (*to speak*), you drop **-su** and attach **shite**. So, you get **hanashite**.

Next, let's look at the **te**-form of Class II verbs. Compared to Class I verbs, the formation of the **te**-form of Class II verbs is much simpler. You just need to drop **-ru** from the dictionary form and attach **-te**. So, for instance, the **te**-form of **taberu** (*to eat*), **miru** (*to see*), **neru** (*to sleep*), and **iru** (*to exist*) are **tabete, mite, nete**, and **ite** respectively.

Finally, the **te**-forms of the two Class III verbs **suru** (*to do*) and **kuru** (*to come*) are **shite** and **kite** respectively.

## PRACTICE 1
What are the **te**-forms of the following Class I verbs?

1. yomu

2. iku

3. asobu

4. kaku

5. hanasu

6. kaeru

7. tsukau

8. tatsu

9. aru

10. modoru

## PRACTICE 2
What are the **te**-forms of the following Class II verbs?

1. neru

2. taberu

3. miru

4. deru

5. iru

## PRACTICE 3
What are the te-forms of the following Class III verbs?

1. suru

2. kuru

## SENTENCE GROUP 2

| | |
|---|---|
| **Amerika no kaisha de hataraite imasu.** | *I am working at a company in the U.S.A.* |
| **Hantoshikan Nihon de benkyooshimasu ga, mata Amerika no kaisha e/ni modorimasu.** | *I will study in Japan for half a year but will go back to the company in the U.S.A. again.* |
| **Dooshite Nihongo o benkyooshi ni Nihon e/ni kita n desu ka?** | *Why did you come to Japan to study Japanese?* |
| **Booekigaisha de Nihon no tantoo na node, shigoto de Nihongo o tsukau n desu.** | *It's that I'm in charge of Japan at my trading company, so I use Japanese a lot for my work.* |
| **Shoorai donna shigoto o shimasu ka?** | *What kind of job will you do in the future?* |
| **Mada wakarimasen kedo, tabun maaketingu no shigoto o shimasu.** | *I don't know yet, but perhaps I will take a marketing job.* |
| **Dooshite Tookyoo de hatarakanai n desu ka?** | *Why won't you work in Tokyo?* |
| **Kazoku ga Koobe ni imasu kara, Koobe de shigoto o sagasu n desu.** | *I have a family in Kobe, so I will look for a job in Kobe.* |

## NUTS & BOLTS 2
### THE PROGRESSIVE FORM OF VERBS

Let's look at the progressive form of Japanese verbs; this form corresponds to the English present progressive tense, as in *I'm eating breakfast now*. In Japanese, the progressive form is made using the **te**-form of verbs and **imasu**.

**Lisa-san wa hon o yonde imasu.**

*Lisa is reading a book.*

**John-san wa ima nete imasu.**

*John is sleeping now.*

**Mariko-san wa Furansugo o benkyooshite imasu.**

*Mariko is studying French.*

Just like the English present progressive, the Japanese progressive form, **-te imasu**, describes the currently ongoing action. For instance, the examples above describe what Lisa and John are doing at this moment. Depending on the context, the progressive form can also describe a continuing action in a longer term. For instance, the last example has two different interpretations. One is that Mariko is studying French at this moment, and the other is that she has been studying French for some certain period of time, say, for three years. Also, the negative form of the progressive form can be used with two different interpretations—to refer to an ongoing action or an action that hasn't been completed yet.

Q. **Ima hon o yonde imasu ka?**

*Are you reading a book now?*

A. **Iie, yonde imasen.**

*No, I am not reading.*

Q. **Kono hon o yomimashita ka?**

*Did you read this book?*

**A. Iie, mada yonde imasen.**
*No, I haven't read it yet.*

As shown in the fourth example above, the construction -**te/-de imasen** can also describe the action that has not been completed yet, in which case it can be translated using the English present perfect.

## PRACTICE 4
Translate into English.

1. Ima nani o shite imasu ka?
2. Sushi o tabete imasu.
3. Mainichi Nihongo o benkyooshite imasu.
4. Mada hirugohan o tabete imasen.
5. John-san wa ima seminaa ni dete imasu.
6. Mada shukudai o shite imasen.

### Culture note
Japanese company employees tend to have a strong sense of loyalty to the company they work for and a special bond with their co-workers. For example, sometimes, even if people finish their work, they remain at the office doing some other work to show solidarity with their co-workers who are still finishing their job. Also, co-workers often go to a restaurant or a bar together to have dinner or drinks after the work. Even though, compared to twenty or so years ago, individualism is more respected in the workplace, the traditional way of thinking about the company as a big family has not completely disappeared yet.

## ANSWERS
**PRACTICE 1: 1.** yonde; **2.** itte; **3.** asonde; **4.** kaite; **5.** hanashite; **6.** kaette; **7.** tsukatte; **8.** tatte; **9.** atte; **10.** modotte

PRACTICE 2: **1.** nete; **2.** tabete; **3.** mite; **4.** dete; **5.**ite

PRACTICE 3: **1.** shite; **2.** kite

PRACTICE 4: **1.** *What are you doing now?* **2.** *I am eating sushi.* **3.** *I am studying Japanese every day.* **4.** *I haven't eaten lunch yet.* **5.** *John is attending the seminar now.* **6.** *I haven't done the homework yet.*

──────────── Lesson 16 (conversations) ────────────

## CONVERSATION 1

Jim is talking with his Japanese friend Akira about their education.

Jim: Akira-san wa Nihon no daigaku de benkyooshimashita ka?

Akira: Hai. Nihon no daigaku o sotsugyooshimashita. Sore kara, daigakuin ni itte, shinrigaku o benkyooshimashita.

Jim: Soo desu ka.

Akira: Jim-san wa Amerika no daigaku o sotsugyooshimashita ka?

Jim: Boku wa shoogakkoo kara kookoo made wa Amerika deshita ga, Igirisu no daigaku ni nyuugakushimashita. Ima wa Amerika no daigakuin de keieigaku wo benkyooshite imasu.

Akira: MBA desu ne.

Jim: Ee. Ichinenkan Nihongo o benkyooshi ni Nihon e kimashita ga, mata Amerika no daigakuin ni modorimasu.

Akira: Soo desu ka. MBA no kurasu wa doo desu ka?

Jim: Repooto ya happyoo ga takusan arimasu kara, totemo taihen desu yo. Guruupu happyoo mo arimasu kara, yoku miitingu ni demasu.

Akira: Soo desu ka. Taihen desu ne.

| Jim: | Akira, did you study at a Japanese university? |
|---|---|
| Akira: | Yes. I graduated from the Japanese university and then went to graduate school and studied psychology. |
| Jim: | I see. |
| Akira: | Jim, did you graduate from a university in the United States? |
| Jim: | From elementary school to high school, I went to school in the United States, but I started college (lit., entered the university) in England. Now, I am studying business management in a graduate school in the United States. |
| Akira: | MBA, right? |
| Jim: | Yes. I came to Japan to study Japanese for one year but will go back to graduate school in the United States again. |
| Akira: | I see. How are MBA classes? |
| Jim: | It's very hard. There are many papers, presentations and so on, so it's very hard. There are also group presentations, so I often attend meetings. |
| Akira: | I see. It's hard, isn't it? |

NOTE 1

To say *(I) know* in Japanese, the progressive form of the verb **shitte imasu** is used. So, when asking someone, *Do you know?*, say **Shitte imasu ka?**, instead of **Shirimasu ka?** In case of the negative form, say **Shirimasen** (*I don't know*).

## NUTS & BOLTS 1
### THE PLAIN PAST TENSE FORM OF VERBS

The plain non-past tense form of verbs was introduced in Lesson 13. Now, let's look at the plain past tense form, first, of Class I verbs.

| Class I | | | | |
|---|---|---|---|---|
| Dictionary form | Non-past negative | Te-form | Past affirmative | Past negative |
| **hanasu** *(to speak)* | hanasanai | hanashite | hanashita | hanasanakatta |
| **yomu** *(to read)* | yoma hai | yonde | yonda | yomanakatta |
| **iku** *(to go)* | ikanai | itte | itta | ikanakatta |
| **aru** *(to have, there is)* | nai | atte | atta | nakatta |

As you can see in the chart, the plain past affirmative form of Class I verbs is very similar to the **te**-form. Since you are already familiar with the **te**-form of verbs, you just need to remember to replace **-te/-de** of the **te**-form with **-ta/-da** in order to get the plain past affirmative form. As for the plain past negative form, you just need to replace the **-nai** ending of the plain non-past negative form with the ending **-nakatta**. Next, let's look at the plain past tense form of Class II verbs.

| Class II | | | | |
|---|---|---|---|---|
| Dictionary form | Non-past negative | Te-form | Past affirmatitve | Past negative |
| **taberu** *(to eat)* | tabenai | tabete | tabeta | tabenakatta |
| **neru** *(to sleep)* | nenai | nete | neta | nenakatta |
| **miru** *(to see)* | minai | mite | mita | minakatta |
| **iru** *(to be)* | inai | ite | ita | inakatta |

As shown in the chart, you just need to drop **-ru** on the dictionary form and attach **-ta** in order to get the plain past affirmative form. As for the plain past negative form, as in the case of Class I verbs, you just need to change **-nai** of the plain non-past negative form to **-nakatta**. Finally, let's look at the plain past form of Class III verbs.

| Class III | | | | |
|---|---|---|---|---|
| Dictionary form | Non-past negative | Te-form | Past affirmatitve | Past negative |
| **suru** *(to do)* | **shinai** | **shite** | **shita** | **shinakatta** |
| **kuru** *(to come)* | **konai** | **kite** | **kita** | **konakatta** |

It is the best to memorize the conjugation of Class III verbs because there are only two verbs in this class. Note that you just need to replace -**te** in the **te**-form of the verbs with -**ta** in order to get their plain past tense form counterpart. Also, as for the plain past negative form, just like Class I and II verbs, you just need to change -**nai** of the plain non-past negative form to -**nakatta**.

## PRACTICE 1
Give the plain past tense form of the following verbs.

Ex. hanasu hanashita
    hanasanai hanasanakatta

1. taberu _____

2. yomanai _____

3. suru _____

4. konai _____

5. kaku _____

6. tsukawanai _____

7. deru _____

8. kaeru _____

9. inai _____

10. aru _____

## CONVERSATION 2

Jane and her Japanese friend Hiromi are talking about their work.

Hiromi: Jane-san wa Amerika no kaisha de hataraite
imasu ka?

Jane: Ee, booekigaisha de hataraite imasu. Watashi
wa hantoshikan Nihon de Nihongo o
benkyooshimasu ga, mata Amerika no kaisha
ni modorimasu.

Hiromi: Soo desu ka. Dooshite Nihongo o benkyooshi
ni kita n desu ka?

Jane: Booekigaisha de Nihon no tantoo na node,
shigoto de Nihongo o tsukau n desu.

Hiromi: Soo desu ka.

Jane: Hiromi-san wa mada daigakusee desu kedo,
shoorai donna shigoto o shimasu ka?

Hiromi: Mada wakarimasen kedo, tabun maaketingu no
shigoto o shimasu.

Jane: Tookyoo de hatarakimasu ka?

Hiromi: Iie.

Jane: Dooshite Tookyoo de hatarakanai n desu ka?

Hiromi: Kazoku ga Koobe ni imasu kara, Koobe de
shigoto o sagasu n desu.

Jane: Soo desu ka.

Hiromi: *Jane, are you working at a company in the U.S.A.?*

Jane: *Yes, I'm working at a trading company. I will study
Japanese in Japan for half a year, but will go back to the
company in the U.S.A. again.*

Hiromi: *I see. Why did you come to study Japanese?*

Jane: *It's that I'm in charge of Japan at my trading company,
so I use Japanese for my work.*

Hiromi: *I see.*

Jane: *Hiromi, you are still a college student, but what kind of
work will you do in the future?*

Hiromi: *I don't know yet, but perhaps I will take a marketing
job.*

> Jane: *Will you work in Tokyo?*
> Hiromi: *No.*
> Jane: *Why won't you work in Tokyo?*
> Hiromi: *It's that I have a family in Kobe, so I will look for a job in Kobe.*
> Jane: *I see.*

NOTE 2

In a casual setting, such as talking with your family and close friends, you will use the plain form instead of the **masu**-form of verbs. Also, when asking questions in informal speech, you don't usually attach the question marker **ka** to the end of the questions; instead, ask a question using rising intonation. For example, if you want to ask your close friend if he/she wants to eat something, you can just say **Taberu?** with a rising intonation.

NOTE 3

When **kaisha** (*company*) is combined with another word such as **booeki** (*trading*) or **seeyaku** (*pharmaceutical*), it becomes **gaisha**. So, a trading company is **booekigaisha**, and a pharmaceutical company is **seeyakugaisha**.

## NUTS & BOLTS 2
### THE EXPRESSION N DESU

Let's learn about the expression **n desu**. It is a colloquial expression used when stating a reason or asking for a reason or an explanation. Remember that the plain form of verbs appears before **n desu** and that **n desu** always remains the same, that is, doesn't change its form for the tense or the affirmative and negative distinction; these features are expressed on the main verb which precedes **n desu**.

A: **Dooshite Nihon e iku n desu ka?**

*Why do you go to Japan?*

B: **Nihongo o benkyoosuru n desu.**

*It's that I will study Japanese.*

A: **Dooshite daigaku e konakatta n desu ka?**

*Why didn't you come to the university?*

B: **Amerika kara tomodachi ga kita n desu.**

*It's that my friend(s) came from the U.S.A.*

Note that you can ask for a reason or seek an explanation without using **n desu**, but if you use it, your curiosity about knowing the reason will be emphasized. Compare the following sentences.

**Dooshite daigaku e kimasen deshita ka?**

*Why didn't you come to the university?*

**Dooshite daigaku e konakatta n desu ka?**

*Why didn't you come to the university?*

Since there's no English equivalent for **n desu**, these sentences have the same English translations. **N desu** expresses a nuance of a meaning. For instance, suppose a teacher is asking a student for a reason of his/her absence. If a teacher asks for a reason using **n desu**, it sounds like he/she cares about a student and really wants to know the reason for the absence.

## PRACTICE 2
Give the plain form counterpart of the following **masu**-forms of verbs.

Ex. mimasu *(non-past/affirmative)*—miru
    yomimashita *(past/affirmative)*—yonda

1. tabemasu *(non-past/affirmative)*

2. kakimashita *(past/affirmative)*

3. kimasen deshita *(past/negative)*

4. demasen *(non-past/negative)*

5. nemashita *(past/affirmative)*

6. shimashita (*past/affirmative*)

7. yomimasen deshita (*past/negative*)

8. kimashita (*past/affirmative*)

9. mimasen (*non-past negative*)

10. aru (*non-past/negative*)

## PRACTICE 3
Change the verbs inside parentheses if necessary, and complete the sentences.

1. A: Dooshite Amerika e/ni _____ n desu ka? (iku)

   *Why did you go to the U.S.A.?*

   B: Eego o _____ n desu. (benkyoosuru)

   *It's that I studied English.*

2. A: Dooshite _____ n desu ka? (neru)

   *Why don't you go to bed?*

   B: Shukudai ga takusan _____ n desu. (aru)

   *It's that there is a lot of homework.*

3. A: Dooshite Supeingo o _____ n desu ka? (hanasu)

   *Why do you speak Spanish?*

   B: Supein ni juunen _____ n desu. (iru)

   *It's that I was in Spain for ten years.*

4. A: Dooshite terebi o _____ n desu ka? (miru)

   *Why don't you watch T.V.?*

   B: Nihongo ga _____ n desu. (wakaru)

   *It's that I don't understand Japanese.*

5. A: Dooshite seminaa ni _____ n desu ka? (deru)

*Why didn't you attend the seminar?*

B: Mekishiko kara kazoku ga _____ n desu. (kuru)

*It's that my family came from Mexico.*

## Tip!

There's a good way to memorize the **te**-form of Class I and Class III verbs. It consists of remembering it while singing a song. One song you can use for this is *Mary Had a Little Lamb*. You can try singing the following with the tune of the song: **ku-ite gu-ide u, tsu, ru-tte mu, nu, bu-nde su, suru-shite kuru-kite iku-itte.** For instance, **ku-ite** means that if the dictionary form of Class I verbs ends with **ku**, like **kaku** (*to write*) and **kiku** (*to listen*), you need to replace -**ku** with -**ite** in order to get the **te**-form of the verbs, **kaite** and **kiite** respectively. Likewise, **su, suru-shite** means that in the case of Class I verbs, whose dictionary forms end in -**su**, like **hanasu** (*to speak*), and the Class III verb **suru** (*to do*), you replace -**su** and **suru** with **shite** in order to get the **te**-form of the verbs. So, in the case of **hanasu** and **suru**, you get **hanashite** and **shite** respectively.

## ANSWERS
**PRACTICE 1: 1.** tabeta; **2.** yomanakatta; **3.** shita; **4.** konakatta; **5.** kaita; **6.** tsukawanakatta; **7.** deta; **8.** kaetta; **9.** inakatta; **10.** atta

**PRACTICE 2: 1.** tabeta; **2.** kaita; **3.** konakatta; **4.** denai; **5.** neta; **6.** shita; **7.** yomanakatta; **8.** kita; **9.** minai; **10.** nai

**PRACTICE 3: 1.** itta, benkyooshita; **2.** nenai, aru; **3.** hanasu, ita; **4.** minai, wakaranai; **5.** denakatta, kita

# UNIT 5
## *Telephone and making appointments*

Welcome to Unit 5! You're almost halfway through the course. Good job! In this unit you will learn how to make an appointment on the phone. Key expressions used in telephone conversations and when making appointments, such as telling time and date or making a request, will be introduced. You will also learn more polite expressions in this unit.

——————————— Lesson 17 (words) ———————————

## WORD LIST 1

| | |
|---|---|
| biyooin | *beauty salon* |
| biyooshi | *hairdresser* |
| yoyaku | *reservation, appointment* |
| katto | *haircut* |
| karaa | *hair dye, hair color* |
| paama | *perm* |
| (o)denwabangoo (*polite with* o) | *telephone number* |
| zero, ree | *zero* |
| Gogatsu | *May* |
| mikka | *third day of the month* |
| sanji | *three o'clock* |
| juugofun | *fifteen minutes* |
| yoroshii | *good* (polite) |
| shibaraku | *for a while* |
| daijoobu | *all right* |
| taihen | *hard, very* |
| ippai | *full* |

| denwashimasu/denwasuru | *to make a phone call* |
|---|---|
| yoyakushimasu/yoyakusuru | *to make a reservation, to make an appointment* |
| okuremasu/okureru | *to be late* |
| kakarimasu/kakaru | *to take time* |

## NUTS & BOLTS 1

### Telling time, days of the week and months

First, let's learn how to ask and tell time.

**Ima nanji desu ka?**

*What time is it now?*

**Kuji nijuugofun desu.**

*It's nine twenty-five.*

Note that **ji** corresponds to English *o'clock* and **fun** corresponds to English *minute(s)*. Because you already know how to count to twelve, let's see how you can tell time from one o'clock to twelve o'clock. But, first, let's point out some variations in the numbers when used to tell time. For instance, *four o'clock* is not **yonji** but **yoji**, and *nine o'clock* is not **kyuuji** but **kuji**.

| one o'clock | two o'clock | three o'clock | four o'clock | five o'clock | six o'clock |
|---|---|---|---|---|---|
| ichiji | niji | sanji | yoji | goji | rokuji |
| seven o'clock | eight o'clock | nine o'clock | ten o'clock | eleven o'clock | twelve o'clock |
| shichiji | hachiji | kuji | juuji | juuichiji | juuniji |

To express minutes, just attach **fun** to any number, but note that in some cases **fun** becomes **pun**. For instance, *one minute* is

**ippun**, *three minutes* is **sanpun**, *six minutes* is **roppun**, *eight minutes* is **happun** (also, **hachifun**), and *ten minutes* is **juppun**. Now, let's count from one minute to ten minutes in Japanese.

| one minute | two minutes | three minutes | four minutes | five minutes |
|---|---|---|---|---|
| **ippun** | **nifun** | **sanpun** | **yonpun, yonfun** | **gofun** |
| *six minutes* | *seven minutes* | *eight minutes* | *nine minutes* | *ten minutes minutes* |
| **roppun** | **nanafun** | **happun** or **hachifun** | **kyuufun** | **juppun** |

You could continue counting all the way up to twenty minutes since you know all the numbers up to twenty, but you haven't learned yet how to count from twenty-one on. It is actually very simple because you can just combine two numbers you already know. For instance, *twenty-five* is the combination of *twenty* and *five*, so you will get **nijuugo**. *Thirty, forty, fifty*, and *sixty* are made the same way, so **sanjuu, yonjuu, gojuu**, and **rokujuu**. Because *ten minutes* is **juppun**, *thirty minutes, forty minutes, fifty minutes*, and *sixty minutes* will be **sanjuppun, yonjuppun, gojuppun**, and **rokujuppun**. It is important to note that *thirty minutes past the hour* can be **sanjuppun** or **han**. So, for instance, *1:30* is **ichiji sanjuppun** or **ichiji han**, and *6:30* is **rokuji sanjuppun** or **rokuji han**.

To distinguish between *a.m.* and *p.m.*, use **gozen** for *a.m.* and **gogo** for *p.m.* So, 1:30 *a.m.* is **gozen ichiji han**, and 1:30 *p.m.* is **gogo ichiji han**. Note the position of **gozen** and **gogo**. Unlike English *a.m.* and *p.m.*, **gozen** and **gogo** appear before the time. It is also important to remember that **nanji** translates as the English *what time*, and **nanpun** corresponds to the English *what minute(s)*.

Now, let's learn how to ask about and tell the date.

**Kyoo wa nangatsu nannichi desu ka?**
*What month and what day is it today?*

**Gogatsu mikka desu.**
*It is May 3rd.*

As shown in the examples above, you just need to attach **gatsu** to a number in order to tell months. April, July, and September require special attention because their names are **Shigatsu**, **Shichigatsu**, and **Kugatsu**. Now, let's say all the months from January to December.

| January | February | March | April | May | June |
|---|---|---|---|---|---|
| Ichigatsu | Nigatsu | Sangatsu | Shigatsu | Gogatsu | Rokugatsu |
| July | August | September | October | November | December |
| Shichigatsu | Hachigatsu | Kugatsu | Juugatsu | Juuichigatsu | Juunigatsu |

To say the day of the month, you have to memorize the terms for the *first day of the month* to the *tenth day of the month*.

| first | second | third | fourth | fifth |
|---|---|---|---|---|
| tsuitachi | futsuka | mikka | yokka | itsuka |
| sixth | seventh | eighth | ninth | tenth |
| muika | nanoka | yooka | kokonoka | tooka |

From the eleventh day of the month on, **nichi** is attached to a number, as in **juuichinichi** (*eleventh day*), **nijuusannichi** (*twenty-third day*) or **sanjuuichinichi** (*thirty-first day*), but the numbers *fourteenth, twen-*

*tieth,* and *twenty-fourth* require special attention. *Fourteenth* is **ju-uyokka,** *twentieth* is **hatsuka,** and *twenty-fourth* is **nijuuyokka.** It is also important to remember that **nangatsu** means *what month,* and **nannichi** translates as *what day.*

## PRACTICE 1
Give the following times in Japanese.

1. 7:10 _____

2. 8:05 a.m. _____

3. 12:30 p.m. _____

4. 4:20 _____

5. 6:48 _____

6. 9:16 _____

7. 11:55 _____

8. 3:29 _____

9. 1:11 a.m. _____

10. 2:53 p.m. _____

## PRACTICE 2
Give the following dates in Japanese.

1. January 1 _____

2. December 31 _____

3. April 3 _____

4. May 5 _____

5. November 20 _____

6. February 14 _____

7. June 6 _____

8. August 10 _____

9. March 7 _____

10. September 8 _____

11. July 4 _____

12. October 9 _____

## WORD LIST 2

| | |
|---|---|
| shinbun | *newspaper* |
| kyuujin | *job posting* |
| kookoku | *advertisement* |
| jinjibu | *human resources department* |
| uketsuke | *reception desk, information desk* |
| uketsukegakari | *receptionist* |
| sofuto | *software* |
| keeken | *experience* |
| depaato | *department store* |
| gozen | *morning, a.m.* |
| gogo | *afternoon, p.m.* |
| yoji | *four o'clock* |
| Kugatsu | *September* |
| hatsuka | *twentieth* |
| Kin'yoobi | *Friday* |
| gokai | *fifth floor* |
| rirekisho | *curriculum vitae* |
| mensetsu | *interview* |
| tanjoobi | *birthday* |
| yasumi | *day off, holiday, vacation* |
| kotoshi | *this year* |
| rainen | *next year* |
| kyonen | *last year* |
| haru | *spring* |

**natsu**
*summer*

**aki**
*fall, autumn*

**fuyu**
*winter*

**natsu yasumi**
*summer vacation*

**hoka**
*other*

**gonenkan**
*for five years*

**shooshoo**
*a little*

**ichido**
*once*

**kawarimasu/kawaru**
*to change*

**machimasu/matsu**
*to wait*

**matasemasu/mataseru**
*to keep someone waiting*

## NUTS & BOLTS 2
### POSTPOSITION NI

Postposition **ni** was already discussed in Lessons 10 and 14. It is used when describing a location of a person or a thing and a direction of a movement. It is also used when expressing a purpose. Now, let's learn another function of **ni**, which is marking time, month, and day.

**Shichiji han ni okimasu.**
*I wake up/get up at 7:30.*

**Hachigatsu ni Nihon e/ni ikimasu.**
*I will go to Japan in August.*

**Ichigatsu tsuitachi ni paatii o shimasu.**
*We will have a party on January 1.*

**Nan-yoobi ni gakkoo e/ni ikimasu ka?**
*What day(s) of the week do you go to school?*

Note that **ni** is not used with adverbs, such as **kyoo** (*today*), **ashita** (*tomorrow*), **kinoo** (*yesterday*), **konshuu** (*this week*), **kyonen** (*last year*), or **rainen** (*next year*), as shown in the following examples.

**Ashita Kyooto e/ni ikimasu.**
*I will go to Kyoto tomorrow.*

**Kyonen daigaku o sotsugyooshimashita.**
*I graduated from the university last year.*

It is also important to remember that the copula **desu** does not combine with **ni** as shown in the following examples.

**Ima shichiji han desu.**
*It's seven thirty now.*

**Kyoo wa Gogatsu itsuka desu.**
*Today is May fifth.*

**Ashita wa Kin'yoobi desu.**
*Tomorrow is Friday.*

## PRACTICE 3
Complete the sentences using the Japanese equivalents of the expressions in parentheses.

1. Kyoo wa _____ desu ka? (*what day of the week*)

2. _____ eega o mimashita. (*on Saturday*)

3. _____ otooto ga nihon e/ni kimasu. (*on June 20*)

4. Ane no tanjoobi wa _____ desu. (*February 3*)

5. _____ uchi e/ni kaerimasu. (*at 6:30 p.m.*)

6. _____ nemasu ka? (*what time*)

7. _____ Amerika e/ni ikimasu ka? (*what day*)

8. Ima _____ desu. (*9:10 a.m.*)

---

### Culture note

New Year's is a major holiday in Japan. Traditionally, at the end of December, people prepare special New Year's food, called **os-echiryoori**, which is meant to last throughout the holidays, and clean the entire house. On December 31, the Japanese usually eat **soba**, buckwheat noodles, wishing that they can live long and stay thin. Usually, people are off from their work for the first several days in January. In the past, most stores, shops and restaurants were closed for the first three days in January, but nowadays many major stores and shops are open even on January 1.

---

**ANSWERS**

**PRACTICE 1: 1.** shichiji juppun; **2.** gozen hachiji gofun; **3.** gogo juuniji sanjuppun/han; **4.** yoji nijuppun; **5.** rokuji yonjuuhappun/yonjuuhachifun; **6.** kuji juuroppun; **7.** juuichiji gojuugofun; **8.** sanji nijuukyuufun; **9.** gozen ichiji juuippun; **10.** gogo niji gojuusanpun

**PRACTICE 2: 1.** Ichigatsu tsuitachi; **2.** Juunigatsu sanjuuichinichi; **3.** Shigatsu mikka **4.** Gogatsu itsuka; **5.** Juuichigatsu hatsuka; **6.** Nigatsu juuyokka; **7.** Rokugatsu muika **8.** Hachigatsu tooka; **9.** Sangatsu nanoka; **10.** Kugatsu yooka; **11.** Shichigatsu yokka; **12.** Juugatsu kokonoka

**PRACTICE 3: 1.** nan-yoobi; **2.** Doyoobi ni; **3.** Rokugatsu hatsuka ni; **4.** Nigatsu mikka; **5.** (gogo) rokuji sanjuppun/han ni; **6.** nanji ni; **7.** nannichi ni; **8.** gozen kuji juppun

## PHRASE LIST 1

| | |
|---|---|
| Moshi moshi. | *Hello.* (on the phone) |
| Mooshiwake gozaimasen. | *I'm very sorry. (lit., I have no excuse.)* (polite) |
| Omachi kudasai. | *Please, wait.* (polite) |
| Omachishite orimasu. | *I/We will be waiting for you.* (polite) |
| Omatase itashimashita. | *I have kept you waiting.* (polite) |
| Kashikomarimashita. | *Certainly.* (polite) |
| Shitsureeshimasu. | *Good-bye.* (polite) |
| katto to karaa | *haircut and color* |
| onamae to odenwabangoo | *name and telephone number* |
| ashita no sanji goro | *around three o'clock tomorrow* |
| asatte no gogo yoji goro | *the day after tomorrow, around four o'clock p.m.* |
| Gogatsu mikka no sanji ni | *at three o'clock on May 3rd* |
| Kugatsu hatsuka Kin'yoobi no yoji ni | *at four o'clock on Friday, September 20th* |
| juugofun gurai | *for about fifteen minutes* |
| dono gurai | *how long, how much* |
| Nijikan gurai kakarimasu. | *It takes about two hours.* |
| okureru kamoshiremasen | *may be late* |
| soredewa | *then* |
| Hare desu./Harete imasu. | *It's sunny.* |
| Ame desu./Ame ga futte imasu. | *It's raining.* |
| Kumori desu. | *It's cloudy.* |
| Yuki desu./Yuki ga futte imasu. | *It's snowing.* |
| Kaze ga tsuyoi desu. | *The wind is strong.* |

## NOTE 1

**Shitsuree** means *impoliteness* or *rudeness*, but the expression **Shitsureeshimasu** is a polite expression and is used as a kind of greeting in a formal setting. For instance, if you're leaving after finishing a conversation with your superior at work, you will say **Shitsureeshimasu.** Also, you can use this phrase as you enter your superior's office: You will knock on the door and wait for your superior to say **Doozo.** After you open the door, say **Shitsureeshimasu** as you enter the office.

## NOTE 2

**Goro** and **gurai** both translate as *about*, but **goro** is used to indicate the approximate time, e.g., *at about five o'clock*, and **gurai** is used when telling the approximate duration, e.g., *for about ten minutes*. Pay attention to the position of these words as it is different from the position of English *about*. **Goro** and **gurai** follow the noun expressing time and duration, e.g., **goji goro** (*around five o'clock*) and **juppun gurai** (*for about ten minutes*).

## NUTS & BOLTS 1
### EXPRESSING PROBABILITY AND CONJECTURE

You can express probability and conjecture using **deshoo** and **kamoshiremasen. Deshoo** corresponds roughly to English *will probably*, and **kamoshiremasen** corresponds to English *may*.

**Rainen Nihon e iku deshoo.**

*I will probably go to Japan next year.*

**Rainin Nihon e iku kamoshiremasen.**

*I may go to Japan next year.*

It is important to remember that the plain form of verbs and adjectives is used before **deshoo** and **kamoshiremasen.** Look at the following sentences.

**Chris wa rainen Nihon e iku deshoo.**

*Chris will probably go to Japan next year.*

**Chris wa rainen Nihon e ikanai deshoo.**
*Chris will probably not go to Japan next year.*

**Chris wa kyonen Nihon e itta deshoo.**
*Chris probably went to Japan last year.*

**Chris wa kyonen Nihon e ikanakatta deshoo.**
*Chris probably didn't go to Japan last year.*

**Chris wa rainen Nihon e iku kamoshiremasen.**
*Chris may go to Japan next year.*

**Chris wa rainen Nihon e ikanai kamoshiremasen.**
*Chris may not go to Japan next year.*

**Chris wa kyonen Nihon e itta kamoshiremasen.**
*Chris may have been to Japan last year.*

**Chris wa kyonen Nihon e ikanakatta kamoshiremasen.**
*Chris may not have been to Japan last year.*

Notice that **deshoo** and **kamoshiremasen** are invariable; the plain form of verbs is conjugated for tense. Nouns can also appear before **kamoshiremasen** and **deshoo**. Look at the following sentences.

**Yamada-san wa sensee deshoo.**
*Mr./Ms. Yamada is probably a teacher.*

**Yamada-san wa sensee ja nai deshoo.**
*Mr./Ms. Yamada is probably not a teacher.*

**Yamada-san wa sensee datta deshoo.**
*Mr./Ms. Yamada was probably a teacher.*

**Yamada-san wa sensee ja nakatta deshoo.**
*Mr./Ms. Yamada was probably not a teacher.*

**Yamada-san wa sensee kamoshiremasen.**
*Mr./Ms. Yamada may be a teacher.*

**Yamada-san wa sensee ja nai kamoshiremasen.**
*Mr./Ms. Yamada may not be a teacher.*

**Yamada-san wa sensee datta kamoshiremasen.**
*Mr./Ms. Yamada may have been a teacher.*

**Yamada-san wa sensee ja nakatta kamoshiremasen.**
*Mr./Ms. Yamada may not have been a teacher.*

Note that in case of the non-past tense affirmative, the plain form of the copula, **da,** does not appear, and that **deshoo** and **kamoshiremasen** immediately follow a noun.

## PRACTICE 1
Change the verbs in parentheses into the appropriate forms to fill in the blanks.

1. Rainen chuugokugo o _____ kamoshiremasen. (benkyooshimasu)

2. Ashita tomodachi ga _____ deshoo. (kimasu)

3. Andy wa _____ kamoshiremasen. (daigakusee desu)

4. Brown-san wa nihongo o _____ deshoo. (hanashimasu)

5. Ashita paatii e _____ kamoshiremasen. (ikimasen)

6. Hayashi-san wa kinoo uchi ni _____ deshoo. (imashita)

7. Taroo wa shukudai o _____ kamoshiremasen. (shimasen deshita)

8. Smith-san wa kyoo shinbun o _____ deshoo. (yomimasen deshita)

9. Ashita wa _____ deshoo. (ame desu)

10. Sapporo wa _____ kamoshiremasen. (yuki ga futte imasu)

## PHRASE LIST 2

| | |
|---|---|
| **shinbun no kyuujin kookoku** | *a job posting in the newspaper* |
| **tantoo no mono** | *a person in charge* |
| **tantoo no mono ni/to kawarimasu** | *transfer/transfers (a phone line) to a person in charge* |

| jinjibu no Tanaka | *Tanaka in the human resources department* |
| webudezainaa no shigoto no ken de | *regarding the job of the web designer* |
| hoka no kaisha de | *at another company* |
| gokai no jinjibu ni | *to the human resources department on the fifth floor* |
| kuru toki (ni) | *when you come* |
| motte kimasu/motte kuru | *to bring something* (inanimate object) |
| motte ikimasu/motte iku | *to take something* (inanimate object) |
| Rirekisho o motte kite kudasai. | *Please bring your resume.* |
| tsurete kimasu/tsurete kuru | *to bring someone or animal* (animate object) |
| tsurete ikimasu/tsurete iku | *to take someone or animal* (animate object) |
| Tomodachi o tsurete kite kudasai. | *Please bring your friends.* |

## PRACTICE 2
Answer the following questions using **deshoo** or **kamoshiremasen** as indicated in parentheses.

1. A: Ashita paatii e ikimasu ka?

   B: _____. (*may not go*)

2. A: Shuumatsu uchi ni imasu ka?

   B: Ee, tabun _____. (*will probably be*)

3. A: John-san wa ototoi kyooto e ikimashita ka?

   B: Wakarimasen ga, _____ ne. (*may have been*)

4. A: Kyoo kanji no kuizu ga arimasu ka?

   B: Kinoo kuizu ga atta kara, kyoo wa _____. (*probably there won't be*)

5. A: Angela-san wa amerika e kaerimashita ka?

   B: _____ ne. (*may have returned*)

6. A: Junko-san wa biyooin ni denwashimashita ka?

   B: _____. (*may not have called*)

7. A: Tookyoo wa kyoo hare desu ka?

   B: _____. (*probably not sunny*) _____. (*probably be cloudy*)

8. A: Nyuuyooku wa kinoo yuki deshita ka?

   B: Wakarimasen ga, _____ ne. (*may have snowed*)

---

*Tip!*

A good way to practice some of the vocabulary you learned in this unit is to check the calendar every morning and say the month, the date, the day of the week in Japanese. Also, whenever you have a chance, you can check your watch and try telling the time in Japanese. This will help you to learn to tell dates and time without thinking.

---

## ANSWERS

**PRACTICE 1: 1.** benkyoosuru; **2.** kuru; **3.** daigakusee; **4.** hanasu; **5.** ikanai; **6.** ita; **7.** shinakatta; **8.** yomanakatta; **9.** ame; **10.** yuki ga futte iru

**PRACTICE 2: 1.** ikanai kamoshiremasen; **2.** iru deshoo; **3.** itta kamoshiremasen; **4.** nai deshoo; **5.** kaetta kamoshiremasen; **6.** denwashinakatta kamoshiremasen; **7.** hare ja nai deshoo, kumori deshoo; **8.** yuki datta/yuki ga futta kamoshiremasen

---

———————— Lesson 19 (sentences) ————————

## SENTENCE GROUP 1

| | |
|---|---|
| Lemon de gozaimasu. | *This is Lemon.* (polite) |
| Yoyakushitai n desu kedo . . . | *I want to make an appointment, but . . .* |
| Itsu ga yoroshii desu ka? | *What (lit., when) is good for you?* |
| Ashita no sanji goro ga ii n desu kedo . . . | *Around three o'clock tomorrow is good, but . . .* |

| | |
|---|---|
| Shibaraku omachi kudasai. | *Please wait for a moment.* (polite) |
| Taihen omatase itashimashita. | *I have kept you waiting for long time.* (polite) |
| Sanji wa yoyaku ga ippai desu. | *There's no opening around three o'clock.* |
| Niji han wa ikaga desu ka? | *What about two thirty?* |
| Katto to karaa o onegaishitai n desu kedo . . . | *I want (to ask for) a haircut and color, but . . .* |
| Dono gurai kakarimasu ka? | *How long will it take?* |
| Nijikan gurai deshoo. | *It will probably take about two hours.* |
| Onamae to odenwabangoo o onegaishimasu. | *Your name and telephone number, please.* |
| Asu Gogatsu mikka no sanji ni omachishite orimasu. | *We will be waiting for you at three o'clock tomorrow, on May 3rd.* |

### NOTE 1
The expression **ikaga desu ka** is a polite version of **doo desu ka**. Both expressions have two meanings: *How is X?* and *What about X?*

### NOTE 2
Note that **asu** (*tomorrow*) is a more formal version of **ashita** you learned earlier.

## NUTS & BOLTS 1
### MAKING REQUESTS WITH -TE KUDASAI
Making request in Japanese is very simple. They are made by adding **kudasai** to the **te**-form of verbs.

**Yoyakushite kudasai.**
*Please make an appointment/a reservation.*

**Denwashite kudasai.**
*Please make a phone call.*

**Namae to denwabangoo o kaite kudasai.**
*Please write your name and phone number.*

**Uchi ni kite kudasai.**

*Please come to my house.*

**Shukudai o shite kudasai.**

*Please do your homework.*

## PRACTICE 1
Make a request using the verbs in parentheses.

1. _____ kudasai. (kuru)

2. _____ kudasai. (iku)

3. _____ kudasai. (taberu)

4. _____ kudasai. (nomu)

5. _____ kudasai. (kiku)

6. _____ kudasai. (kaku)

7. _____ kudasai. (miru)

8. _____ kudasai. (iu)

9. _____ kudasai. (okiru)

10. _____ kudasai. (hanasu)

## PRACTICE 2
Make a request in the following situations.

1. *You want Mr. King to come to the party.*

King-san, _____.

2. *You want Ms. Tanaka, who is fluent in English, to speak English.*

Tanaka-san, _____.

3. *You want Ms. Lopez to teach you Spanish.*

Lopez-san, _____.

4. *You want your roommate, John, to wake up.*

John-san, _____.

5. *You want Ms. Suzuki to call you tomorrow.*

Suzuki-san, _____.

## SENTENCE GROUP 2

| | |
|---|---|
| Shinbun no kyuujinkookoku o mita n desu kedo . . . | *I saw the job posting in the newspaper, but . . .* |
| Tantoo no mono ni kawarimasu node, shooshoo omachi kudasai. | *I will transfer you to the person in charge, so please wait for a moment.* |
| Webudezainaa no shigoto no ken de odenwa shiteiru n desu ga. | *I am calling you regarding the job of the web designer.* |
| Keeken wa arimasu ka? | *Do you have any work experience?* |
| Hoka no kaisha de gonenkan uebu dezain no shigoto o shite imashita. | *I had (lit., was doing) a web-design job at another company for five years.* |
| Ichido ohanashishishitai n desu kedo. | *I want to talk with you once, but . . .* |
| Gokai no jinjibu ni kite kudasai. | *Please come to the human resources department on the fifth floor.* |
| Kuru toki ni, rirekisho o motte kite kudasai. | *Please bring your resume when you come.* |
| Nijuppun gurai deshoo. | *It will probably be about twenty minutes.* |

## NUTS & BOLTS 2
### POLITE EXPRESSIONS

Japanese polite expressions can be divided into five categories. There are polite forms of nouns and adjectives, but different degrees of politeness are often expressed by using different forms of verbs.

In informal situations, such as when talking to close friends and family members, people use the plain form of verbs or the copula **da** instead of the **masu**-form of verbs or the copula **desu**. The **masu**-form of verbs and the copula **desu** are used in a variety of more formal social settings, including the workplace.

Even though the **masu**-form of verbs is considered a polite form, you can come out as even more polite by using honorific and humble forms of verbs. An honorific form is used when describing actions taken by someone you need or want to pay respect to, like a superior at work, a teacher or a customer. When describing actions taken by the speaker himself/herself or members of his/her in-group, such as his/her family members, a speaker must use the humble form. By humbling yourself or your family member, you express respect toward the person you're speaking to.

The honorific and humble forms of verbs will be discussed in Lesson 31, but let's look at some of the polite expressions that will be used in the dialogues in Lesson 20 of this unit now. In the table below, the **masu**-form of verbs and the copula **desu**, as well as other expressions with the same level of politeness are called standard forms in order to distinguish them from the even more polite expressions.

| POLITE FORM | STANDARD FORM | |
| --- | --- | --- |
| X de gozaimasu. | X desu. | *(It) is X.* |
| Omachi kudasai. | Matte kudasai. | *Please wait.* |
| Omatase itashimashita. (humble) | Matasemashita. | *I kept you waiting.* |
| Omachishite orimasu. (humble) | Matte imasu. | *I'm waiting for you.* |
| Ohanashishitai desu. (humble) | Hanashitai desu. | *I want to talk.* |
| irasshaimasu (honorific) | imasu/ikimasu/ kimasu | *exist(s)/come(s)/ go(s)* |
| Shitsuree itashimasu. (humble) | Shitsureeshimasu. | *Good-bye.* |
| Mooshiwake gozaimasen./Mooshiwake arimasen. (humble) | Gomennasai./ Sumimasen. | *I am sorry.* |
| Yoroshii desu ka? | Ii desu ka? | *Is it okay?* |

At this stage, you should simply concentrate on recognizing these polite expressions.

## PRACTICE 3
Give the polite form of the following expressions.

1. Matte imasu.

2. Hanashitai desu.

3. Ken-san wa imasu ka?

4. Matte kudasai.

5. Suzuki desu.

6. Ii desu ka?

7. Matasemashita.

8. Mooshiwake arimasen.

9. Shitsureeshimasu.

## PRACTICE 4
Choose the appropriate polite expressions from the list below to complete the sentences.

de gozaimasu, omachi kudasai, omatase itashimashita, omachishite orimasu, ohanashishitai desu, shitsuree itashimasu, mooshiwake gozaimasen

1. A: Moshi moshi, tanaka-san irasshaimasu ka?

   B: Hai, shooshoo _____.

   *Please wait for a little moment. (lit., a minute later)*

   C: Doomo_____. Tanaka desu.

   *I have kept you waiting. This is Tanaka.*

2. A: Ichido _____ kara, mensetsu ni kite kudasai.

   *I want to talk with you once, so please come for an interview.*

   B: Hai.

3. A: Hai, Rainbow Soft _____.

   *Yes, this is Rainbow Soft.*

   B: Moshi moshi, Tanaka-san onegaishitai n desu kedo?

   *Hello, I want to ask for Mr./Ms. Tanaka, but . . .*

4. A: Ashita no sanji ni yoyakushitai n desu kedo.

   *I want to make an appointment for three o'clock tomorrow.*

   B: _____ ga, ashita no sanji wa yoyaku ga ippai desu.

   *We're sorry, but there's no opening at three o'clock tomorrow.*

5. A: Kin'yoobi no goji ni yoyakushitai n desu kedo.

   *I want to make an appointment for five o'clock on Friday, but . . .*

   B: Hai, kashikomarimashita. Dewa, goji ni _____.

   *Yes, certainly. Then, we will be waiting for you at five o'clock.*

---

### *Tip!*

Suppose you have a robot, and you can make five requests to him every day. You tell your robot to do those things using the **-te ku-dasai** structure. Since your vocabulary is still limited, you can make the same requests repeatedly. Alternatively, you can use the same verbs but change the direct objects. If you practice this task for a week or so, you will become comfortable with this structure and will be able to use it in a real-life setting.

## ANSWERS

PRACTICE 1: 1. kite; 2. itte; 3. tabete; 4. nonde; 5. kiite;
6. kaite; 7. mite; 8. itte; 9. okite; 10. hanashite

PRACTICE 2: 1. paatii ni kite kudasai; 2. Eego o hanashite
kudasai; 3. Supeingo o oshiete kudasai; 4. okite kudasai;
5. ashita denwashite kudasai

PRACTICE 3: 1. Omachishite orimasu. 2. Ohanashishitai desu.
3. Ken-san wa irasshaimasu ka? 4. Omachi kudasai. 5. Suzuki de
gozaimasu. 6. Yoroshii desu ka? 7. Omatase itashimashita.
8. Mooshiwake gozaimasen. 9. Shitsuree itashimasu.

PRACTICE 4: 1. omachi kudasai, omatase itashimashita;
2. ohanashishitai desu; 3. de gozaimasu; 4. mooshiwake
gozaimasen; 5. omachishite orimasu

————— Lesson 20 (conversations) —————

## CONVERSATION 1

Randy is making an appointment with her hairdresser on the
phone.

Uketsuke: Lemon de gozaimasu.
  Randy: Ah, moshi moshi. Ano, yoyakushitai n desu
           kedo.
Uketsuke: Hai, itsu ga yoroshii desu ka?
  Randy: Ashita no sanji goro ga ii n desu kedo.

Uketsuke: Shibaraku omachi kudasai.
(One minute later.)
Uketsuke: Taihen omatase itashimashita. Mooshiwake
           gozaimasen ga, sanji wa yoyaku ga ippai desu.
           Ni ji wa ikaga desu ka?
  Randy: Juugofun gurai okureru kamoshiremasen ga,
           daijoobu desu ka?
Uketsuke: Hai, daijoobu desu yo.
  Randy: Sore jaa, ni ji han ni onegai shimasu.

Uketsuke: Katto desu ka?

Randy: Katto to karaa o onegaishitai n desu kedo.

Uketsuke: Hai, kashikomarimashita.

Randy: Dono gurai jikan ga kakarimasu ka?

Uketsuke: Soo desu nee. Nijikan gurai deshoo. Yoroshii desu ka?

Randy: Hai.

Uketsuke: Dewa, onamae to odenwabangoo o onegaishimasu.

Randy: Namae wa Randy Simpson desu. Denwabangoo wa 03–3977–5081 desu.

Uketsuke: Hai, soredewa, asu Gogatsu mikka no ni ji han ni omachishite orimasu.

Randy: Ja, shitsureeshimasu.

Uketsuke: Hai, shitsuree itashimasu.


Receptionist: *This is (the) Lemon (Beauty Salon).*

Randy: *Oh, hello. Well, I want to make an appointment, but . . .*

Receptionist: *Yes, when is a good time for you?*

Randy: *Around three o'clock tomorrow is good for me.*

Receptionist: *Please wait for a moment.*

(One minute later.)

Receptionist: *I'm sorry for keeping you waiting for a long time. We are sorry, but there's no opening at three o'clock. What about two o'clock?*

Randy: *I may be late for about fifteen minutes, but is it okay?*

Receptionist: *Yes, that's fine.*

Randy: *Then, at two thirty, please.*

Receptionist: *Hair cut?*

Randy: *I want (to ask for) a hair cut and color.*

Receptionist: *Yes, certainly.*

Randy: *Ah, about how long will it take?*

Receptionist: *Let me see. It will probably be for about two hours. Is it okay?*

Randy: *Yes.*

Receptionist: *Then, your name and telephone number, please.*

| Randy: | My name is Randy Simpson, and my phone number is 03–3977–5081. |
|---|---|
| Receptionist: | Yes, then, we will be waiting for you at two thirty tomorrow, May 3rd. |
| Randy: | Good-bye then. |
| Receptionist: | Yes, good-bye. |

## NOTE 1

Conjunctions **kedo** (*but*) and **ga** (*but*) often appear at the end of unfinished sentences in Japanese. They are used as an indirect and more polite way of switching a turn in a conversation to the addressee. In the sentence like **Ohanashishitai n desu kedo** (*I want to talk, but* . . . ), the speaker waits to hear the addressee's response without asking overtly whether or not it is okay for the addressee to talk with the speaker. This style is less direct and, therefore, more polite, and frequently used in everyday conversation.

## NOTE 2

When telling a telephone number, you can separate the numbers with **no**, in this case corresponding to the English hypen, or you can pause for a moment instead of saying **no**, just like you would in English. For instance, 03–3954–6782 is **zero san no san kyuu go yon no roku nana hachi ni**.

## NUTS & BOLTS 1
### EXPRESSING WANTS AND DESIRES

Let's learn how to express your wants and desires now. Use the "conjunctive" form of the verb, obtained by dropping the ending **masu** from the **masu**-form of a verb, and attach **tai desu**.

> the conjunctive form of verbs (**masu**-form minus **masu**)
> + **tai desu**

**Sushi ga tabetai desu.**
*I want to eat sushi.*

**Koohii ga nomitai desu.**
*I want to drink coffee.*

**Eega ga mitai desu.**
*I want to see a movie.*

**Itaria e ikitai desu.**
*I want to go to Italy.*

Notice that the direct object marker **o** is replaced by **ga** in this construction. However, this is not a rigid rule. Even though **ga** is preferred, it is also okay to use **o**. The conjugation of **tai** is the same as that of **i**-adjectives. The non-past negative form and the past affirmative and negative forms of **tai** will be introduced in Lesson 31 after the conjugation of **i**-adjectives is discussed.

## PRACTICE 1
Change the following sentences using + **tai desu.**

1. Koohii o nomimasu.

2. Kyooto e ikimasu.

3. Chuugokugo o benkyooshimasu.

4. Hon o yomimasu.

5. Tomodachi ni denwashimasu.

6. Uchi e kaerimasu

7. Eego o hanashimasu.

8. Kanji o kakimasu.

9. Konpyuutaa o kaimasu.

10. Juuji han ni nemasu.

11. Nihon no eega o mimasu.

12. Juuniji ni okimasu.

## CONVERSATION 2

Mark is on the phone making an appointment for his job interview at a computer software company.

Uketsuke: ABC Sofuto de gozaimasu.
Mark: Ano, shinbun no kyuujin kookoku o mita n desu kedo.
Uketsuke: Dewa, tantoo no mono ni kawarimasu kara, shooshoo omachi kudasai.
(A little later.)
Tanaka: Jinjibu no Tanaka desu.
Mark: Webu dezainaa no shigoto no ken de odenwa shite iru n desu ga.
Tanaka: Keeken wa arimasu ka?
Mark: Hai. Hoka no kaisha de gonenkan webu dezain no shigoto o shite imashita.
Tanaka: Soo desu ka. Dewa, ichido ohanashishitai n desu kedo.
Mark: Hai.
Tanaka: Asatte no gogo yoji goro wa ikaga desu ka?
Mark: Hai, daijoobu desu.
Tanaka: Sore dewa, asatte Kugatsu hatsuka Kin'yoobi no yoji ni gokai no jinjibu ni kite kudsai.
Mark: Gokai desu ne.
Tanaka: Hai. Kuru toki ni, rirekisho o motte kite kudasai ne.
Mark: Hai, wakarimashita.
Tanaka: Sore dewa, asatte.
Mark: Arigatoo gozaimasu. Shitsureeitashimasu.

Receptionist: *ABC Software.*
Mark: *Well, I saw your job posting in the newspaper, but . . .*
Receptionist: *Then, I will transfer you to the person in charge, so wait a moment, please.*
(A little later.)
Tanaka: *I'm Tanaka in the human resources department.*
Mark: *I'm calling regarding the job of web designer.*

| Tanaka: | Do you have any experience? |
|---|---|
| Mark: | Yes. I had (lit., was doing) a web-designing job at another company for five years. |
| Tanaka: | I see. Then, I'd like (lit., want) to talk to you. |
| Mark: | Yes. |
| Tanaka: | What about the day after tomorrow around four o'clock? |
| Mark: | Yes, that's fine. |
| Tanaka: | Then, please come to the human resources department on the fifth floor at four o'clock in the afternoon, the day after tomorrow, Friday, September twentieth. |
| Mark: | Fifth floor, right? |
| Tanaka: | Yes. When you come, please bring your resume, okay? |
| Mark: | Yes, okay. |
| Tanaka: | Then, I'll see you the day after tomorrow. |
| Mark: | Thank you very much. Good-bye. |

## NUTS & BOLTS 2

### THE TOKI-CLAUSES

The **toki**-clause corresponds to the English *when*-clause, i.e., it is a clause describing the time of an action or state. **Toki** can follow the plain forms of verbs, nouns followed by **no**, **i**-adjectives, or **na**-adjectives followed by **na**. See the summary below.

---

Plain form of verbs + **toki**, . . .
Noun + **no** + **toki**, . . .
Plain/Non-past form of **i**-adjectives + **toki**, . . .
Stem of **na**-adjectives + **na** + **toki**, . . .

---

Let's look at the sentences containing the **toki**-clause. Note that the postposition **ni** and the topic marker **wa** can be added after **toki**.

The plain form of verbs appears before the **toki**-clause. Verbs can be either non-past or past tense and either affirmative or negative. Note that the **toki**-clause precedes the main clause and is separated from it by a comma.

**Uchi ni kuru toki, denwashite kudasai.**

*Please call me when you come to my house.*

**Wakaranai toki wa, kiite kudasai.**

*Please ask me when you don't understand.*

**Benkyooshite ita toki ni, tomodachi ga kimashita.**

*My friend came when I was studying.*

**Kanji ga wakaranakatta toki, sensee ni kikimashita.**

*When I didn't know kanji, I asked the teacher.*

With nouns, the noun + **no** appears before **toki** regardless of the tense, and in negative sentences, it is the noun + **ja nai** instead.

**Gakusee no toki, takusan benkyooshimashita.**

*When I was a student, I studied a lot.*

**Kurasumeeto ja nai toki wa, Yamada-san no namae o shirimasen deshita.**

*When he/she was not a classmate, I didn't know Mr./Ms. Yamada's name.*

As with nouns, the non-past tense form of adjectives is used in the **toki**-clause regardless of what tense is used in the main clause.

**Tenki (*weather*) ga ii toki, tenisu o shimasu.**

*I play tennis when the weather is nice.*

**Tenki ga ii toki, tenisu o shimashita.**

*I played tennis when the weather was nice.*

In the case of **na**-adjectives, **na** is attached to an adjective before **toki**. This is a special form of adjectives that will be discussed in Lesson 21.

**Hima na toki, yoku eega o mimasu.**

*When I am free, I often see a movie.*

**Hima na toki, tomodachi ni denwashimashita.**
*I called my friend when I was free.*

Now compare the following two sentences.

**Nihon e iku toki, Nyuu Yooku no depaato de kamera o kaimashita.**
*I bought a camera at a department store in New York when I was going to Japan.*

**Nihon e itta toki, Tookyoo no depaato de kamera o kaimashita.**
*I bought a camera at a department store in Tokyo when I went to Japan.*

The tense of a verb in a **toki**-clause indicates a time relative to the event mentioned in the main clause, i.e., it answers the question, "Does the event in the **toki**-clause happen before or after the event in the main clause?" So, if you look at the above two examples, the use of the non-past tense form **iku** in the **toki**-clause in the first example indicates you bought a camera before you went to Japan; the use of the past tense form **itta** in the **toki**-clause in the second example indicates that you bought a camera after you got to Japan.

## PRACTICE 2
Choose the appropriate **toki**-clause on the right side to complete the sentences on the left side.

1. _____, supeingo o benkyooshimashita.

a. Nihon e itta toki

2. _____, watashi ga bangohan o tsukurimasu.

b. Mensetsu ni iku toki

3. _____, Fujisan (*Mt. Fuji*) o mimashita.

c. Haha ga inai toki

4. _____, goji ni uchi e kaerimashita.

d. Daigakusee no toki

5. _____, rirekisho o kakimashita.

e. Toshokan ga shizukana toki wa

6. _____, toshokan de hon o yomimasu.

7. _____, nihonjin no tomodachi ni kikimasu.

f. Nihongo no shukudai ga muzukashii toki

g. Senshuu seminaa ni denakatta toki

---

## Cool links

To get much interesting information about Japanese annual holidays, as well as about Japanese society, culture and modern life in general, visit the following website: http://www.japan-zone.com/culture/holiday.shtml.

You can also get current news and weather info there. Finally, you can browse pictures of Japanese landmarks, nature, people, etc., on this website.

---

## ANSWERS

**PRACTICE 1: 1.** Koohii ga nomitai desu. **2.** Kyooto e ikitai desu. **3.** Chuugokugo ga benkyooshitai desu. **4.** Hon ga yomitai desu. **5.** Tomodachi ni denwashitai desu. **6.** Uchi e kaeritai desu. **7.** Eego ga hanashitai desu. **8.** Kanji ga kakitai desu. **9.** Konpyuutaa ga kaitai desu. **10.** Juujihan ni netai desu. **11.** Nihon no eega ga mitai desu. **12.** Juuniji ni okitai desu.

**PRACTICE 2: 1.** d; **2.** c; **3.** a; **4.** g; **5.** b; **6.** e; **7.** f

# UNIT 6
## *Asking directions*

In Unit 6 you will learn how to ask and give directions. You will also learn some essential vocabulary for getting around town and using transportation. Two types of conditional forms, the **to**-conditional and **tara**-conditional, will be introduced.

——————————— Lesson 21 (words) ———————————

## WORD LIST 1

| | |
|---|---|
| densha | *train* |
| chikatetsu | *subway* |
| basu | *bus* |
| takushii | *taxi* |
| eki | *station* |
| machi | *town* |
| tokoro | *place* |
| michi | *street, road* |
| kado | *corner* |
| migi | *right* |
| hidari | *left* |
| migigawa | *right side* |
| hidarigawa | *left side* |
| biru | *high-rise building* |
| ookii | *big, large* |
| shiroi | *white* |
| hitotsume | *first* |
| futatsume | *second* |
| mittsume | *third* |
| yukkuri | *slowly* |

| massugu | straight |
| shibaraku | for a while |
| magarimasu/magaru | to turn |
| arukimasu/aruku | to walk |
| hashirimasu/hashiru | to run |

NOTE 1
The word **tokoro** (*place*) is always accompanied by a modifier, such as an adjective.

## NUTS & BOLTS 1
### ADJECTIVES IN THE PRENOMINAL POSITION
There are two different types of adjectives in Japanese: the **i**-adjectives and the **na**-adjectives. I-adjectives end in **-i**, like **ookii** (*big*) and **atarashii** (*new*); adjectives that do not end with **-i** are **na**-adjectives. Let's look at some examples.

| I-adjectives | | | |
|---|---|---|---|
| **ookii** | *big* | **chiisai** | *small* |
| **atarashii** | *new* | **furui** | *old* |
| **takai** | *high, expensive* | **hikui** | *low* |
| **omoshiroi** | *interesting* | **tsumaranai** | *boring* |
| **oishii** | *delicious* | **mazui** | *distasteful* |
| **chikai** | *near* | **tooi** | *far* |
| **yasashii** | *easy, kind, gentle* | **muzukashii** | *difficult* |

| Na-adjectives | | | |
|---|---|---|---|
| kiree | *beautiful, pretty, clean* | yuumee | *famous* |
| benri | *convenient* | fuben | *inconvenient* |
| shinsetsu | *kind, generous* | kantan | *easy, simple* |
| nigiyaka | *lively* | shizuka | *quiet* |
| hima | *have a lot of free time* | taisetsu | *important* |

Adjectives appear before nouns in Japanese, just like in English. Na-adjectives have the ending -na added to them, e.g., **shinsetsuna** hito (*kind person*). Take a look at these examples.

**ookii daigaku**
*a big university*

**atarashii densha**
*a new train*

**takai biru**
*a tall building*

**omoshiroi hon**
*an interesting book*

**furui eega**
*an old movie*

**benrina konpyuutaa**
*a convenient computer*

**nigiyakana machi**
*a lively town*

**kantanna shukudai**
*an easy homework*

**shinsetsuna hito**
*a kind person*

**yuumeena kaisha**
*a famous company*

Now, let's look at sentences containing adjectives. Note that some of the sentences contain multiple adjectives.

**Nyuu Yooku wa nigiyakana machi desu.**
*New York is a lively town.*

**Kinoo atarashii konpyuutaa o kaimashita.**
*I bought a new computer yesterday.*

**Tanaka-san wa shinsetsuna hito desu.**
*Mr./Ms. Tanaka is a kind person.*

**Ane wa chiisai akai kuruma o kaimashita.**
*My older sister bought a small red car.*

**Furui omoshiroi eega ga mitai desu.**
*I want to see an interesting old movie.*

Note that -**na** is added to a **na**-adjective even if it doesn't immediately precede a noun, being separated from it by another adjective, e.g., **yuumeena ii resutoran** (*a/the famous good restaurant*).

## PRACTICE 1
Choose the appropriate adjectives from the list below to complete the sentences. English equivalents are given in parentheses.

atarashii, shinsetsuna, kantanna, oishii, omoshiroi, yuumeena

1. _____ sushi ga tabetai desu. (*delicious*)

2. Ani wa _____ daigaku de benkyooshite imasu. (*famous*)

3. _____ eega ga mitai desu. (*interesting*)

4. Chichi wa _____ kuruma o kaimashita. (*new*)

5. Mori-san wa _____ hito desu. (*kind*)

6. _____ shigoto desu ga, sanjikan kakarimashita. (*easy*)

## PRACTICE 2

Fill in the blanks with Japanese equivalents of the English adjectives in parentheses.

1. _____ heya desu ne. (*clean*)

2. Shuumatsu eega o mimashita ga, _____ eega deshita. (*boring*)

3. Suzuki-san wa _____ kaisha de hataraite imasu. (*famous*)

4. Shinjuku ya shibuya wa _____ tokoro desu. (*lively*)

5. _____ koohii ga nomitai desu. (*delicious*)

## WORD LIST 2

| | |
|---|---|
| yuubinkyoku | *post office* |
| ginkoo | *bank* |
| byooin | *hospital* |
| resutoran | *restaurant* |
| kissaten | *coffee shop* |
| eegakan | *movie theater* |
| depaato | *department store* |
| suupaa | *supermarket* |
| konbini | *convenience store* |
| kooen | *park* |
| kooban | *police booth* |
| tatemono | *building* |
| koosaten | *intersection* |
| shingoo | *traffic light* |
| meetoru | *meter* |
| kaban | *bag* |

| koko | *here* |
| soko | *there* (closer to the addressee) |
| asoko | *over there* (far from both the speaker and the addressee) |
| temae | *before, this side* |
| atarashii | *new* |
| kiree | *beautiful, pretty* |
| watarimasu/wataru | *to cross* |
| miemasu/mieru | *to be able to be seen, to be visible* |
| narimasu/naru | *to become* |

## NUTS & BOLTS 2
### WORDS INDICATING LOCATION

Let's learn some words (postpositions) indicating location in Japanese.

| **X no mae** | *in front of X* |
|---|---|
| **X no ue** | *on /above X* |
| **X no yoko** | *the side of X* |
| **X no naka** | *inside X* |
| **X to Y no aida** | *between X and Y* |
| **X no ushiro** | *behind X* |
| **X no shita** | *under X* |
| **X no tonari** | *next to X* |
| **X no mukai** | *across from X* |
| **X no mawari** | *around X* |

Now, let's look at words indicating location used in sentences.

A: Ginkoo wa doko desu ka?
*Where is a bank?*

B: Ginkoo wa yuubinkyoku no <u>mae</u> desu yo.
*The bank is in front of the post office.*

A: Eegakan no mae ni nani ga arimasu ka?
*What's in front of the movie theater?*

B: Eegakan no <u>mae</u> ni resutoran ga arimasu.
*There's a restaurant in front of the movie theater.*

A: Kaban no <u>naka</u> ni nani ga arimasu ka?
*What's in the bag?*

B: Kaban no <u>naka</u> ni hon to nooto ga arimasu.
*There are a book/books and a notebook/notebooks in the bag.*

A: Jisho wa doko desu ka?
*Where is a dictionary?*

B: Jisho wa tsukue no <u>ue</u> ni arimasu yo.
*The dictionary is on the desk.*

A: Depaato to eegakan no aida ni nani ga arimasu ka?
*What's between the department store and the movie theater?*

B: Depaato to eegakan no <u>aida</u> ni resutoran ga arimasu.
*There's a restaurant between the department store and the movie theater.*

## PRACTICE 3
Choose the appropriate words indicating location to complete the sentences. You also need to insert the appropriate particles into parentheses.

mae, ushiro, ue, shita, tonari, mukai, aida, naka

1. *The post office is in front of the bank.*

   Yuubinkyoku wa ginkoo ( ) _____ ( ) arimasu.

2. *There's a movie theater next to the station.*

   Eki ( ) _____ ( ) eegakan ga arimasu.

3. *There are books and pens on the desk.*

   Tsukue ( ) _____ ( ) hon to pen ga arimasu.

4. *The restaurant is behind the department store.*

   Resutoran wa depaato ( ) _____ desu.

5. *Ken is between Kate and Bill.*

   Ken wa Kate ( ) Bill ( ) _____ ( ) imasu.

---

## *Culture note*

In the US every street has a name. In Japan, on the other hand, only major roads have names and most streets don't. Of course, this can make getting around a Japanese town or a city a bit of a challenge. The best thing to do if you're lost is to ask a passerby or a police officer for help with finding the place you're looking for. You'll find a police officer at a police booth, a small structure where police officers are located. In big cities like Tokyo, there are many such police booths, and people often refer to the police to ask for directions and report lost and found items.

## ANSWERS
**PRACTICE 1: 1.** oishii; **2.** yuumeena; **3.** omoshiroi; **4.** atarashii; **5.** shinsetsuna; **6.** kantanna

**PRACTICE 2: 1.** kireena; **2.** tsumaranai; **3.** yuumeena; **4.** nigiyakana; **5.** oishii

**PRACTICE 3: 1.** no, mae, ni; **2.** no, tonari ni; **3.** no, ue, ni; **4.** no, ushiro; **5.** to, no, aida, ni

## PHRASE LIST 1

| | |
|---|---|
| chikatetsu no eki | *subway station* |
| kono michi | *this street* |
| hitotsume no kado | *the first corner* |
| hidari ni magarimasu | *turn left* |
| moo sukoshi yukkuri | *a little more slowly* |
| Sooka. | *I see. (casual)* |
| sorekara | *after that, then* |
| massugu iku to | *if you go straight* |
| shiroi ookii biru | *a big white building (lit., a white big building)* |
| sono biru | *that building* (closer to the addressee) |
| sono biru no mae | *in front of that building* |
| aruite gofun gurai | *about five minutes walking* |
| Nihon ni tsukimasu | *arrive in Japan* |

## NUTS & BOLTS 1

### DEMONSTRATIVES

Now, let's learn Japanese demonstratives corresponding to English *this* and *that*.

| kore | *this* (closer to the speaker) |
|---|---|
| sore | *that* (closer to the addressee) |
| are | *that* (far from both the speaker and the addressee) |
| dore | *which one* |

Note that two Japanese words, **sore** and **are**, correspond to English *that*. **Sore** refers to something closer to the addressee, and **are** refers to something far from both the speaker and the addressee. Also, **dore** corresponds to English *which (one)*. Look at the following short dialogues.

A: **Kore wa nan desu ka?**
*What's this?*

B: **Sore wa Nihongo no jisho desu yo.**
*That's a Japanese dictionary.*

A: **Are wa nan desu ka?**
*What's that?*

B: **Are wa yuubinkyoku desu.**
*That's a post office.*

A: **Dore o kaimasu ka?**
*Which one will you buy?*

B: **Kore to sore o kaimasu.**
*I will buy this (one) and that (one).*

Remember that when these demonstratives appear before nouns, they become **kono, sono,** and **ano; dore** becomes **dono.**

| | |
|---|---|
| **kono hon** | *this book* |
| **sono hon** | *that book* (closer to the addressee) |
| **ano hon** | *that book* (far from both the speaker and the addressee) |
| **dono hon** | *which book* |

Now, let's look at some example sentences.

**Kono hon wa omoshiroi desu ga, sono hon wa tsumaranai desu.**
*This book is interesting, but that book is boring.*

A: **Ano kireena tatemono wa nan desu ka?**
*What's that beautiful building?*

B: **Are wa atarashii depaato desu.**
*That's a new department store.*

A: **Dono eega ga mitai desu ka?**
*Which movie do you want to see?*

B: **Kono eega ga mitai desu.**
*I want to see this movie.*

It is important to know that the demonstratives **kore, sore,** and **are** cannot be used when referring to people. For instance, when introducing **Suzuki-san** (*Mr./Ms. Suzuki*), it would be very rude to say, **Kore wa Suzuki-san desu** (*This is Mr./Ms. Suzuki*). In this situation, you have to use demonstrative words **kochira, achira,** and **sochira.** These words mean *this way, that way (closer to the addressee),* and *that way (far from both the speaker and the addressee)* respectively, and are used when pointing the direction. They can also be used when making introductions.

**Kochira e doozo.**
*Please come this way.*

**Kochira wa Suzuki-san desu.**
*This is Suzuki-san.*

On the other hand, **kore** (*this*) and **kono hito** (*this person*) can be used when referring to a person in a picture. Next, let's look at Japanese expressions corresponding to English *here* and *there*.

| koko | *here* |
|------|--------|
| soko | *there* (closer to the addressee) |
| asoko | *there* (far from both the speaker and the addressee) |
| doko | *where* |

The following short dialogues illustrate how these demonstratives are used.

A: **Ichiroo-san no nooto wa doko desu ka?**
*Where's Ichiro's notebook?*

B: **Ichiroo-san no nooto wa koko ni arimasu yo.**
*Ichiro's notebook is here.*

A: **Soko ni nani ga arimasu ka?**
*What's there?*

B: **Shinbun ga arimasu.**
*There's newspaper.*

A: **Eki wa doko desu ka?**
*Where is a station?*

B: **Asoko desu.**
*It's over there.*

## PRACTICE 1
Fill in the blanks with the appropriate demonstrative words.

1. _____ wa Ben no kuruma desu.

*This is Ben's car.*

2. A: Dore ga ii desu ka?

*Which (one) is good?*

B: _____ ga ii desu.

*That one (over there) is good.*

3. _____ tatemono wa yuubinkyoku desu.

*That building (closer to you) is a post office.*

4. A: Byooin wa doko desu ka?

*Where is a hospital?*

B: _____ desu.

*It's over there.*

5. _____ eega wa omoshiroi desu.

*This movie is interesting.*

6. _____ ni kite kudasai.

*Please come here.*

## PHRASE LIST 2

| | |
|---|---|
| kono hen ni | *in this area* |
| koko kara | *from here* |
| doo yatte | *how* |
| futatsume no koosaten | *the second intersection* |
| gojuu meetoru gurai | *about fifty meters* |
| Supein ryoori no resutoran | *Spanish restaurant* |
| atarashii kireena tatemono | *nice new building* |
| shingoo no temae | *before the traffic light* |
| meeru de kiku, e-meru de kiku | *inquire by e-mail* |
| Shigatsu ni narimasu. | *April has come. (lit., April became.)* |

The phrase, **doo yatte**, is a combination of **doo** (*how*) and the **te**-form of **yarimasu** (*do*) and can be translated as *how*. This may be a little confusing because **doo** by itself also means *how*, as in **Doo desu ka?** (*How is it?*). The difference is that **doo yatte** is used only when asking about how to do something or how to get to a certain destination.

## NUTS & BOLTS 2
### "BECOME" NOUNS AND NA-ADJECTIVES

It is possible to express the concept of becoming, e.g., *to become a teacher* or *to become famous*, in Japanese using the structure with **ni narimasu/ni naru**.

---

noun + **ni narimasu/naru**
stem of **na**-adjective + **ni narimasu/naru**

---

Look at the examples below.

**daigakusee ni naru**
*become(s) a college student*

**kaishain ni naru**
*become(s) a company employee*

**haru ni naru**
*become(s) spring (i.e., it's spring/spring has arrived)*

**yuumee ni naru**
*become(s) famous*

**joozu ni naru**
*become(s) good at, become(s) skillful*

**benri ni naru**
*become(s) convenient*

Now, let's look at the sentences containing these structures.

**Kenji-san wa rainen daigakusee ni narimasu.**
*Kenji will become a college student next year.*

**A: Shoorai nani ni naritai desu ka?**
*What do you want to be (lit., become) in the future?*

**B: Eego no sensee ni naritai desu.**
*I want to be (lit., become) an English teacher.*

**Kuruma o kaimashita kara, benri ni narimashita.**
*I bought a car, so it became convenient.*

**Kono hen wa shuumatsu totemo nigiyaka ni narimasu.**
*This area becomes very lively on a weekend.*

**Mainichi renshuushite imasu kara, tenisu ga joozu ni narimashita.**
*Since I'm practicing every day, I became good at tennis.*

## PRACTICE 2
Translate into English.

1. Shoorai nani ni naritai desu ka?
2. Isha ni naritai desu.
3. Sono kaisha wa saikin (*recently*) yuumee ni narimashita.
4. Kono hen wa yoru totemo shizuka ni narimasu.
5. Juuniji han ni narimashita kara, hirugohan o tabe ni ikimasen ka?

## PRACTICE 3
Fill in the blanks with the appropriate expressions from the list below.

sono kado, kono hen, ano tatemono, kono michi, koko kara

1. _____ o massugu itte kudasai.

*Please go straight along this street.*

2. _____ ni ginkoo wa arimasu ka?

*Is there a bank in this area?*

3. Chikatetsu no eki wa _____ no temae ni arimasu.

*The subway station is before that building over there.*

4. _____ daigaku made aruite nijuppun gurai kakarimasu.

*It takes about twenty minutes walking from here to the university.*

5. _____ o hidari ni magatte, massugu ikimasu.

*Turn left at that corner (closer to you), and go straight ahead.*

## Tip!

The best way to practice demonstratives is to practice them in real situations by pointing to objects around you and refering to them using appropriate demonstratives. For instance, if you are in the living room, you can point to a sofa, a table, a television set, and whatever other objects you see, and then, make sentences using demonstratives. You can say **Kore wa sofaa** (*sofa*) **desu** or **Kono sofaa wa ii desu**. Then, you can change your location in the living room and try referring to the same objects from a new perspective.

## ANSWERS

**PRACTICE 1: 1.** Kore; **2.** Are; **3.** Sono; **4.** Asoko; **5.** Kono; **6.** Koko

**PRACTICE 2: 1.** What do you want to be in the future? **2.** I want to be a doctor. **3.** That company has recently become famous. **4.** This area becomes very quiet in the evening. **5.** It became twelve thirty, so why don't we go to have lunch?

**PRACTICE 3: 1.** kono michi; **2.** kono hen; **3.** ano tatemono; **4.** koko kara; **5.** sono kado

## SENTENCE GROUP 1

| | |
|---|---|
| Chikatetsu no eki e ikitai n desu kedo. | *I want to go to the subway station, but . . .* |
| Chikatetsu no eki dattara, kono michi o massugu ikimasu. | *If you're looking for a subway station, go straight on this street.* |
| Hitotsume no kado o hidari ni magarimasu. | *Turn left at the first corner.* |
| Moo sukoshi yukkuri onegaishimasu. | *A little more slowly, please.* |
| Massugu iku to, migigawa ni ookii biru ga arimasu. | *If you go straight, there's a big building on your right.* |
| Biru no mae ni chikatetsu no eki ga arimasu. | *There's a subway station in front of the building.* |
| Aruite gofun gurai deshoo. | *It will probably be about five minutes walking.* |

## NUTS & BOLTS 1

### THE TARA-CONDITIONAL

Conditional sentences express the condition for some outcome to happen, as in the English conditional sentence *If I buy a car, it will be easier to get to work*. Japanese has two different types of conditional sentences: the **tara**-conditionals and the **to**-conditionals. Let's discuss the **tara**-conditionals first, which correspond to English clauses starting in *if* or *when*. The structure of **tara**-conditional sentences is represented below.

Plain past tense form of verbs/adjectives/copula + **ra**, . . .

The clause expressing the condition (corresponding to the English *if-* or *when-*clause) ends in **ra**. Since **ra** is preceded by the plain past tense form of verbs, adjectives, or a copula, all of which end with -ta—e.g., **kita** (*came, arrived*), **gakusee datta** (*was a student*), and **takakatta** (*was expensive*)—the *if-*clause always ends with **-ta + ra**, which explains the name of this construction. Now, let's see how the **tara**-conditional is used.

**Nihon ni tsuitara, denwashite kudasai.**
*When you arrive in Japan, please call me.*

**Kuruma o kattara, kuruma de kaisha ni ikimasu.**
*If/When I buy a car, I will go to work (lit., the company) by car.*

**Daigaku ni densha de ittara, sanjuppun gurai kakarimasu.**
*If I go to the university by train, it will take about thirty minutes.*

**Gakusee dattara, motto benkyooshite kudasai.**
*If you are a student, please study more.*

Note that the clauses that follow the **tara**-clauses above are all in the non-past tense; they can also be in the past tense, as shown in the examples below.

**Uchi ni kaettara, ie no mae de tomodachi ga matte imashita.**
*When I went home, my friend was/my friends were waiting in front of the house.*

**Kaisha ni aruite ittara, ichijikan kakarimashita.**
*When I went to the office on foot (lit., by walking), it took one hour.*

**Kurasu ni ittara, sensee mo gakusee mo imasen deshita.**
*When I went to class, neither the teacher nor students were there.*

Note that when the second (main) clause is in the past tense, the event or the action described in this clause is something the speaker was not expecting, and therefore, it is beyond the speaker's control. The following sentences show that the **tara**-conditionals can be used to express counter-factuality, a situation where the speaker knows that the condition expressed is not true.

**Gakusee dattara, natsu yasumi ga nagai n desu kedo . . .**

*If I were a student, I would have a long summer vacation, but . . .*

**Nihonjin dattara, motto takusan kanji o shitte iru n desu ga . . .**

*If I were Japanese, I would know more kanji, but . . .*

**Okane ga attara, atarashii kuruma o kau deshoo.**

*If I had money, I would probably buy a new car.*

The **tara**-conditionals are also used when asking for or giving advice, as shown in the examples below.

A: **Nihongo o benkyooshitai n desu kedo, doo shitara ii desu ka?**

*I want to study Japanese; what shall I do?*

B: **Nihon ni ryuugakushitara ii desu yo.**

*It would be good if you went to Japan to study.*

A: **Tookyoo eki ni ikitai n desu kedo, doo yatte ittara ii desu ka?**

*I want to go to the Tokyo Station; how should I get there?*

B: **Densha de ittara ii deshoo.**

*It would probably be good if you go by train.*

A: **Hiroshi-san no denwabangoo ga wakaranai n desu ga, doo shitara ii deshoo ka?**

*I don't know Hiroshi's phone number; what should I do?*

B: **Meeru de kiitara doo desu ka?**

*How about if you inquire by e-mail?*

NOTE 1
Notice that **doo** translates as both *what* and *how* in English.

## PRACTICE 1

Match the Japanese sentences and the English translations.

1. Nihon e ittara, sumoo ga mitai desu.

   a. *If I had money, I would buy a new computer, but . . .*

2. Jikan ga attara, eega ga mitai desu.

   b. *If I had siblings, it would be nice, but . . .*

3. Wakaranakattara, kiite kudasai.

   c. *If I go to Japan, I want to see sumoo.*

4. Yamada-san ga kitara, oshiete kudasai.

   d. *When I went to the new Italian restaurant, Ken and Mari were there.*

5. Eki ni aruite ittara, nijuppun kakarimashita.

   e. *Please tell me when Yamada-san comes.*

6. Times Square e ittara, hito ga takusan imashita.

   f. *If you don't understand, please ask me.*

7. Okane ga attara, atarashii konpyuutaa o kau n desu ga . . .

   g. *When I walked to the station, it took twenty minutes.*

8. Kyoodai ga itara, ii n desu kedo . . .

   h. *I don't have time today, but if it's tomorrow, it will be okay.*

9. Atarashii Itaria ryoori no resutoran e ittara, Ken-san to Mari-san ga imashita.

   i. *When I went to Times Square, there were many people.*

10. Kyoo wa jikan ga arimasen ga, ashita dattara, daijoobu desu.

    j. *If I have time, I want to see a movie.*

## SENTENCE GROUP 2

| | |
|---|---|
| Kono hen ni yuubinkyoku wa arimasu ka? | *Is there a post office in this area?* |
| Koko kara aruite juugofun gurai kakarimasu. | *It takes about fifteen minutes walking from here.* |
| Dooyatte ittara ii deshoo ka? | *How should I go/get there?* |
| Futatsume no koosaten o watatte, gojuumeetoru gurai ikimasu. | *Cross the second intersection, and go for about fifty meters.* |
| Gojuumeetoru gurai iku to, hidarigawa ni resutoran ga arimasu. | *If you go for about fifty meters, there will be a restaurant on your left.* |
| Atarashii kireena tatemono desu. | *It's a nice new building.* |
| Sono resutoran no kado o migi ni magatte, shibaraku massugu ikimasu. | *Turn right at the corner of that restaurant, and go straight for a while.* |
| Shibaraku massugu iku to, hidarigawa ni yuubinkyoku ga miemasu. | *If you go straight for a while, you will see a post office on your left.* |
| Shingoo no temae desu. | *It's before the traffic light.* |

## PRACTICE 2

Match the appropriate suggestions on the right with the questions on the left.

1. Kono kanji ga wakaranai n desu ga, doo shitara ii desu ka?

    a. Kaisha ni denwashitara doo desu ka?

2. Shibuya e ikitai n desu kedo, dooyatte ittara ii deshoo ka?

    b. Jisho o mitara doo desu ka?

3. Mori-san to hanashitai n desu kedo, doo shitara ii desu ka?

    c. Eegakan no mae no resutoran ni ittara doo desu ka?

4. Nihongo ga joozu ni naritain desu ga, doo shitara ii deshoo ka?

d. Chikatetsu de ittara ii desu yo.

5. Oishii Supein ryoori ga tabetai n desu kedo, doko e ittara ii desu ka?

e. Mainichi nijikan gurai benkyooshitara ii desu yo.

## Discovery activities

First, think of and write down a few different sets of street directions using Japanese equivalents of expressions like go *straight*, *turn right at the first corner*, and *cross the intersection*. Next, get out of the house and follow the first set of directions and see where it will take you. You can try another set of directions on some other day, when you have time. As you do this, try saying the given directions in Japanese repeatedly for practice.

## ANSWERS
**PRACTICE 1: 1.** c; **2.** j; **3.** f; **4.** e; **5.** g; **6.** i; **7.** a; **8.** b; **9.** d; **10.** h

**PRACTICE 2: 1.** b; **2.** d; **3.** a; **4.** e; **5.** c

—————— Lesson 24 (conversations) ——————

## CONVERSATION 1
Carlos is in Tokyo trying to find the way to the subway station.

Carlos: **Sumimasen. Chikatetsu no eki e ikitai n desu kedo.**

Tsuukoonin: **Chikatetsu no eki desu ka? Chikatetsu no eki dattara, kono michi o massugu itte, hitotsume no kado o hidari ni magatte . . .**

Carlos: **Ano, sumimasen ga, moo sukoshi yukkuri onegaishimasu.**

Tsuukoonin: **Ah, soo ka. Etto, kono michi o massugu itte, hitotsume no kado o hidari ni magarimasu.**

Carlos: Massugu itte, hidari desu ne?

Tsuukoonin: Ee. Sore kara, shibaraku massugu iku to, migigawa ni shiroi ookii biru ga arimasu.

Carlos: Shiroi ookii biru desu ne?

Tsuukoonin: Ee. Sono biru no mae ni chikatetsu no eki ga arimasu yo.

Carlos: Biru no mae desu ne?

Tsuukoonin: Tabun aruite juugofun gurai deshoo.

Carlos: Doomo arigatoo gozaimashita.

Carlos: *Excuse me, I want to go to the subway station, but . . .*

Passerby: *Subway station? If you're looking for the subway station, go straight along this street, and turn left at the first corner, and . . .*

Carlos: *Oh, I'm sorry, but a little more slowly, please.*

Passerby: *Oh, I see. Well, go straight on this street, and turn left at the first corner.*

Carlos: *Go straight and left, right?*

Passerby: *Yes. After that, if you go straight for a while, there will be a big white building on your right.*

Carlos: *Big white building, right?*

Passerby: *Yes. There will be a subway station in front of that building.*

Carlos: *In front of the building, right?*

Passerby: *Perhaps, it will be about fifteen minutes walking.*

Carlos: *Thank you very much.*

NOTE 1

People often confirm the information they heard by repeating it. For instance, when listening to street directions, you'll probably want to make sure you understood the directions correctly. One way to check your understanding is to repeat the whole sentence, as in **Kono michi o massugu itte, hidari ni magaru n desu ne?** If the sentence ends with a verb, **n desu** is used and the sentential particle **ne** is added, as in **Hidari ni magaru n desu ne?** Alternatively, you can repeat the key part of the sentence or expression, as in **Hidari desu ne?** In all cases, the final sentential particle **ne** is used when confirming information.

## NUTS & BOLTS 1
### To-CONDITIONAL

Now, let's learn another conditional form, the **to**-conditional. Unlike the **tara**-conditional, the **to**-conditional uses the plain non-past tense form of verbs, adjectives, and the copula. This structure is summarized below.

> plain non-past form of verbs/adjectives/copula + **to**, . . .

The **to**-conditional is often used when describing a natural consequence of an act or action. For instance, sentences like *When spring comes, it gets warm* and *If you press this button, the door opens* describe a natural sequence of events and therefore use the **to**-conditional. The **to**-conditional often also expresses the meaning of the English *whenever*. Look at the following sentences.

**Shigatsu ni naru to, sakura ga kiree desu.**
*When April comes, cherry blossoms are beautiful.*

**Nihon e iku to, itsumo kabuki o mimasu.**
*When I go to Japan, I always see kabuki.*

Note that the above sentences can also be translated using *whenever*. Just as with the **tara**-conditional, when the second (main) clause is in the past tense, it describes an unexpected event.

**Yuubinkyoku e iku to, Saito-san ga imashita.**
*When I went to the post office, Mr./Ms. Saito was there.*

In this sentence the speaker did not expect that Mr./Ms. Saito would be at the post office. Since the **to**-conditional describes a natural sequence of events, it is often used when giving street directions.

**Massugu iku to, ginkoo ga arimasu.**

*If you go straight, there's a bank.*

**Koosaten o wataru to, eegakan ga arimasu.**

*If you cross the intersection, there's a movie theater.*

It is important to remember that in directions, the **to**-conditional can be used only once, as shown in the following example.

**Kono michi o massugu itte, hitotsume no kado o hidari ni magatte, shibaraku iku to, migigawa ni ginkoo ga arimasu.**

*Go straight on this street, turn left at the first corner, and if you go for a while, there will be a bank on your right.*

Also, since the **to**-conditional describes a natural sequence of events, the second (main) clause cannot contain expressions describing the speaker's will and wish, an invitation, request, permission, obligation, or command. In this sense, we can say that the **to**-conditional has more restrictions than the **tara**-conditional on its use.

## PRACTICE 1
Translate into English.

1. Sono michi o massugu iku to, ginkoo ga arimasu.

2. Ano biru ni hairu to, Furansu ryoori no resutoran ga arimasu.

3. Ima ni iku to, chichi ga nete imashita.

4. Koosaten o watatte, hidari ni magaru to, eegakan ga arimasu.

5. Densha de iku to, yonjuppun gurai kakaru deshoo.

## CONVERSATION 2

Karin, who is in Kyoto, is trying to find a post office.

Karin: Sumimasen. Kono hen ni yuubinkyoku wa
arimasu ka?

Tsuukoonin: Ee. Demo, koko kara aruite juugofun gurai
kakarimasu yo.

Karin: Dooyatte ittara ii deshoo ka?

Tsuukoonin: Etto, kono michi o massugu itte, futatsume no
koosaten o watatte, gojuu meetoru gurai iku to,
hidarigawa ni supein ryoori no resutoran ga
arimasu. Namae wa Casa desu.

Karin: Casa desu ne.

Tsuukoonin: Ee. Atarashii kireena tatemono desu. Sono
resutoran no kado o migi ni magatte, shibaraku
massugu iku to, hidarigawa ni yuubinkyoku ga
miemasu yo.

Karin: Resutoran no kado o migi ni magatte, massugu
iku to, hidarigawa desu ne.

Tsuukoonin: Ee. Shingoo no temae desu.

Karin: Wakarimashita. Doomo arigatoo gozaimashita.


Karin: *Excuse me. Is there a post office in this area?*

Passerby: *Yes. But, it will take about fifteen minutes (to get there)
walking from here.*

Karin: *How should I get there?*

Passerby: *Well, go straight on this street, cross the second
intersection, and if you go straight for about fifty
meters, there will be a Spanish restaurant on your left.
Its name is Casa.*

Karin: *Casa, right?*

Passerby: *Yes. It's a nice new building. Turn right at the corner of
that restaurant, and if you go straight for a while, you
will see a post office on your left.*

Karin: *Turn right at the corner of the restaurant, and if I go
straight, (it will be) on my left, right?*

> *Passerby:* Yes. It's before the traffic light.
> *Karin:* I got it. Thank you very much.

### NOTE 2

Often the listener uses different expressions, the so-called **aizuchi** (*back-channel expressions*), to show to the speaker that he/she is listening to what the speaker is saying. Expressions like **Soo desu ka** (*I see*) and **Soo desu ne** (*That's right*), as well as **Ee** (*Yes*) and **Hai** (*Yes*), are used in such a way. Of course, the listener can also show that he/she is participating in a conversation nonverbally, just by nodding.

## PRACTICE 2

Choose the right expressions to fill in the blanks.

1. Sono kado o migi ni _____, daigaku ga arimasu.

    a. magaru

    b. magaru to

2. Eki ni _____, denwashite kudasai.

    a. tsuitara

    b. tsuku to

3. Uchi ni _____, haha no tomodachi ga imashita.

    a. kaettara

    b. kaeru toki

4. Depaato e _____, kono kaban o kaimashita.

    a. iku to

    b. itta toki

5. A: Kono kanji ga wakaranai n desu ga . . .

    B: Sensee ni _____ doo desu ka?

    a. kiitara

    b. kiku to

## ANSWERS

**PRACTICE 1: 1.** If you go straight on that street, there's a bank. **2.** If you enter that building, there's a French restaurant. **3.** When I went to the living room, my father was sleeping. **4.** If you cross the intersection and turn left, there's a movie theater. **5.** It will probably take about forty minutes if you go by train.

**PRACTICE 2: 1.** b; **2.** a; **3.** a; **4.** b; **5.** a

# UNIT 7
## Shopping

In Unit 7, you will learn some key expressions and vocabulary related to shopping for food and clothes. You will also learn how to use color words and numbers up to 1,000,000.

—————————— Lesson 25 (words) ——————————

## WORD LIST 1

| | |
|---|---|
| ten'in | *store clerk* |
| seetaa | *sweater* |
| shatsu | *shirt* |
| burausu | *blouse* |
| zubon, pantsu | *pants* |
| jiipan, jiinzu | *jeans* |
| sukaato | *skirt* |
| nekutai | *necktie* |
| uuru | *wool* |
| men | *cotton* |
| shima | *stripes* |
| muji | *solid* (of color) |
| dezain | *design* |
| saizu | *size* |
| ninki | *popularity* |
| (o)shiharai (polite with o) | *payment* |
| genkin | *cash* |
| kaado, kurejitto kaado | *credit card* |
| otsuri | *change* |
| okaeshi | *return, change* (polite) |
| sen en | *1,000 yen* |
| ichiman en | *10,000 yen* |

| | |
|---|---|
| **aka** (noun), **akai** (adjective) | *red* |
| **ao** (noun), **aoi** (adjective) | *blue* |
| **midori** (noun, adjective) | *green* |
| **kiiro** (noun), **kiiroi** (adjective) | *yellow* |
| **chairo** (noun), **chairoi** (adjective) | *brown* |
| **guree** (noun, adjective) | *gray* |
| **pinku** (noun, adjective) | *pink* |
| **jimi** | *sober, quiet* (of color) |
| **hade** | *showy, loud* |
| **akarui** | *bright* |
| **kurai** | *dark* |
| **karui** | *light* |
| **omoi** | *heavy* |
| **atsui** | *hot* |
| **samui** | *cold* |
| **atatakai** | *warm* |
| **suzushii** | *cool* |
| **omoimasu/omou** | *to think* |
| **sagashimasu/sagasu** | *to look for* |
| **azukarimasu/azukaru** | *to keep* |
| **gozaimasu/gozaru** | *to be, to exist (polite)* |

Note 1

Japanese color names have both an i-adjective form and a noun form. For instance, *white sweater* can be either **shiroi seetaa** or **shiro no seetaa**.

## NUTS & BOLTS 1
### LOANWORDS

Japanese has many English loanwords, used for words like *coffee, television, radio, computer, building, sweater,* or *skirt*. Since the Japanese pronunciation of these loanwords is usually very different from the original pronunciation, English speakers often cannot recognize these words easily. Also, in some cases, the meaning of these loanwords is different from the original meaning. For instance, Japanese word **biru** comes from English *building*, but **biru** can refer only to high-rise buildings.

Loanwords are always written in **katakana,** one of the three types of Japanese characters mentioned in Lesson 1. The following chart represents some of the loanwords written in katakana.

| Katakana | Romanization | English |
|---|---|---|
| コーヒー | **koohii** | *coffee* |
| チーズ | **chiizu** | *cheese* |
| ピザ | **piza** | *pizza* |
| ケーキ | **keeki** | *cake* |
| チョコレート | **chokoreeto** | *chocolate* |
| ビール | **biiru** | *beer* |
| レタス | **retasu** | *lettuce* |
| キャベツ | **kyabetsu** | *cabbage* |
| トマト | **tomato** | *tomato* |
| バナナ | **banana** | *banana* |
| ワイン | **wain** | *wine* |
| ジュース | **juusu** | *juice* |
| コンピュータ or コンピューター | **konpyuuta** or **konpyuutaa** | *computer* |
| テレビ | **terebi** | *television* |

| | | |
|---|---|---|
| ラジオ | **rajio** | *radio* |
| ビル | **biru** | *building* |
| セーター | **seetaa** | *sweater* |
| ブラウス | **burausu** | *blouse* |
| シャツ | **shatsu** | *shirt* |
| パンツ | **pantsu** | *pants* |
| ジーンズ | **jiinzu** | *jeans* |
| ウール | **uuru** | *wool* |
| ピンク | **pinku** | *pink* |
| オレンジ | **orenji** | *orange* |
| グレー | **guree** | *gray* |

When writing in Katakana, long vowels are represented by a horizontal line like コー ヒー if you are writing horizontally, and by a vertical line, if you are writing vertically.

## PRACTICE 1
Which words do you think are written in katakana?

1. midori (*green*)

2. aka (*red*)

3. pinku (*pink*)

4. chairo (*brown*)

5. guree (*gray*)

6. konpyuutaa (*computer*)

7. zasshi (*magazine*)

8. tamanegi (*onion*)

9. sarada (*salad*)

10. kyuuri (*cucumber*)

11. retasu (*lettuce*)

12. sushi (*sushi*)

13. chiizu (*cheese*)

14. sake (*liquor*)

15. wain (*wine*)

16. seetaa (*sweater*)

17. kutsu (*shoes*)

18. sukaato (*skirt*)

19. tatemono (*building*)

20. biru (*high-rise building*)

## WORD LIST 2

| paatii | *party* |
| biiru | *beer* |
| wain | *wine* |
| (o)sake | *liquor, alcoholic beverage* |
| juusu | *juice, soft drink* |
| mizu | *water* |
| yasai | *vegetable* |
| retasu | *lettuce* |
| kyabetsu | *cabbage* |
| kyuuri | *cucumber* |
| tomato | *tomato* |

| | |
|---|---|
| jagaimo | *potato* |
| tamanegi | *onion* |
| hamu | *ham* |
| tamago | *egg* |
| yudetamago | *boiled egg* |
| pan | *bread* |
| chiizu | *cheese* |
| bataa | *butter* |
| sarada | *salad* |
| piza | *pizza* |
| choomiryoo | *seasoning* |
| koshoo | *pepper* |
| shio | *salt* |
| satoo | *sugar* |
| daasu | *dozen* |
| kaato | *shopping cart* |
| nedan | *price* |
| bukka | *prices (of commodities)* |
| amai | *sweet* |
| karai | *spicy, salty* |
| suppai | *sour* |
| onaji | *same* |
| zenbu | *all* |
| moshi | *if, in case* |
| tsukurimasu/tsukuru | *to make* |
| tarimasen/tarinai | *be insufficient, be short* |

## NUTS & BOLTS 2

### ADJECTIVES: NON-PAST AFFIRMATIVE AND NEGATIVE FORMS

We've talked about different types of adjectives earlier; now, let's learn how they conjugate. In this lesson, we'll discuss the non-past tense form. The past tense form of adjectives will be introduced in Lesson 30.

First, let's look at the conjugation of i-adjectives. The following chart shows both the polite and the plain form of the non-past tense.

| Plain non-past tense | | Polite non-past tense | |
|---|---|---|---|
| Affirmative | Negative | Affirmative | Negative |
| takai (*expensive,* *high*) | takaku nai<br>takaku arimasen | takai desu | takaku nai desu |
| ookii (*big*) | ookiku nai<br>ookiku arimasen | ookii desu | ookiku nai desu |
| omoshiroi desu (*interesting*) | omoshiroku nai<br>omoshiroku arimasen | omoshiroi desu | omoshiroku nai |
| akarui (*bright*) | akaruku nai<br>akaruku arimasen | akarui desu | akaruku nai desu |
| atatakai (*warm*) | atatakaku nai<br>atatakaku arimasen | atatakai desu | atatakaku nai desu |
| ii (*good*) | yoku nai<br>yoku arimasen | ii desu | yoku nai desu |

In order to make a plain non-past negative form, drop the final -i and attach -**ku nai**. For the polite form, drop the final -i and attach -**ku nai desu** or -**ku arimasen**. Note that the negative form of **ii** (*good*) is **yoku nai**. Now, let's look at the sentences containing i-adjectives.

A: **Kono seetaa wa takai desu ka?**

*Is this sweater expensive?*

B: **Iie, takaku nai desu yo. Yasui desu.**

*No, it's not expensive. It's cheap.*

A: **Sono piza wa oishii desu ka ?**

*Is that pizza delicious?*

B: **Ie, amari oishiku arimasen.**

*No, it's not so delicious.*

Next, let's look at the conjugation of **na**-adjectives, which is the same as that of nouns.

| Plain non-past tense | | Polite non-past tense | |
|---|---|---|---|
| Affirmative | Negative | Affirmative | Negative |
| **kiree da** (*beautiful* or *clean*) | **kiree ja nai** | **kiree desu** | **kiree ja arimasen** |
| **shizuka da** (*quiet*) | **shizuka ja nai** | **shizuka desu** | **shizuka ja arimasen** |
| **yuumee da** (*famous*) | **yuumee ja nai** | **yuumee desu** | **yuumee ja arimasen** |
| **benri da** (*convenient*) | **benri ja nai** | **benri desu** | **benri ja arimasen** |

In Lessons 11 and 14, the conjugation of the copula **desu** and its plain-form counterpart **da** were introduced. Once you know the conjugation of the copula **desu** and **da**, you can conjugate **na**-adjectives easily. Now, let's look at some sentences containing **na**-adjectives.

**Chikatetsu wa benri desu.**

*The subway is convenient.*

**Ano kooen wa amari shizuka ja arimasen.**

*That park is not so quiet.*

**Sono depaato wa totemo yuumee desu.**

*That department store is very famous.*

**Watashi no heya wa amari kiree ja arimasen.**

*My room is not so clean.*


## PRACTICE 2

Fill in the blanks with **i**-adjectives from the list below, then change them into an appropriate form to complete the sentences. Use polite forms.

omoi, omoshiroi, nagai, takai, oishii, hiroi, akarui, atatakai

1. A: Sono kaban wa _____ ka?

   *Is that bag heavy?*

   B: Iie, _____. Karui desu.

   *No, it isn't heavy. It's light.*

2. A: Kono eega wa _____ ka?

   *Is this movie long?*

   B: Iie, _____. Mijikai desu yo.

   *No, it isn't long. It's short.*

3. A: Sono seetaa wa _____ ka?

   *Is that sweater expensive?*

   B: Iie, _____. Yasui desu yo.

   *No, it isn't expensive. It's cheap.*

4. A: Sono sarada wa _____ ka?

   *Is that salad delicious?*

   B: Iie, amari_____. Mazuku arimasen kedo.

5. A: Ima wa _____ ka?

   *Is the living room bright?*

B: Iie,_____. Chotto kurai desu.

*No, it isn't bright. It's a little dark.*

## PRACTICE 3

Fill in the blanks with **na**-adjectives from the list below, then change them into an appropriate form to complete the sentences. Use the polite forms.

shizuka, nigiyaka, benri, kiree, yuumee

1. Shinjuku wa totemo _____.

   *Shinjuku is very lively.*

2. Sono kaisha wa amari _____.

   *That company is not so famous.*

3. Watashi no apaato wa amari _____.

   *My apartment is not so clean.*

4. Kono konpyuutaa wa totemo _____.

   *This computer is very convenient.*

5. Ano kooen wa amari _____.

   *That park is not so quiet.*

## NUTS & BOLTS 3

### SAYING "BECOME" WITH I-ADJECTIVES

You learned how to say *become a teacher* and *become famous* in Lesson 22. *Teacher* is a noun, and *famous* in Japanese is a **na**-adjective. Now, let's learn how to say *become/get expensive* or *become/get cold*. *Expensive* and *cold* in Japanese are **i**-adjectives. You can use the structure below.

**ku**-form of **i**-adjectives + **narimasu/naru**

The **ku**-form of adjectives is the form used in negatives, like **takaku nai** and **ookiku nai**. Here are some examples.

| takaku naru | become(s) expensive | ookiku naru | become(s) big |
|---|---|---|---|
| atsuku naru | become(s) hot | samuku naru | become(s) cold |
| furuku naru | become(s) old | karuku naru | become(s) light |

Let's see how these expressions can be used in sentences.

**Saikin bukka ga takaku narimashita.**
*Recently, prices got (lit., became) high.*

**Shichigatsu ni naru to, atsuku narimasu.**
*When July comes (lit., it becomes July), it gets (lit., becomes) hot.*

**Watashi no konpyuutaa wa furuku natta node, atarashii konpyuutaa ga kaitai desu.**
*My computer got (lit., became) old, so I want to buy a new computer.*

## PRACTICE 4
Translate into English.

1. Watashi no kuruma wa furuku narimashita.

2. Heya ga akaruku narimashita.

3. Kono hon wa omoshiroku narimashita.

4. Haru ni natte, atatakaku narimashita.

5. Juunigatsu ni naru to, samuku narimasu.

## Culture note

Department stores in Japan are much bigger than their American counterparts. Many of them have five, six, seven, or even more floors, and you can buy almost anything there. Usually, they have groceries, such as meat, fish, and vegetables, and snack bars in the basement. A large restaurant and a few smaller specialty restaurants can be found on the upper floors, and coffee shops may be found in the same building. Some stores even have playgrounds for children on the roof. In the summer, the roof is converted to a "beer garden" serving popular Japanese food such as *yaki-tori* (skewered grilled chicken), beer, and other drinks. These are popular after-work and evening spots in larger cities.

## ANSWERS

**PRACTICE 1:** 3; 5; 6; 9; 11; 13; 15; 16; 18; 20

**PRACTICE 2: 1.** omoi desu, omoku nai desu *or* omoku arimasen; **2.** nagai desu, nagaku nai desu *or* nagaku arimasen; **3.** takai desu, takaku nai desu *or* takaku arimasen; **4.** oishii desu, oishiku nai desu *or* oishiku arimasen; **5.** akarui desu, akaruku nai desu *or* akaruku arimasen

**PRACTICE 3: 1.** nigiyaka desu; **2.** yuumee ja arimasen; **3.** kiree ja arimasen; **4.** benri desu; **5.** shizuka ja arimasen

**PRACTICE 3: 1.** *My car got old.* **2.** *The room became bright.* **3.** *This book became interesting.* **4.** *Spring has come, and it got warm.* **5.** *When December comes (lit., when December becomes), it gets cold.*

—————————— Lesson 26 (phrases) ——————————

## PHRASE LIST 1

| | |
|---|---|
| **Irasshaimase.** | *Welcome.* (in a store) |
| **Omataseitashimashita.** | *We have kept you waiting.* (polite) |
| **Ikaga desu ka?** | *How is it?* |
| **hontoo ni** | *really* |

| | |
|---|---|
| sore dewa | *then* |
| korede | *with this* |
| Emu de ii. | *Medium is okay.* |
| donna seetaa | *what kind of sweater* |
| uuru hyakupaasento | *100% wool* |
| kochira no chairoi seetaa | *this brown sweater* |
| sono guree to aka no shima no | *that one with gray and red stripes* |
| chairo ka guree | *brown or gray* |
| moo sukoshi akarui chairo | *a little brighter brown* |
| ao ka pinku | *blue or pink* |
| kiree na iro | *pretty color* |
| sukoshi mijikai | *a little short* |
| chotto jimi | *a little sober* (of color) |
| muji no mo | *the one in solid color, too* |
| ii dezain | *good design* |
| ninki ga arimasu | *is/are popular* |
| jiinzu ni mo pantsu ni mo aimasu | *match(es) with both jeans and pants* |
| sanzen nihyakuen no okaeshi | *three thousand, two hundred yen change* |
| Oikura desu ka? | *How much is it?* |
| oyasuku natte imasu | *has/have been priced down* |
| Kore (o) kudasai. | *Please give me this.* |

NOTE 1

**A ka B** means *A or B*. So, **wain ka biiru** means *wine or beer*, and **ashita ka asatte** means *tomorrow or the day after tomorrow*.

NOTE 2

Honorific prefix **o** can sometimes be attached to adjectives like **oyasui** (*cheap*) and **okiree** (*beautiful, clean*).

# NUTS & BOLTS 1
## STATING REASONS

You can state reasons using the following structure.

> **A shi, B shi, Y.**
> *A and B, and so Y.*

In the above structure, A and B are expressing the reasons, and Y is expressing the conclusion. Let's look at examples.

**Kono seetaa wa karui shi, atatakai shi, totemo ii desu.**
*This sweater is light and warm, and so very nice.*

**Watashi no apaato wa furui shi, eki kara tooi shi, amari yoku arimasen.**
*My apartment is old, and furthermore, far from the station, and so not so good.*

**Tanaka-san wa shinsetsu da shi, majime (*earnest*) da shi, totemo ii hito desu.**
*Mr./Ms. Tanaka is kind and earnest, and so he/she is a very good person.*

**Ano kooen wa kiree da shi, shizuka da shi, ii desu yo.**
*That park is clean and quiet, and so it's good.*

**Sono resutoran wa oishii shi, amari takaku nai shi, mata ikitai desu.**
*That restaurant is delicious and not so expensive, and so I want to go there again.*

As you can see, the plain form of verbs, i-adjectives, and the copula appears before **shi**.

Note that you can state three or more reasons using the same structure. It can also be used to give just one reason.

**Kyoo wa ame da shi, samui shi, kaze ga tsuyoi shi, dekaketaku nai desu.**
*Today it's raining, cold, and furthermore, the wind is strong, and so I don't want to go out.*

**Yuki ga futte iru shi, kyoo wa uchi ni imashoo.**

*It's snowing, and so let's stay at home.*

## PRACTICE 1
Fill in the blanks with the appropriate words, and complete the sentences.

1. Watashi no kuruma wa _____ shi, _____ shi, atarashii kuruma ga kaitai desu.

   *My car is old and small, and so I want to buy a new car.*

2. Mari-san wa _____ shi, ii hito desu.

   *Mari is kind, and so she is a good person.*

3. Kono seetaa wa iro ga _____ shi, _____ shi, _____ shi, kaimasen.

   *As for this sweater, it has a subdued color (lit., the color is quiet), it is large, and furthermore, expensive, and so I won't buy it.*

4. Kyoo wa _____ shi, ii hi desu ne.

   *Today is warm, and so it's a nice day.*

5. Kono hon wa _____ shi, _____ shi, yomimasen.

   *This book is long and boring, and so I won't read it.*

## PHRASE LIST 2

| | |
|---|---|
| kyoo no paatii | *today's party* |
| nannin gurai | *about how many people* |
| biiru o sandaasu | *three dozen bottles of beer* |
| wain o roppon | *six bottles of wine* |
| shiro wain to aka wain o sanbon zutsu | *white wine and red wine three bottles each* |
| nihon no o nidaasu | *two dozen bottles of the Japanese one* |
| amerika no o ichidaasu | *a dozen bottles of the American one* |
| nihon no to amerika no | *Japanese one and American one* |

| | |
|---|---|
| ippon gosen en | *five thousand yen for one bottle* |
| onaji nedan | *same price* |
| onaji nedan no aka wain | *red wine of the same price* |
| chotto takasugimasu | *a little too expensive* |
| moo sukoshi yasui no | *a slightly cheaper one* |
| sarada ni iremasu | *put/puts into a salad* |
| zenbu de ikura gurai | *about how much all together* |
| uchi o demasu | *leave/leaves home* |
| Soo dese ne. | *That's right.* |

NOTE 1

Note the expressions **shiro wain** (*white wine*) and **aka wain** (*red wine*). Here the color word precedes the noun directly without **no**, as one might expect. This is only allowed in well-established compound terms.

NOTE 2

The word **zutsu** has no direct English translation, but here are examples of its use: **A to B o hitotsu zutsu kau** means *buy one A and one B each*, and **hon o issatsu zutsu yomu** means *read one book at a time*. Also, the phrase **sukoshi zutsu** means *little by little*.

## NUTS & BOLTS 2
### NUMBERS FROM 21 TO 1,000,000

You have already learned how to count from 1 to 20 in Lesson 6. Now, let's learn how to count from 21 to 1,000,000. First, let's learn the tens: 30, 40, 50, 60, 70, 80, and 90.

| 30 | 40 | 50 | 60 | 70 | 80 | 90 |
|---|---|---|---|---|---|---|
| sanjuu | yonjuu | gojuu | rokujuu | nanajuu | hachijuu | kyuujuu |

To say 21, combine words for *twenty* and *one*: **nijuu ichi**. Similarly, 34, 55, 76, 82, and 99 are: **sanjuu yon** or **sanjuu shi**, **gojuu**

**go, nanajuu roku, hachijuu ni,** and **kyuujuu kyuu** or **kyuujuu
ku.** Next, let's learn how to count from 100 to 999.

| 100 | 200 | 300 | 400 | 500 |
|---|---|---|---|---|
| hyaku | nihyaku | sanbyaku | yonhyaku | gohyaku |
| 600 | 700 | 800 | 900 | |
| roppyaku | nanahyaku | happyaku | kyuuhyaku | |

100 is **hyaku,** but note the variations in the word when it combines
with other elements, such as in words for 300, 600, and 800. If you
want to say 150, you just need to combine **hyaku** and **gojuu** to get
**hyaku gojuu.** If you want to say 158, you just need to combine
**hyaku, gojuu,** and **hachii** to get **hyaku gojuu hachi.** In this way,
263, 312, 408, 579, 633, 791, 837, and 999 will be as follows.

| 263 | nihyaku rokujuu san | 312 | sanbyaku juuni |
|---|---|---|---|
| 408 | yonhyaku hachi | 579 | gohyaku nanajuu kyuu |
| 633 | roppyaku sanjuu san | 791 | nanahyaku kyuujuu ichi |
| 835 | happyaku sanjuu go | 999 | kyuuhyaku kyuujuu kyuu |

Next, let's learn how to count from 1000 to 9000.

| 1000 | 2000 | 3000 | 4000 | 5000 |
|---|---|---|---|---|
| sen | nisen | sanzen | yonsen | gosen |
| 6000 | 7000 | 8000 | 9000 | |
| rokusen | nanasen | hassen | kyuusen | |

1000 is **sen**, but there are variations of it in 3000 and 8000. If you want to say 1600, you just need to combine **sen** and **roppyaku** to get **sen roppyaku**. If you want to say 1652, you just need to combine **sen**, **roppyaku**, **gojuu**, and **ni** to get **sen roppyaku gojuu ni**. In this way, 2310, 3875, 4966, 5245, 6801, 7432, 8916, and 9999 will be as follows.

| 2310 | nisen sanbyaku juu | 6801 | rokusen happyaku ichi |
|------|--------------------|------|------------------------|
| 3875 | sanzen happyaku nanajuu go | 7432 | nanasen yonhyaku sanjuu ni |
| 4966 | yonsen kyuuhyaku rokujuu roku | 8916 | hassen kyuuhyaku juu roku |
| 5245 | gosen nihyaku yonjuu go | 9999 | kyuusen kyuuhyaku kyuujuu kyuu |

Now, let's learn how to count from 10,000 to 10,000,000.

| 10,000 | 20,000 | 30,000 | 40,000 | 50,000 |
|--------|--------|--------|--------|--------|
| ichiman | niman | sanman | yonman | goman |
| 60,000 | 70,000 | 80,000 | 90,000 | 100,000 |
| rokuman | nanaman | hachiman | kyuuman | juuman |
| 200,000 | 300,000 | 400,000 | 500,000 | 600,000 |
| nijuuman | sanjuuman | yonjuuman | gojuuman | rokujuuman |
| 700,000 | 800,000 | 900,000 | 1,000,000 | |
| nanajuuman | hachijuuman | kyuujuuman | hyakuman | |

If you want to say 56,700, you just need to combine **goman, rokusen,** and **nanahyaku** to get **goman rokusen nanahyaku.** Likewise, if you want to say 716,892, you just need to combine **nanajuuichiman, rokusen, happyaku, kyuujuu,** and **ni** to get **nanajuu ichiman rokusen happyaku kyuujuuni.** In this way, 601,321, 715,430 and 999,999 will be as follows.

| | |
|---|---|
| 601,321 | **rokujuuman sen sanbyaku nijuu ichi** |
| 715,430 | **nanajuuichiman gosen yonhyaku sanjuu** |
| 999,999 | **kyuujuukyuuman kyusen kyuuhyaku kyuujuu kyuu** |

Note that 61,000 is **rokuman issen,** not **rokuman sen,** and 11,977 and 331,680 are **ichiman issen kyuuhyaku nanajuu nana** and **sanjuu sanman sen roppyaku hachijuu** respectively.

## PRACTICE 2
Give the following numbers in Japanese.

1. 27 _____
2. 38 _____
3. 56 _____
4. 303 _____
5. 685 _____
6. 899 _____
7. 971 _____
8. 1,320 _____
9. 2,007 _____
10. 3,866 _____

11. 8,682 _____
12. 11,100 _____
13. 24,318 _____
14. 83,688 _____
15. 90,877 _____
16. 101,134 _____
17. 265,359 _____
18. 773,823 _____
19. 859,754 _____
20. 999,999 _____

## ANSWERS

**PRACTICE 1: 1.** furui, chiisai; **2.** shinsetsu da *or* yasashii; **3.** jimi da, ookii, takai; **4.** atatakai; **5.** nagai, tsumaranai

**PRACTICE 2: 1.** nijuu nana/nijuu shichi; **2.** sanjuu hachi; **3.** gojuu roku; **4.** sanbyaku san; **5.** roppyaku hachijuu go; **6.** happyaku kyuujuu kyuu; **7.** kyuuhyaku nanajuu ichi; **8.** sen sanbyaku nijuu; **9.** nisen nana; **10.** sanzen happyaku rokujuu roku; **11.** hassen roppyaku hachijuu ni; **12.** ichiman sen hyaku; **13.** niman yonsen sanbyaku juu hachi; **14.** hachiman sanzen roppyaku hachijuu hachi; **15.** kyuuman happyaku nanajuu nana; **16.** juuman sen hyaku sanjuu yon; **17.** nijuu rokuman gosen sanbyaku gojuu kyuu; **18.** nanajuu nanaman sanzen happyaku nijuu san; **19.** hachijuu goman kyuusen nanahyaku gojuu yon; **20.** kyuujuu kyuuman kyuusen kyuuhyaku kyuujuu kyuu

--------- Lesson 27 (sentences) ---------

## SENTENCE GROUP 1

Seetaa wa dochira desu ka? — *Where are the sweaters?* (polite)

Nekutai wa sochira ni gozaimasu. — *The neckties are there.* (polite)

Donna seetaa o osagashi desu ka? — *What kind of sweater are you looking for?* (polite)

Uuru hyakupaasento de, chairo ka guree no wa arimasu ka? — *Do you have one made of 100% wool and either brown or gray?*

| | |
|---|---|
| Kochira no chairoi seetaa wa ikaga desu ka? | *What about this brown sweater?* |
| Moo sukoshi akarui chairo ga ii n desu kedo. | *I prefer a little brighter brown, but . . .* |
| Sono guree to aka no shima no wa ii dezain desu ne. | *That one with gray and red stripes has a nice design, doesn't it?* |
| Kono seetaa wa ninki ga aru n desu yo. | *This sweater is popular.* |
| Karuishi, totemo atatakaishi, ii desu yo. | *It's light, very warm, and so, it's good.* |
| Mijikaku arimasen ka? | *Isn't it short?* |
| Sukoshi mijikai kamoshiremasen. | *It may be a little short.* |
| Jiinzu ni mo pantsu ni mo aimasu. | *It matches with both jeans and pants.* |
| Sukaato ni au to omoimasu. | *I think it matches with a skirt.* |
| Muji no mo arimasu ka? | *Do you also have one in a solid color?* |
| Ao ka pinku dattara gozaimasu. | *If it's blue or pink, we have it.* |
| Aoi no wa kireena iro desu ne. | *Blue is a pretty color.* |
| Kochira wa ichiman rokusen happyaku en desu. | *This one is 16,800 yen.* |
| Niman en deshita ga, seeru na node oyasuku natte imasu. | *It was 20,000 yen, but it has been priced down because it's on sale.* |
| Saizu wa emu de ii desu ka? | *As for size, is medium okay?* |
| Goman yen motte imasu. | *I have 50,000 yen.* |
| Oshiharai wa genkin desu ka? | *Are you paying cash? (lit., As for payment, is it by cash?)* |
| Kaado de onegaishimasu. | *With a card, please.* |
| Niman en oazukarishimasu. | *I'll keep 20,000 yen.* |
| Sanzen nihyakuen no okaeshi desu. | *It's 3,200 yen change.* |

## NUTS & BOLTS 1
### USING SUGIRU/SUGIMASU (TOO, TOO MUCH)
Sugiru/sugimasu (*too, too much*) is used in the following structure.

> stem of an **i**-adjective/**na**-adjective/
> conjunctive form of the verb + **sugiru/sugimasu**

The stem of an **i**-adjective is its form without the final **-i**: so the stems of **akarui, yasashii,** and **takai** are **akaru, yasashi,** and **taka** respectively. The stem of a **na**-adjective is its form without the copula: so the forms **kiree, yuumee,** and **benri** are stems. The conjunctive form of a verb is the **masu**-form of the verb minus **masu**: so the conjunctive forms of **tabemasu, nomimasu,** and **ikimasu** are **tabe, nomi,** and **iki** respectively. Now, let's see how the expression **sugiru/sugimasu** is used in sentences.

**Tookyoo no eegakan wa takasugimasu.**
*Movie theaters in Tokyo are too expensive.*

**Kono hon wa muzukashisugimasu.**
*This book is too difficult.*

**Kono burausu wa chotto hadesugimasu ne.**
*This blouse is a little too showy, isn't it?*

**Ima no apaato wa fubensugimasu kara, atarashii apaato o sagashite imasu.**
*The current apartment is too inconvenient, so I am looking for a new apartment.*

**Nichiyoobi wa ohiru made nemashita. Chotto nesugimashita.**
*I slept until noon on Sunday. I slept a little too much.*

**Kinoo biiru o nomisugimashita kara, kyoo wa osake o nomimasen.**
*I drank too much beer yesterday, so I won't drink liquor today.*

## PRACTICE 1

Complete the sentences using the expression **sugiru/sugimasu**. Pay attention to the tense. Use polite form with **masu** or **desu**.

1. Kyoo no shukudai wa _____. (kantan)

   *Today's homework is too easy.*

2. Kono zasshi wa _____. (tsumaranai)

   *This magazine is too boring.*

3. Kono iro wa _____. (akarui)

   *This color is too bright.*

4. Eega wa _____. (mijikai)

   *The movie was too short.*

5. Kono kooen wa _____. (shizuka)

   *This park is too quiet.*

6. Shinjuku wa _____. (nigiyaka)

   *Shinjuku is too lively.*

7. Kinoo wain o _____. (nomimasu)

   *I drank too much wine yesterday.*

8. Kyoo wa _____. (tabemasu)

   *I ate too much today.*

9. Shuumatsu _____. (benkyooshimasu)

   *I studied too much on weekend.*

10. _____. (Kaimasu)

    *I bought too much.*

## SENTENCE GROUP 2

| | |
|---|---|
| Kyoo no paatii wa nannin gurai kuru n desu ka? | *As for today's party, about how many people are coming?* |
| Juunin gurai da to omoimasu kedo . . . | *I think about ten people, but . . .* |
| Biiru o sandaasu kattara ii desu ne? | *It will be okay if we buy three dozen bottles of beer, right?* |
| Biiru wa Nihon no o nidaasu kattara doo desu ka? | *As for beer, how about buying two dozen bottles of Japanese beer?* |
| Sore wa ii kangae desu ne. | *That's a good idea.* |
| Kono shiro wain wa doo desu ka? | *What about this white wine?* |
| Sore wa ippon gosen en desu yo. | *That's 5,000 yen for a bottle.* |
| Chotto takasugiru to omoimasu. | *I think it's a little too expensive.* |
| Moo sukoshi yasui no wa arimasen ka? | *Isn't there one that's a little cheaper?* |
| Onaji nedan no aka wain mo arimasu yo. | *There's red wine at the same price, too.* |
| Sono shiro wain to kono aka wain o sanbon zutsu kaato ni iremasu ne. | *I will take three bottles each of that white wine and this red wine.* |
| Retasu to kyuuri to tomato to hamu o katte, sarada o tsukuttara doo desu ka? | *What about if we buy lettuce, cucumbers, tomatoes, and ham, and make a salad?* |
| Tamago mo katte, yudetamago o tsukutte, sarada ni iretara ii desu ne. | *It will be good if we also buy eggs, make boiled eggs, and put them into the salad, right?* |
| Sushi to piza o kaimasu kara, zenbu de ikura gurai desu ka? | *Since we will buy sushi and pizza, about how much will it be all together?* |
| Boku wa sanman en gurai motte imasu kedo . . . | *I have about 30,000 yen, but . . .* |

Moshi tarinakattara,
kurejitto kaado o tsukaimasu
kara, daijoobu desu yo.

*If it's not enough, I will use a credit card,
so it will be okay.*

## NUTS & BOLTS 2
### INDEFINITE PRONOUN NO

The indefinite pronoun **no** usually corresponds to English *one* and replaces a noun which has already been introduced in a prior speech. Look at the following English sentences.

*I like this red shirt, but I don't like that blue one.*
*This sweater is short. Do you have a long one?*

Now take a look at Japanese sentences with **no**.

**Kono akai shatsu wa suki desu ga, ano aoi no wa suki ja arimasen.**
*I like this red shirt, but I don't like that blue one.*

**Kono seetaa wa mijikai desu.**
*This sweater is short.*

**Nagai no wa arimasu ka?**
*Do you have a long one?*

The indefinite pronoun **no**, like the English *one*, is always accompanied by modifiers, such as an adjective or a demonstrative, or a combination of the two. Also, a possessor word can appear before **no**.

**John-san no kuruma wa atarashii desu ga, Jim-san no wa furui desu.**
*John's car is new, but Jim's is old.*

**Watashi no kaban wa omoi desu ga, imooto no wa karui desu.**
*My bag is heavy, but my younger sister's bag is light.*

Note that **no** cannot replace a noun that refers to a person.

Notice that the possessive marker **no**, which you learned about at the beginning of this course, and the indefinite pronoun **no** have the same form. As illustrated by the last two examples above, when they would be required to appear next to each other in a sentence (as in . . . **Jim-san no no wa furui desu** or . . . **imooto no no wa karui desu** above), they merge to avoid repetition and only one **no** is actually used.

## PRACTICE 2
Translate into English.

1. Kono guree no zubon wa nagasugimasu ga, ano kuroi no wa mijikasugimasu.

2. Suzuki-san no konpyuuta wa atarashii desu ga, Mori-san no wa furui desu.

3. Sono akai kireena seetaa wa kaimasu ga, ano chairo no jimina no wa kaimasen.

4. Kono chiisai keeki wa oishii desu ga, sono ookii no wa amari oishiku arimasen.

5. Sono orenji no shatsu wa ii desu kedo, kono pinku no wa chotto hade desu ne.

### *Discovery activities*

Look around your bedroom, living room, kitchen, yard, or another area of your house, and describe the objects you see using adjectives you've learned so far. For instance, you can describe your sofa, table, bookshelf, refrigerator, flowers, and so on. Of course, you can also do this task at your workplace or school for more practice.

## ANSWERS

**PRACTICE 1: 1.** Kyoo no shukudai wa kantansugimasu.
**2.** Kono zasshi wa tsumaranasugimasu. **3.** Kono iro wa
akarusugimasu. **4.** Eega wa mijikasugimashita. **5.** Kono kooen
wa shizukasugimasu. **6.** Shinjuku wa nigiyakasugimasu. **7.** Kinoo
wain o nomisugimashita. **8.** Kyoo wa tabesugimashita.
**9.** Shuumatsu benkyooshisugimashita. **10.** Kaisugimashita.

**PRACTICE 2: 1.** These gray pants are too long, but those black
ones are too short. **2.** Mr./Ms. Suzuki's computer is new, but
Mr./Ms. Mori's is old. **3.** I will buy that pretty red sweater, but I
won't buy that brown plain one over there. **4.** This small cake is
delicious, but that big is not so good. **5.** That orange shirt is
nice, but this pink one is a little showy.

———————— Lesson 28 (conversations) ————————

## CONVERSATION 1
Cathy has come to the women's section of a department store in
Tokyo to buy a sweater.

> Ten'in: Irasshaimase.
> Cathy: Seetaa wa dochira desu ka?
> Ten'in: Sochira ni gozaimasu ga, donna seetaa o
> osagashi desu ka?
> Cathy: Uuru hyaku paasento de, chairo ka guree no wa
> arimasu ka?
> Ten'in: Sore dewa, kochira no chairoi seetaa wa ikaga
> desu ka?
> Cathy: Etto, moo sukoshi akarui chairo ga ii n desu
> kedo. Ah, sono guree to aka no shima no wa ii
> dezain desu ne.
> Ten'in: Kochira desu ka? Kono seetaa wa ninki ga aru
> n desu yo. Karuishi, totemo atatakaishi, ii desu
> yo.
> Cathy: Mijikaku arimasen ka?

Ten'in: Sukoshi mijikai kamoshiremasen ga, jiinzu ni mo pantsu ni mo au to omoimasu.

Cathy: Muji no mo arimasu ka?

Ten'in: Ao ka pinku dattara gozaimasu ga. Kochira ga ao de, kochira ga pinku desu.

Cathy: Aoi no wa kiree na iro desu ne. Kore, oikura desu ka?

Ten'in: Etto, kochira wa ichiman rokusen happaku en desu. Niman en deshita ga, seeru na node oyasuku natte imasu.

Cathy: Jaa, kore kudasai.

Ten'in: Saizu wa emu de ii desu ka?

Cathy: Hai.

Ten'in: Oshiharai wa genkin desu ka? Kaado desu ka?

Cathy: Kore de onegaishimasu.

Ten'in: Hai. Niman en oazukarishimasu. Shooshoo omachi kudasai.

(Three minutes later.)

Ten'in: Omataseitashimashita. Sanzen nihyaku en no okaeshi desu. Doomo arigatoo gozaimashita.


*Salesperson:* Welcome to our store.

*Cathy:* Where are the sweaters?

*Salesperson:* Sweaters are there, but what kind of sweater are you looking for?

*Cathy:* Do you have one that's made of 100% wool, and brown or gray?

*Salesperson:* Then, what about this brown one?

*Cathy:* Well, I'd prefer a little brighter brown. Oh, that one with gray and red stripes has a nice design.

*Salesperson:* This one? This sweater is popular. It's light, very warm, and so it's good.

*Cathy:* Isn't it short?

*Salesperson:* It may be a little short, but I think it will match with both jeans and pants.

*Cathy:* Do you also have one in solid color?

| Salesperson: | If it's a blue one or pink one, we have it. This is blue, and this is pink. |
| Cathy: | As for the blue one, the color is pretty, isn't it? How much is this? |
| Salesperson: | Well, this one is 16,800 yen. It was 20,000 yen, but it has been priced down because it's on sale. |
| Cathy: | Then, I will take this one. |
| Salesperson: | Is medium size okay? |
| Cathy: | Yes. |
| Salesperson: | Are you paying cash or with a credit card? |
| Cathy: | With this one, please. |
| Salesperson: | Okay, that's (lit., I'll keep) 20,000 yen. Please wait for a moment. |

(Three minutes later.)

| Salesperson: | I'm sorry to keep you waiting. It's 3,200 yen change. Thank you very much. |

NOTE 1

When you enter stores and restaurants, salespeople and waitresses/ waiters will say **irasshaimase** (*welcome*) to you. You will also often hear **(Donna no o) osagashi desu ka?** (*What [kind of item] are you looking for?*) and **Omachi kudasai** (*Please wait*).

## NUTS & BOLTS 1
### DESCRIBING A SEQUENCE OF EVENTS AND ACTIONS
The te-form of verbs was introduced in Lesson 15, where you learned about two structures that use this form of verbs: the progressive form, in Lesson 15, and requests, in Lesson 19. The te-form of verbs is also used to describe a sequence of events and actions. Take a look at the following sentences.

**Suupaa e itte, retasu to kyuuri o kaimashita.**

*I went to a supermarket and bought lettuce and cucumbers.*

**Nihon e itte, ichinenkan Nihongo o benkyooshimashita.**

*I went to Japan and studied Japanese for a year.*

You can theoretically connect any number of events or actions using the te-form of verbs, but very long sequences would be hard to process, so they are usually divided up into two or more sentences. For instance, if you want to describe your daily routine, you need to make several sentences in order to list all the activities you engage in every day.

**Rokuji han ni okite, asagohan o tabete, shinbun o yonde, hachiji ni uchi o dete, kaisha ni ikimasu. Juuniji made shigoto o shite, hirugohan o tabete, ichiji ni miitingu ni demasu. Sore kara, repooto o kaite, rokuji ni kaisha o dete, shichiji ni ie ni tsukimasu. Bangohan o tabete, terebi o mite, ofuro ni haitte** (*take a bath*), **juuichiji han ni nemasu.**

*I wake up at six thirty, eat breakfast, read a newspaper, leave home at eight, and go to work (lit., the company). I work until twelve, eat lunch, and attend the meeting at one. After that, I write a report, leave the company at six, and arrive home at seven. I eat dinner, watch TV, take a bath, and go to bed at eleven thirty.*

Note that the te-form of verbs cannot appear at the end of a sentence. Also, since the te-form does not express the tense, the tense is determined by the last verb in a sequence, appearing at the end of the sentence.

## PRACTICE 1
Choose the appropriate verbs from the list below and fill in the blanks with their te-form.

benkyoosuru, ryuugakusuru, sotsugyoosuru, hanasu, au, kau, yomu, miru, kiku, taberu, iku

1. Sensee to _____, koko ni kimashita.

   *I talked to a teacher and then came here.*

2. Wain o nihon _____, paatii ni ikimashita.

   *I bought two bottles of wine and then went to a party.*

3. Zasshi o _____, ongaku o _____, sore kara nemashita.

   *I read a magazine, listened to music, and then went to bed.*

4. Ginza de tomodachi ni _____, eega o _____, sore kara resutoran
   e _____, bangohan o tabemashita.

   *I met my friend in Ginza, saw a movie, and then went to a restaurant,
   and had dinner.*

5. Daigaku o _____, Nihon ni _____, ninenkan Nihongo o _____,
   sore kara Eego o oshiemashita.

   *I graduated from a university, studied abroad in Japan, studied
   Japanese for two years, and then taught English.*


## CONVERSATION 2

Alex has come to a supermarket with his new Japanese roommate
Ken to get some food and beverages for their house party.

**Alex:** Kyoo no paatii wa nannin gurai kuru n desu ka?

**Ken:** Etto, juunin gurai da to omoimasu kedo.

**Alex:** Jaa, biiru o sandaasu to wain o roppon kattara
ii desu ne?

**Ken:** Soo desu ne. Biiru wa Nihon no o nidaasu to
Amerika no o ichidaasu kattara doo desu ka?

**Alex:** Sore wa ii kangae desu ne. Sore kara, wain wa
shiro to aka o sanbon zutsu kattara ii desu ne.

**Ken:** Ee. Jaa, kono shiro wain wa doo desu ka?

**Alex:** Demo, sore wa ippon gosen en desu yo.
Chotto takasugiru to omoimasu. Moo sukoshi
yasui no wa arimasen ka?

**Ken:** Jaa, kore wa doo desu ka? Ippon sennihyaku en
desu yo. Onaji nedan no akawain mo arimasu yo.

**Alex:** Ee. Jaa, sono shiro wain to kono aka wain o
sanbon zutsu kaato ni iremasu ne.

**Ken:** Sore kara, retasu to kyuuri to tomato to hamu
o katte, sarada o tsukuttara doo desu ka?

Alex: Ee. Jaa, tamago mo katte, yudetamago o tsukutte, sarada ni iretara ii desu ne.

Ken: Sore kara, sushi to piza o kaimasu kara, zenbu de ikuragurai desu ka?

Alex: Boku wa kyuusen en gurai motte imasu kedo.

Ken: Boku wa ichiman nisen en gurai desu. Moshi tarinakattara, kurejitto kaado o tsukaimasu kara daijoobu desu yo.

Alex: Soo desu ne.


*Alex: About how many people are coming to today's party?*

*Ken: Well, I think about ten people, but . . .*

*Alex: Then, it will be okay if we buy three dozen bottles of beer and six bottles of wine, right?*

*Ken: Yes. As for beer, how about buying two dozen bottles of Japanese beer and one dozen bottles of American beer?*

*Alex: That's a good idea. And then, as for wine, it will be okay if we buy three bottles of white wine and three bottles of red wine, right?*

*Ken: Yes. Then, what about this white wine?*

*Alex: But, that's five thousand yen for a bottle. That's a little too expensive. Isn't there a slightly cheaper one?*

*Ken: Then, what about this? It's one thousand two hundred yen for one. There is also red wine at the same price.*

*Alex: Okay. Then, I will put that white wine and this red wine, three bottles each, into the cart.*

*Ken: And then, what about buying lettuce, cucumber, tomato, and ham, and making a salad?*

*Alex: Okay. Then, it will be good if we also buy eggs, make boiled eggs, and put them in the salad.*

*Ken: And, since we will buy sushi and pizza, how much will it be all together?*

*Alex: I have about 9,000 yen.*

*Ken: As for me, about 12,000 yen. If it's not enough, I will use a credit card, so it's okay.*

*Ken: That's right.*

## NUTS & BOLTS 2
### STATING ONE'S OPINION WITH TO OMOIMASU/OMOU (*I think that*)
Now, let's learn the expression you can use to state your opinion.

Plain form of verbs/adjectives/copula + **to omoimasu/omou**

Note that the plain form appears before **to omoimasu/omou**.
Look at the following sentences.

A: **Kono sushi wa doo desu ka?**
*How's this sushi?*

B: **Totemo oishii to omoimasu.**
*I think it's very delicious.*

A: **Andy wa daigakusee desu ka?**
*Is Andy a college student?*

B: **Iie, daigakusee ja nai to omoimasu. Kyonen daigaku o
sotsugyooshita to omoimasu.**
*No, I think he is not a college student. I think he graduated last year.*

A: **Kyoo Hayashi-san wa kaisha ni kuru to omoimasu ka?**
*Do you think Mr./Ms. Hayashi will come to the office (lit., company) today?*

B: **Ee, kuru to omoimasu.**
*Yes, I think he/she will come.*

A: **Mari-san wa kyoo isogashii to omoimasu ka?**
*Do you think Mari is busy today?*

B: **Iie, isogashiku nai to omoimasu kedo.**
*No, I think she is not busy, but . . .*

A: **Yamada-san wa kinoo miitingu ni demashita ka?**
*Did Mr./Ms. Yamada attend the meeting yesterday?*

B: **Ee, deta to omimasu kedo.**
*Yes, I think he/she attended, but . . .*

In negative sentences, you can negate either the verb **omou** or the other verb, as in English; the latter is more common.

**Lopez-san wa Amerikajin ja nai to omoimasu.**
*I think Mr./Ms. Lopez is not American.*

**Lopez-sa wa Amerikajin da to omoimasen.**
*I don't think Mr./Ms. Lopez is American.*

**Kono seetaa wa yasukunai to omoimasu.**
*I think this sweater is not cheap.*

**Kono seetaa wa yasui to omoimasen.**
*I don't think this sweater is cheap.*

**Chen-san wa kuruma o kawanakatta to omoimasu.**
*I think Mr./Ms. Chen didn't buy a car.*

**Chen-san wa kuruma o katta to omoimasen.**
*I don't think Mr./Ms. Chen bought a car.*

## PRACTICE 2
Translate into English.

1. Lisa-san wa Chuugokujin da to omoimasu ka?

2. Kono wain wa amari takakunai to omoimasu.

3. Taroo-san wa kyoo gakkoo e ikanakatta to omoimasu.

4. Watashi no apaato wa chotto fuben da to omoimasu.

5. Sono eega wa omoshiroi to omoimasen.

6. Kono hon wa nagasugiru to omoimasu.

7. Kono keeki wa amasugiru to omoimasen ka?

8. Sono karee *(curry)* wa zenzen karaku nai to omoimasu.

## ANSWERS

**PRACTICE 1: 1.** hanashite; **2.** katte; **3.** yonde, kiite; **4.** atte, mite, itte; **5.** sotsugyooshite, ryuugakushite, benkyooshite

**PRACTICE 2: 1.** *Do you think Lisa is Chinese?* **2.** *I think this wine is not so expensive.* **3.** *I think Taro didn't go to school today.* **4.** *I think my apartment is slightly inconvenient.* **5.** *I don't think that movie is interesting.* **6.** *I think this book is too long.* **7.** *Don't you think this cake is too sweet?* **8.** *I think that curry is not hot at all.*

# UNIT 8
## *At a restaurant*

In Unit 8, you will learn the expressions you can use when dining out at a restaurant. You will also learn how to describe and talk about food. Honorific and humble polite forms of verbs will be also introduced.

## —————— Lesson 29 (words) ——————

### WORD LIST 1

| | |
|---|---|
| **nimeesama** (*polite*) | *two people* |
| **menyuu** | *menu* |
| **teishoku** | *prix fixe meal* |
| **tenpura** | *tempura (fried shrimp, vegetables, etc.)* |
| **unagi** | *eel* |
| **unajuu** | *broiled eel on rice* |
| **korokke** | *croquette* |
| **katsu** | *cutlet* |
| **karee** | *curry* |
| **miso** | *soy bean paste* |
| **(o)miso shiru** (*polite with* o) | *miso soup* |
| **gohan** | *cooked rice, meal* |
| **okazu** | *dish eaten with cooked rice* |
| **tabemono** | *food* |
| **nomimono** | *beverage* |
| **doressingu** | *dressing* |
| **ryoo** | *amount* |
| **hanbun** | *half* |
| **okanjoo** | *bill* |
| **tabako** | *tobacco, cigarette* |
| **amai** | *sweet* |

| | |
|---|---|
| karai | *spicy, salty* |
| shiokarai | *salty* |
| suppai | *sour* |
| ichido | *once* |
| chuumonshimasu/ chuumonsuru | *to order* |
| agemasu/ageru | *to give* |
| moraimasu/morau | *to receive* |

### NOTE 1

**Nimeesama** is a polite form of **nimee**, and it is used to talk about customers in restaurants, clubs, or bars. **Nimee** means *two people*, and **sama**, the polite form of **san** (*Mr./Ms.*), is added to it. At a restaurant, waitresses and waiters usually use **ichimeesama** (*one person*), **nimeesama** (*two people*), **sanmeesama** (*three people*), **yonmeesama** (*four people*), **gomeesama** (*five people*), and so on.

## NUTS & BOLTS 1
### GIVING AND RECEIVING VERBS

**Agemasu** (*to give*), **moraimasu** (*to receive*), and **kuremasu** (*to give*) are the so-called giving and receiving verbs. They are special in that they can be used as main verbs or can be attached to the **te-**form of other verbs. In this lesson, the giving and receiving verbs functioning as main verbs will be introduced. Take a look at the following structures.

---

**A ga/wa B ni X o agemasu/ageru.**

(humble polite form: **sashiagemasu/sashiageru**)

*A gives B X./A gives X to B.*

---

**B ga/wa A ni/kara X o moraimasu/morau.**

(humble polite form: **itadakimasu/itadaku**)

*B receives X from A.*

---

> **A ga/wa B ni X o kuremasu/kureru.**
> (honorific form: **kudasaimasu/kudasaru**)
> (B is a speaker or a speaker's in-group member, e.g., family.)
> *A gives B X./A gives X to B.*

First, let's look at the sentences containing **agemasu**.

**Watashi wa haha ni sukaafu o agemashita.**
*I gave my mother a scarf.*

**Lisa-san wa Hiroshi-san ni chokoreeto o agemashita.**
*Lisa gave Hiroshi chocolates.*

**Morita-san ni kono hon o agetai n desu ga.**
*I want to give Mr./Ms. Morita this book, but . . .*

If the receiver is an animal or a plant, you can use **yarimasu** instead of **agemasu**.

**Watashi wa inu (*dog*) ni kukkii o agemasu/yarimasu.**
*I give cookies to a dog/dogs.*

**Hana ni mizu o agemasu/yarimasu.**
*I give water to plants.*

**Yarimasu** is less polite than **agemasu**. Even though **yarimasu** may be used in informal situations when the receiver is a person, it is always better to use it only when the receiver is an animal or a plant. **Sashiagemasu** is a humble polite form of **agemasu**, and it is used when the receiver is someone you need or want to pay respect to.

**Watashi wa sensee ni boorupen o sashiagemashita.**
*I gave a teacher a ballpoint pen.*

**Haha wa Yamada-sensee ni wain o sashiagemashita.**
*My mother gave Professor Yamada a bottle of wine.*

**Buchoo (*division manager*) ni nekutai o sashiagetara doo desu ka?**
*How about if you give a necktie to the division manager?*

Note that when **sashiagemasu** is used, the giver is always a speaker or a speaker's in-group member, such as a family member. Also, it is important to remember that a humble polite form, **sashiagemasu**, cannot be used if the receiver is a family member. So, even if you want to pay respect to your parents, you cannot use **sashiagemasu** in the following sentence where **agemasu** is used instead.

**Watashi wa chichi to haha ni seetaa o agemashita.**
*I gave a sweater to my father and mother.*

Next, let's look at sentences with **moraimasu** (*to receive*).

**Watashi wa ani ni furui konpyuutaa o moraimashita.**
*I received an old computer from my older brother.*

**Noriko-san wa Kenji-san kara kireena hana o moraimashita.**
*Noriko received beautiful flowers from Kenji.*

**Watashi wa tomodachi ni akai kaban o moraimashita.**
*I received a red bag from my friend.*

If the giver is someone you need or want to pay respect to, **itadakimasu**, the humble polite form of **moraimasu**, is used.

**Watashi wa sensee ni kono hon o itadakimashita.**
*I received this book from my teacher.*

**Imooto wa Eego no sensee kara jisho o itadakimashita.**
*My younger sister received a dictionary from her English teacher.*

**Watashi wa buchoo kara biiruken o itadakimashita.**

*I received a gift certificate for beer from the division manager.*

It is important to remember that when **itadakimasu** is used, the receiver has to be a speaker or a speaker's in-group member, such as a family member. Also, you cannot use the humble polite form **itadakimasu** if the giver is your in-group member. So, again, even if you want to pay respect to your parents, you cannot use **itadakimasu** in the following sentence.

**Watashi wa chichi to haha ni atarashii kamera o moraimashita.**

*I received a new camera from my father and mother.*

Finally, let's discuss **kuremasu** (*to give*). Both **agemasu** and **kuremasu** are translated as *to give*, but in the case of **kuremasu**, the receiver is always a speaker or a speaker's in-group member.

**Mariko-san ga watashi ni kono hon o kuremashita.**

*Mariko gave me this book.*

**Hayashi-san wa imooto ni kireena nooto o kuremashita.**

*Mr./Ms. Hayashi gave my younger sister a pretty notebook.*

**Mori-san ga watashi to otooto ni pen o ippon zutsu kuremashita.**

*Mr./Ms. Mori gave me and my younger brother one pen for each.*

If the subject of a sentence is someone you need or want to pay respect to, **kudasaimasu**, the honorific form of **kuremasu**, is used.

**Smith-sensee ga watashi to kurasumeeto ni jisho o kudasaimashita.**

*Professor Smith gave me and my classmates a dictionary.*

**Kachoo** (*section manager*) **ga watashi ni Furansu no aka wain o kudasaimashita.**

*The section manager gave me a French red wine.*

**Yamada-sensee ga ani ni sono jisho o kudasaimashita.**
*Professor Yamada gave that dictionary to my older brother.*

## PRACTICE 1
Fill in the blanks with the appropriate giving and receiving verbs listed below. Change them into appropriate forms as necessary.

agemasu, sashiagemasu, moraimasu, itadakimasu, kuremasu, kudasaimasu

1. Watashi wa otooto ni furui konpyuutaa o \_\_\_\_\_.

   *I gave my younger brother an old computer.*

2. Kono jisho wa Ozeki-sensee ni \_\_\_\_\_ n desu.

   *As for this dictionary, I received it from Professor Ozeki.*

3. Masaru-san ga imooto ni chokoreeto o \_\_\_\_\_.

   *Masaru gave my younger sister chocolates.*

4. Ashita watashi to kurasumeeto wa sensee ni hana o \_\_\_\_\_.

   *I and my classmates will give our teacher flowers tomorrow.*

5. Buchoo ni kono wain o \_\_\_\_\_.

   *I received this wine from a division manager.*

6. Kono boorupen wa kachoo ga \_\_\_\_\_ n desu.

   *As for this ballpoint pen, a section manager gave it to me.*

## WORD LIST 2

| | |
|---|---|
| sakana | *fish* |
| yakizakana | *broiled fish* |
| nizakana | *boiled fish* |
| sashimi | *sliced raw fish* |
| niku | *meat* |
| gyuuniku | *beef* |

| | |
|---|---|
| butaniku | *pork* |
| toriniku | *chicken* |
| ebi | *shrimp* |
| ika | *cuttlefish, squid* |
| tako | *octopus* |
| hotate | *scallop(s)* |
| kai | *shellfish* |
| muurugai | *mussel(s)* |
| wafuu | *Japanese style* |
| yoofuu | *Western style* |
| kikai, chansu | *chance* |
| dezaato | *dessert* |
| aisukuriimu | *ice cream* |
| shaabetto | *sherbet* |
| chokoreeto keeki | *chocolate cake* |
| koocha | *(black) tea* |
| kapuchiino | *cappuccino* |
| kafeore | *café au lait* |
| shachoo | *president of a company* |
| buchoo | *division manager* |
| kachoo | *section manager* |
| tsumetai | *cold* |
| meshiagarimasu (*honorific polite*)/meshiagaru | *to eat, to drink* |
| itadakimasu (*humble polite*)/ itadaku | *to eat, to drink, to receive* |
| ome ni kakarimasu (*humble polite*)/ome ni kakaru | *to see, to meet* |

## NUTS & BOLTS 2
### EXPRESSING A COMPLETION OF AN ACTION AND AN ATTEMPT

First, let's learn how to express a completion of an action. Take a look at the following structure.

## te-form of verb + shimaimashita/shimatta

Look at the examples containing this expression. Note that the adverb **moo** (*already*) is often used with this structure.

**Shukudai o shite shimaimashita kara, ongaku o kikimasu.**
*I finished (my) homework, so I will listen to music.*

**Moo hirugohan o tabete shimaimashita.**
*I have already eaten lunch.*

In negative sentences, a combination of the **te**-form of verbs and **imasen** is used.

A: **Moo kono eega o mite shimaimashita ka?**
*Have you already seen this movie?*

B: **Iie, mada mite imasen.**
*No, I haven't seen it yet.*

A: **Moo sono shoosetsu o yonde shimaimashita ka?**
*Have you already read that novel?*

B: **Iie, mada yonde imasen.**
*No, I haven't read it yet.*

Note that the adverb **mada** is often used in negative sentences. **Mada** is translated as *not yet* when it appears in negative sentences and as *still* when it is used in affirmative sentences, as in **Mada tabete imasu** (*I'm still eating*). In some contexts, the combination of the **te**-form of verbs and **shimaimashita** expresses the speaker's regret.

**Kinoo wa biiru o ichi daasu nonde shimaimashita.**
*I ended up drinking one dozen bottles of beer yesterday.*

**Ohiru made nete shimaimashita.**
*I regrettably slept until noon.*

**Chokoreeto keeki o mittsu tabete shimaimashita.**
*I ended up eating three slices of chocolate cake.*

Next, let's learn how to express an attempt. You can use the following structure when expressing an atempt.

> te-form of verbs + **mimasu/miru**

Look at the sentences containing this expression.

**Nihonjin no tomodachi to Nihongo de hanashite mimashita.**
*I tried speaking with my Japanese friend(s) in Japanese (to see how it goes).*

**Shuumatsu atarashii kamera o tsukatte mimasu.**
*I will try using a new camera on weekends (to see how it is).*

**Uchi de sushi o tsukutte mimashita ga, amari oishiku arimasen deshita.**
*I tried making sushi at home (to see how it is), but it was not so good.*

## PRACTICE 2
Translate into English.

1. Kinoo karee o tsukutte mimashita ga, chotto karasugimashita.

2. Kurejitto kaado de juugoman en no kamera o katte shimaimashita.

3. Kono hon wa moo yonde shimatta node, imooto ni agemasu.

4. Rainen Supein e itte mitai desu.

5. Paatii e itte, osake o nomisugite shimaimashita.

## ANSWERS

PRACTICE 1: **1.** agemashita; **2.** itadaita; **3.** kuremashita; **4.** sashiagemasu; **5.** itadakimashita; **6.** kudasatta

PRACTICE 2: **1.** *I tried making curry yesterday, but it was a little too hot.* **2.** *I ended up buying a camera for 150,000 yen with a credit card yesterday.* **3.** *Since I have already read this book, I will give it to my younger sister.* **4.** *I want to try going to Spain next year.* **5.** *I went to a party and ended up drinking too much liquor.*

———————— Lesson 30 (phrases) ————————

## PHRASE LIST 1

| | |
|---|---|
| kireena resutoran | *pretty restaurant* |
| donna ryoori | *what kind of meal* |
| konde imasu | *is/am/are crowded* |
| tenpura teishoku ka korokke teishoku | *prix fixe tempura meal or prix fixe croquette meal* |
| unajuu ka sushi teeshoku | *unajuu or sushi prix fixe meal* |
| koohii demo | *coffee or something like that* |
| gohan no ue | *on top of cooked rice* |
| gohan no ue ni unagi ga notte imasu | *eel is put on cooked rice* |
| jitsu wa | *actually* |
| ato de | *later* |

| **resutoran o deta ato de** | *after leaving a restaurant* |
| **korokke teeshoku ni shimasu** | *have/has a prix fixe croquette meal (lit., make it a prix fixe croquette meal)* |
| **soo shimasu** | *do/does so* |
| **moshi yokattara** | *if it's okay* |
| **hanbun agemasu** | *give(s) half* |
| **tabako o suimasu** | *smoke(s) a cigarette* |

NOTE 1

When attached to a noun, **demo** means *something like that*. For instance, **koohii demo** and **Mori-san demo** mean *coffee or something like that* and *Mr./Ms. Mori or someone like him/her* respectively. **Demo** is used to make speech less direct, and more polite, even if the speaker is actually thinking of a specific thing or person.

NOTE 2

**Moshi** (*if*) can be used in conditional sentences, such as the **tara**- and **to**-conditionals. Adding **moshi** does not change the meaning of a sentence, but rather, emphasizes its meaning.

## NUTS & BOLTS 1
### ADJECTIVES: PAST TENSE, AFFIRMATIVE AND NEGATIVE FORM
In Lesson 25, you learned the non-past tense forms of adjectives. Now, let's learn their past tense forms. First, let's look at **i**-adjectives.

| Plain form, past tense | | Polite form, past tense | |
|---|---|---|---|
| Affirmative | Negative | Affirmative | Negative |
| **yokatta** (*was/were good*) | **yoku nakatta** | **yokatta desu** (*was/were good*) | **yoku nakatta desu** **yoku arimasen deshita** |
| **amakatta** (*was/were sweet*) | **amaku nakatta** | **amakatta desu** (*was/were sweet*) | **amaku nakatta desu** **amaku arimasen deshita** |

| Plain form, past tense | | Polite form, past tense | |
|---|---|---|---|
| karakatta (*was/were spicy*) | karaku nakatta | karakatta desu (*was/were spicy*) | karaku nakatta desu karaku arimasen deshita |
| hirokatta (*was/ were spacious*) | hiroku nakatta | hirokatta desu (*was/were spacious*) | hiroku nakatta desu hiroku arimasen deshita |
| muzukashikatta (*was/were difficult*) | muzukashiku nakatta | muzukashikatta desu nakatta desu (*was/were difficult*) | muzukashiku nakatta desu arimasen deshita muzukashiku |

For the plain affirmative form, drop the final -**i** and attach -**katta**, and for the polite affirmative form, you just need to add **desu**. For the plain negative form, replace final -**i** with -**ku** and add -**nakatta**.

Note that -**nakatta** is the past tense form of **nai**. As you can see, the conjugation of **nai**, the plain form of **arimasen** (*does/do not exist*), is the same as that of **i**-adjectives. For the polite negative form, you just need to add **desu** to -**ku nakatta**; you can also use **arimasen deshita** instead of **nakatta desu**. Let's take a look at some of the sentences containing the past tense forms of **i**-adjectives.

**Kono karee wa totemo karakatta node, mizu o takusan nomimashita.**

*This curry was very hot, so I drank a lot of water.*

**Chokoreeto keeki wa amakatta desu kedo, chiizu keeki wa amari amaku nakatta desu.**

*(The) chocolate cake was sweet, but (the) cheesecake was not so sweet.*

**Sono eega wa totemo yokatta node, moo ichido mitai desu.**

*That movie was very good, so I want to see it again.*

Next, let's look at the past tense forms of **na**-adjectives, which are the same as those of nouns.

| Polite form, past tense | | Plain form, past tense | |
| --- | --- | --- | --- |
| Affirmative | Negative | Affirmative | Negative |
| hima deshita (*had a lot of free time*) | hima ja arimasen deshita | hima datta | hima ja nakatta |
| kiree deshita (*was/were beautiful*) | kiree ja arimasen deshita | kiree datta | kiree ja nakatta |
| shinsetsu deshita (*was/were kind, was/were enerous*) | shinsetsu ja arimasen deshita | shinsetsu datta | shinsetsu ja nakatta |
| fuben deshita (*was/were inconvenient*) | fuben ja arimasen deshita | fuben datta | fuben ja nakatta |

The conjugation of **desu** was introduced in Lesson 11 and its plain form counterpart **da** in Lesson 14, so you won't have any difficulty conjugating the past tense forms and the non-past tense forms of **na**-adjectives. Let's look at some sentences containing the past tense forms of **na**-adjectives.

**Shuumatsu Ginza wa totemo nigiyaka deshita ga, kyoo wa shizuka desu ne.**

*Ginza was very lively on weekends, but it's quiet today, isn't it?*

**Buchoo wa amari shinsetsu ja arimasen deshita ga, saikin wa totemo shinsetsu desu.**

*The division manager used to be not so kind, but lately he/she is very kind.*

**Kyonen made sono kashu (*singer*) wa yuumee ja arimasen deshita ga, ima wa totemo yuumee desu.**

*That singer was not famous until last year, but now he/she is very famous.*

## PRACTICE 1

Fill in the blanks with the appropriate form of the adjectives below. Use the polite forms (**masu-** and **desu-**forms).

muzukashii, benri, ii, urusai (*noisy*), fuben, shizuka, oishii

1. Kono hon wa totemo _____ yo. Yonde mitara ikaga desu ka?

   *This book was very good. How about if you try reading it?*

2. A: Toshokan wa _____ ka?

   *Was the library quiet?*

   B: Iie, _____. Sukoshi _____.

   *No, it was not quiet. It was a little noisy.*

3. Chikaku ni suupaa ga atta toki wa _____ ga, ima wa suupaa ga arimasen kara _____.

   *When there was a supermarket nearby, it was convenient, but now it's inconvenient because there's no supermarket.*

4. Ano resutoran wa _____ ga, kono resutoran wa amari _____.

   *That restaurant was excellent (lit., delicious), but this restaurant was not so excellent.*

5. Sono kaisha no mensetsu wa _____ ga, kono kaisha no mensetsu wa zenzen _____.

   *The interview at that company was difficult, but the interview at this company was not difficult at all.*

## PHRASE LIST 2

| | |
|---|---|
| sono sakana ryoori | *that fish dish* |
| kono wafuu sarada | *this Japanese-style salad* |
| sono hotate no ryoori | *that scallop dish* |
| tsumetai dezaato | *cold dessert* |

| | |
|---|---|
| dezaato to koohii demo | dessert and coffee or something like that |
| Ikaga deshita ka? (polite) | How was it? |
| Doo deshita ka? | How was it? |
| ichido kite mitakatta | wanted to try and come once |
| Mite mimashoo. | Let's try seeing it. |
| nakanaka chansu ga nakatta | didn't have an opportunity |
| muurugai mo haitte imasu | mussels are also added to it |
| ryoo ga ookatta | it was a lot (lit., the amount was a lot) |
| zenbu tabete shimatta | finished eating everthing |
| nomisugite shimatta | ended up drinking too much |
| sukoshi itadaita (humble polite) | ate a little, received a little |
| Sukoshi meshiagarimasen ka? (honorific polite) | Would you like to eat/drink a little? |
| hoteru no chikaku de | near the hotel |
| buchoo ni ome ni kakaru (humble polite) | meet/meets a division manager |
| buchoo ni ome ni kakatta toki ni (humble polite) | when I met a division manager |
| moo ichido | one more time |
| koohii dake de ii | okay with only coffee |
| sorede | so, for that reason |
| zehi | by all means, at any cost |
| yorokonde | is/are/am glad to |

NOTE 2

**Nakanaka**, used in a negative sentence, means *not easily* or *not readily*. So, **nakanaka chansu ga nai** and **nakanaka konai** mean *not have an opportunity* and *not come readily* respectively. In an affirmative context, **nakanaka** means *quite*, so **nakanaka ii** and **nakanaka oishii** mean *quite good* and *quite delicious* respectively.

## NUTS & BOLTS 2
### BEFORE AND AFTER: MAE NI AND ATO DE

A sequence of events and actions can be described using **mae** (*before*) and **ato** (*after*). The postposition **ni** follows **mae**, and **mae ni** follows either a noun + **no** or the plain, non-past, affirmative form of a verb (regardless of the tense in the main clause). **Ato** follows either a noun + **no** or the plain, past, affirmative form of a verb (regardless of the tense in the main clause). The postposition **de** follows **ato**, but it is optional. The following chart summarizes these structures.

---

noun + **no**/verb (plain non-past affirmative) + **mae ni**

*Before . . .*

noun + **no**/ verb (plain past affirmative) + **ato (de)**

*After . . .*

---

Let's see how these expressions are used.

**Paatii no mae ni wain o kaimashita.**
*I bought wine before the party.*

**Paatii e iku mae ni wain o kaimashita.**
*I bought wine before going to the party.*

**Bangohan no mae ni shukudai o shite shimaimashita.**
*I have done my homework before dinner.*

**Bangohan o taberu mae ni shukudai o shite shimaimashita.**
*I have done my homework before eating dinner.*

**Miitingu no ato hirugohan o tabemashita.**
*After the meeting, I ate lunch.*

**Miitingu ni deta ato hirugohan o tabemashita.**
*After attending the meeting, I ate lunch.*

**Eega o mita ato de uchi e kaerimasu.**
*I will go home after seeing a movie.*

**Mori-san no ato de kono konpyuutaa o tsukaimasu.**
*I will use this computer after Mr./Ms. Mori.*

**Daigaku o sotsugyooshita ato ginkoo de hatarakimasu.**
*I will work at a bank after graduating from the university.*

Note that **ni** and **de** are both dropped before the copula **desu** or **da**.

**Tesuto no mae desu kara, takusan benkyooshimasu.**
*Since it's before the test, I study a lot.*

**Jogingu (*jogging*) o shita ato desu kara, mizu ga nomitai desu.**
*Since it's after I jogged, I want to drink water.*

## PRACTICE 2
Fill in the blanks with the appropriate Japanese expressions.

1. _____ tomodachi ni denwashimasu.

   *I will call my friend before dinner.*

2. _____ koohii o nomimasu.

   *I drink coffee after getting up.*

3. _____ Nihongo o benkyooshimashita.

   *I studied Japanese before going to Japan.*

4. _____ kissaten e ikimashita.

   *I went to a café after lunch.*

5. _____ hon o yomimasu.

   *I read a book before going to bed.*

6. _____ Eego o benkyooshimasu.

   *I will study English after going to the U.S.A.*

## Tip!

Keeping a diary in Japanese is a good way to improve your Japanese language skills. You can write about things you do and experience every or almost every day using several sentences. Challenge yourself by putting together more complex sentences using such structures as the **te**-form of verbs, the **to**- and **tara**-conditionals, **toki, no mae ni**, and **no ato (de)**, as well as conjunctions like **ga, kedo, kara**, and **node**.

## ANSWERS

**PRACTICE 1: 1.** yokatta desu; **2.** shizuka deshita, shizuka ja arimasen deshita, urusakatta desu; **3.** benri deshita, fuben desu; **4.** oishikatta desu, oishiku nakatta desu/oishiku arimasen deshita; **5.** muzukashikatta desu, muzukashiku nakatta desu/muzukashiku arimasen deshita

**PRACTICE 2: 1.** Bangohan no mae ni; **2.** Okita ato (de); **3.** Nihon e iku mae ni; **4.** Hirugohan no ato (de); **5.** Neru mae ni; **6.** Amerika e itta ato (de)

---

## Lesson 31 (sentences)

---

### SENTENCE GROUP 1

| | |
|---|---|
| **Kono resutoran wa ninki ga arukara, itsumo konde imasu.** | *This restaurant is very popular; therefore, it's always crowded.* |
| **Nani ga tabetai desu ka?** | *What would you like (lit., do you want) to eat?* |
| **Tenpura teishoku ka korokke teishoku ga ii kashira.** | *I wonder if the prix fixe tempura meal or croquette meal are good.* |
| **Unajuu wa donna ryoori desu ka?** | *What kind of meal is unajuu?* |
| **Gohan no ue ni unagi ga notte imasu.** | *It's eel placed over cooked rice.* |

| | |
|---|---|
| Senshuu koko de unajuu o tabeta n desu ga, totemo oishikatta desu yo. | *I ate unajuu here last week, and it was very delicious.* |
| Ichido tabete mitara doo desu ka? | *How about if you try it out once? (lit., How about if you eat it once?)* |
| Kyoo wa unajuu ni shimasu. | *Today I will have unajuu. (lit., I will make it unajuu.)* |
| Unajuu wa teeshoku ja nai kara, omisoshiru o chuumonshitara doo desu ka? | *Since unajuu is not a prix fixe meal, would you like to order (lit., how about if you order) a miso soup?* |
| Sarada mo chuumonshimashoo ka? | *Shall I order a salad, too?* |
| Moshi yokattara, watashi no o hanbun agemasu. | *If it's okay with you, I will give you half of mine.* |
| Senshuu sarada o chuumonshtiara, totemo ryoo ga ookatta desu. | *When I ordered a salad last week, it was quite large (lit., the amount was a lot).* |
| Koko wa konde iru kara, ato de kissaten ni ikimashoo. | *It's crowded here, so let's go to a café afterwards.* |
| Jikan ga attara, kono resutoran o deta ato de, kissaten de koohii demo nomimasen ka? | *If we have time, after leaving this restaurant, why don't we have coffee or something like that at a café?* |
| Jaa, chuumonshimashoo ka? | *Then, shall we order?* |
| Ee, chuumonshimashoo. | *Yes, let's order!* |

## NUTS & BOLTS 1

### POLITE EXPRESSIONS: HONORIFIC AND HUMBLE POLITE FORMS OF VERBS

Some of the polite expressions were introduced in Lesson 19. Now, let's learn honorific and humble polite forms of verbs.

| Masu-form | Honorific form | Humble form |
|---|---|---|
| ikimasu (*to go*) kimasu (*to come*) | irasshaimasu/irassharu | mairimasu/mairu |
| imasu (*to be/ to exist*) | irasshaimasu/irassharu | orimasu/oru |
| shimasu (*to do*) | nasaimasu/nasaru | itashimasu/itasu |
| tabemasu (*to eat*) nomimasu (*to drink*) | meshiagarimasu/meshiagaru | itadakimasu/itadaku |
| mimasu (*to see*) | goran ni narimasu goran ni naru | haikenshimasu haikensuru |
| iimasu (*to say*) | osshaimasu/ossharu | mooshimasu/moosu |

Not all verbs have special honorific and humble polite forms; in that case, honorific form and humble polite forms can be formed according to the following rules.

Honorific form: **o** + conjunctive form of verb + **ni narimasu/naru**

Humble form: **o** + conjunctive form of verb + **shimasu/suru** or **itashimasu/itasu**

Note that you can use either **shimasu** or **itashimasu** to form a humble polite form, like **okakishimasu** or **okakiitashimasu** (*to write*). Because **itashimasu** is actually the humble polite form of **shimasu**, it is even more polite than **shimasu**. Here are some examples.

| Masu-form | Honorific form | Humble form |
|---|---|---|
| **yomimasu** (*read*) | oyomi ni narimasu/naru | oyomi shimasu/suru<br>oyomi itashimasu/itasu |
| **kikimasu** (*listen*) | okiki ni narimasu/naru | okiki shimasu/suru<br>okiki itashimasu/itasu |
| **tsukurimasu** (*make*) | otsukuri ni narimasu/naru | otsukuri shimasu/suru<br>otsukuri itashimasu/itasu |
| **tsukaimasu** (*use*) | otsukai ni narimasu/naru | otsukai shimasu/suru<br>otsukai itashimasu/itasu |
| **dekakeru** (*go out*) | odckake ni narimasu/naru | odekake shimasu/suru<br>odekake itashimasu/itasu |

There are also verbs which have a special honorific form but do not have a special humble polite form, or vice versa. For instance, the verb **aimasu** (*meet*) has a special humble polite form, **ome ni kakarimasu**, but its honorific form, **oai ni narimasu**, is formed following the above regular rules.

Now, let's look at how an honorific form and a humble polite form of verbs are used. As pointed out in Lesson 19, an honorific form is used when describing actions taken by someone you need to or want to pay respect to, like a superior at work, a teacher, or a customer. On the other hand, a humble form is used when describing actions taken by the speaker himself/herself or his/her in-group members, like a family member. Take a look at the following example mini-dialogues. Assume that A is **buchoo** (*division manager*) and B is **shain** (*company employee*).

A: **Suzuki-san, ashita naniji ni kaisha ni kimasu ka?**
*Mr./Ms. Suzuki, what time are you coming to the office (lit., company) tomorrow?*

B: Hachi ji goro mairimasu. Buchoo wa nanji ni irasshaimasu ka?
*I'll come around eight. What time are you coming, Division Manager?*

A: Watashi wa hachiji han goro kuru to omoimasu.
*I think I'll come around eight-thirty.*

B: Buchoo, moo sukoshi biiru o meshiagarimasen ka?
*Wouldn't you like to have a little more beer, Division Manager?*

A: Jaa, moo sukoshi. Hayashi-san mo moo sukoshi doo desu ka?
*Well, a little more. Would you also like a little more, Mr./Ms. Hayashi?*

B: Dewa, watashi mo moo sukoshi itadakimasu.
*Okay, I will have a little more, too.*

B: Buchoo wa gorufu (*golf*) o nasaimasu ka?
*Division Manager, do you play golf?*

A: Un, tokidoki ne.
*Yes, sometimes.*

B: Ashita no miitingu de buchoo ga kono repooto o oyomi ni narimasu ka?
*Division Manager, will you read this report at tomorrow's meeting?*

A: Soo da naa.
*Let me see.*

B: Yoroshikattara, watashi ga oyomi itashimasu ga.
*If it's okay, I will read it, but . . .*

A: Jaa, onegaishimasu.
*Please do. (lit., Then, please.)*

## PRACTICE 1
Choose the appropriate honorific polite form from the list below to complete the sentences. Change them into the appropriate form if necessary.

meshiagarimasu, irasshaimasu, okaki ni narimasu, nasaimasu, oyomi ni narimasu, osshaimasu, goran ni narimasu

1. Oda sensee ga kono hon o _____.

*Professor Oda wrote this book.*

2. Buchoo wa ashita Amerika e _____.

*The division manager will arrive in the U.S.A. tomorrow.*

3. Shachoo wa tenpura ga suki desu kara, takusan _____ to omoimasu.

*The president likes tempura, so I think he/she'll eat a lot.*

4. Shuumatsu kachoo wa tenisu o _____.

*The section manager will play tennis on weekends.*

5. Buchoo, kono eega o _____ ka?

*Division Manger, did you see this movie?*

## PRACTICE 2
Choose the appropriate humble polite form from the list below to complete the sentences. Change them into an appropriate form if necessary.

ohanashishimasu, itadakimasu, haikenshimasu, mairimasu, okakishimasu, mooshimasu, itashimasu, ome ni kakarimasu

1. Buchoo, sore wa watashi ga _____.

*Division Manager, I'll do it.*

2. Sensee no shashin (*photography*) o _____ ga, totemo yokatta desu.

*I saw the professor's photography, and it was very good.*

3. Paatii de kachoo no ryoori o _____ ga, totemo oishikatta desu.

*I had a dish prepared by the section manager at the party, and it was very delicious.*

4. Shachoo, ashita no yoji goro mata _____.

*President, I'll come again tomorrow around four o'clock.*

5. Buchoo, chotto _____ n desu ga.

*Division Manager, I'd like to talk to you for a little while.*

## SENTENCE GROUP 2

| | |
|---|---|
| Sono sakana ryoori wa ikaga deshita ka? | *How was that fish dish?* |
| Sono hotate no ryoori wa doo deshita ka? | *How was that scallop dish?* |
| Kono wafuu sarada mo oishikatta desu. | *This Japanese-style salad was also good.* |
| Sore wa yokatta. | *That was good.* |
| Ichido kono resutoran e kite mitakatta n desu. | *I wanted to try and come to this restaurant once.* |
| Ebi ya ika ya muurugai mo haitte ite, ryoo ga ookatta n desu ga, zenbu tabete shimaimashita. | *Among other things, shrimp, cuttlefish, and mussels are also in it, and it was a lot, but I finished it all.* |
| Watashi mo Kato-san no ryoori o sukoshi itadakimashita kara. | *I also had a little bit of Mr./Ms. Kato's dish, so . . .* |
| Wain o moo sukoshi meshiagarimasen ka? | *Would you like to have a little more wine?* |
| Jitsu wa kinoo sukoshi nomisugite shimatta n desu. | *Actually, I ended up drinking a little too much yesterday.* |
| Oda-buchoo ni ome ni kakatta toki ni, buchoo ga biiruken o kudasaimashita. | *When I saw the Division Manager Oda, he/she gave me a beer gift certificate.* |
| Dezaato to koohii demo chuumonshimasen ka? | *Why don't we order a dessert and coffee or something like that?* |
| Tsumetai dezaato ga tabetai desu. | *I want to eat a cold dessert.* |

| Moo ichido menu o mite mimashoo. | *Let's try looking at the menu one more time.* |
| Keeki shika nai desu ne. | *There are only cakes.* |
| Aisukuriimu ka shaabetto ga tabetakatta desu. | *I wanted to eat ice cream or sherbet.* |
| Koohii dake de ii desu. | *I'm fine with only coffee.* |
| Chokoreeto keeki to koocha ni shimasu. | *I will have a chocolate cake and tea. (lit., I will make it a chocolate cake and tea.)* |

## NUTS & BOLTS 2
### EXPRESSING DESIRES: TAI IN THE PAST TENSE

In Lesson 20, the non-past tense from of **tai** (*to want to*) was introduced. Let's learn now the past tense form of **tai**. The conjugation of **tai** is the same as that of i-adjectives. Since you have just learned the past tense form of i-adjectives in Lesson 30, forming the past tense of **tai** should be simple.

| Polite form, past tense | | Plain form, past tense | |
|---|---|---|---|
| Affirmative | Negative | Affirmative | Negative |
| takatta desu (*wanted to*) | taku nakatta desu | taku arimasen | taku nakatta deshita |

Let's look at some sentences containing the past tense form of **tai**.

**Miitingu ni detaku arimasen deshita ga, shachoo mo ode ni natta node, demashita.**
*I didn't want to attend the meeting, but I did (lit., attended) because the president also attended.*

**Guree no seetaa ga kaitakatta desu ga, nakatta node, chairo no o kaimashita.**
*I wanted to buy a gray sweater, but they didn't have one, so I bought a brown one.*

## PRACTICE 3

Fill in the blanks with the appropriate expressions to complete the sentences.

1. Kinoo wa sakana ryoori ga _____ ga, kyoo wa nikuryoori ga tabetai desu.

   *I wanted to eat fish yesterday, but today I want to eat meat.*

2. Nichiyoobi ni tenisu ga _____ n desu ga, Getsuyoobi ni tesuto ga atta node, uchi de benkyoo shimashita.

   *I wanted to play tennis on Sunday, but since there was a test on Monday, I studied at home.*

3. Sono eega wa _____ kedo, kono eega wa _____.

   *I wanted to see that movie; I didn't want to see this movie.*

4. Itaria e _____ n desu ga, tomodachi ga iru node, Supein e ikimashita.

   *I wanted to go to Italy, but I went to Spain because I had a friend there.*

5. Sono hon wa nagai shi, muzukashii shi, _____ n desu ga, yondara nakanaka yokatta desu.

   *That book was long and difficult, and so I didn't want to read it (at first), but I liked it (lit., it was quite good) when I read it.*

---

### *Discovery activities*

Japanese food has become well-known and well-liked in the United States and around the world. Many Japanese restaurants exist in big cities. Even in small towns, you're likely to find at least one Japanese restaurant. If there's one in your town, go there and see if you can read the names of dishes in Japanese. The names of the dishes are probably written in both Japanese and English. Also, try ordering your food in Japanese. Maybe you can even have a little chat with Japanese waiters and waitresses.

---

## ANSWERS
PRACTICE 1: **1.** okaki ni narimashita; **2.** irasshaimasu;
**3.** meshiagaru; **4.** nasaimasu; **5.** goran ni narimashita

PRACTICE 2: **1.** itashimasu; **2.** haikenshimashita;
**3.** itadakimashita; **4.** mairimasu; **5.** ohanashishitai

PRACTICE 3: **1.** tabetakatta desu; **2.** shitakatta; **3.** mitakatta
desu, mitaku nakatta desu/mitaku arimasen deshita;
**4.** ikitakatta; **5.** yomitaku nakatta

─────────── Lesson 32 (conversations) ───────────

## CONVERSATION 1
Ellie is having lunch with her Japanese colleague Mari at a Japanese restaurant.

Ueitoresu: Irasshaimase. Nimeesama desu ka?
Mari: Hai.
Ueitoresu: Otabako wa osui ni narimasu ka?
Mari: Iie.
Ueitoresu: Dewa, kochira e doozo. Menyuu de gozaimasu.
Ellie: Chiisai kedo, kireena resutoran desu ne. Kono
resutoran wa totemo ninki ga aru kara, itsumo
konde iru n desu yo.
Mari: Ee. Ellie-san wa nani ga tabetai desu ka?
Ellie: Uun, tenpura teishoku ka korokke teishoku ga
ii kashira.
Mari: Watashi wa unajuu ka sushi teishoku ga ii ka
naa.
Ellie: Unajuu wa donna ryoori desu ka?
Mari: Gohan no ue ni unagi ga notte iru n desu yo.
Jitsu wa senshuu koko de unajuu o tabeta n
desu kedo, totemo oishikatta desu. Ichido
tabete mitara doo desu ka?
Ellie: Soo desu ne. Jaa, kyoo wa unajuu ni shimasu.

Mari: Watashi wa kyoo wa sushi teishoku ni shimasu. Unajuu wa teishoku ja nai kara, omisoshiru o chuumon shitara doo desu ka?

Ellie: Soo desu ne. Sarada mo chuumon shimashoo ka?

Mari: Sarada wa, moshi yokattara, watashi no o hanbun agemasu. Senshuu sarada o chuumonshiara, totemo ryoo ga ookatta n desu.

Ellie: Jaa, soo shimasu. Nomimono mo chuumon shimasu ka?

Mari: Etto, jikan ga attara, kono resutoran o deta ato de, kissaten de koohii demo nomimasen ka?

Ellie: Soo desu ne. Koko wa konde iru kara, ato de kissaten ni ikimashoo.

Mari: Jaa, chuumonshimashoo ka?

Ellie: Ee, chuumonshimashoo.


Waitress: *Welcome. Two people?*

Mari: *Yes.*

Waitress: *Do you (lit., will you) smoke?*

Mari: *No.*

Waitress: *Then, this way, please. Here is the menu.*

Ellie: *It's a small but pretty restaurant, isn't it? This restaurant is very popular, so it's always crowded.*

Mari: *Yes. What do you want to eat, Ellie?*

Ellie: *Well, I wonder if the prix fixe tempura or croquette meals are good.*

Mari: *I wonder if the prix fixe unajuu or sushi meals are good.*

Ellie: *What kind of dish is unajuu?*

Mari: *It's eel placed (served) over rice. Actually, I ate unajuu here last week, and it was very delicious. How about if you try it once?*

Ellie: *Yes, then I will have unajuu today.*

Mari: *I will have the prix fixe sushi meal today. Since unajuu is not a prix fixe meal, how about ordering a miso soup?*

Ellie: *Yes, right. Should I order a salad, too?*

> Mari: *As for the salad, if you'd like (lit., it's okay with you), I'll give you half of mine. When I ordered the salad last week, it was pretty big.*
>
> Ellie: *Yes, then I will do so. Are we going to order drinks, too?*
>
> Mari: *Well, if we have time, after (lit., we leave) the restaurant, why don't we have coffee or something like that at a café?*
>
> Ellie: *That's good. It's crowded here, so let's go to a café later.*
>
> Mari: *Then, shall we order?*
>
> Ellie: *Yes, let's order.*

NOTE 1

**Ka na, ka naa,** or **kashira** are often added to sentences in the course of a conversation. They can be translated as *I wonder*. They are attached to the plain-form of verbs, copula **desu** and **da,** and their past tense counterpart **deshita** and **datta. Kashira** is used only by female speakers.

## NUTS & BOLTS 1

INVITING PEOPLE: *LET'S . . . !, WHY DON'T WE . . . ?, SHALL WE . . . ?*
Now, let's learn how to invite people. There are three different expressions you can use when inviting people as shown in the following chart.

---

Conjunctive form of the verb + **masen ka?**
*Why don't we . . . ?*
Conjunctive form of the verb + **mashoo ka?**
*Shall we . . . ?*
Conjunctive form of the verb + **mashoo!**
*Let's . . . !*

---

Let's look at how these expressions are used.

A: **Doyoobi ni issho ni eega o mimasen ka?**
*Why don't we see a movie together on Saturday?*

B: **Ii desu ne. Nani o mimashoo ka?**
*That's good. What shall we see?*

A: **Kono atarashii eega wa doo desu ka?**
*What about this new movie?*

B: **Ee, jaa sore o mimashoo.**
*Yes, then let's see it!*

A: **Issho ni hirugohan o tabemasen ka?**
*Why don't we eat lunch together?*

B: **Ee, zehi. Doko de tabemashoo ka?**
*Yes, by all means. Where shall we eat?*

A: **Kaisha no mae no Itaria resutoran wa doo desu ka?**
*What about the Italian restaurant in front of the company?*

B: **Soo desu ne. Jaa, soko ni ikimashoo!**
*Okay. Then, let's go there.*

A: **Ashita issho ni tenisu o shimasen ka?**
*Why don't we play tennis together tomorrow?*

B: **Ee, yorokonde. Doko de shimashoo ka?**
*Yes, I'm glad to. Where shall we play?*

A: **Eki no mukai no kooen wa doo desu ka?**
*What about the park across from the station?*

B: **Soo desu ne. Soo shimashoo!**
*Okay. Let's do it!*

Question words such as **nani, doko, dare,** and **itsu** can be combined with **mashoo ka** (*shall we*), but not with **masen ka** (*why don't we*) and **mashoo** (*let's*), just like in English. Also, **mashoo ka** can be translated as *Shall I . . . ?* depending on the context.

A: **Buchoo, sono repooto wa watashi ga okakiitashimashoo ka?**
*Division Manager, shall I write that report?*

B: **Jaa, onegaishimasu.**
*Sure, please.*

## PRACTICE 1
Translate into Japanese using the words in parentheses. You also need to provide the appropriate particles.

1. *Why don't we listen to the music together?* (ongaku, issho ni, kikimasen ka)

2. *What kind of music shall we listen to?* (ongaku, donna, kikimashoo ka)

3. *Let's listen to Japanese music!* (kikimashoo, ongaku, Nihon)

4. *Why don't we talk at a café?* (kissaten, hanashimasen ka)

5. *Which café shall we go?* (ikimashoo ka, kissaten, dono)

6. *Let's go to the café next to the university.* (daigaku, ikimashoo, kissaten, tonari)

7. *Why don't we make sushi together?* (osushi, tsukurimasen ka, issho ni)

8. *When shall we make it?* (tsukurimashoo ka, itsu)

9. *Let's make sushi on Sunday!* (tsukurimashoo, osushi, Nichiyoobi)

10. *Why don't we buy a new TV?* (terebi, kaimasen ka, atarashii)

11. *Where shall we buy it?* (kaimashoo ka, doko)

12. *Let's buy a TV at the department store!* (terebi, depaato, kaimashoo)

## CONVERSATION 2

Mr. Kato has brought his business partner Mr. Smith to a seafood restaurant in Tokyo. They have just finished their meal.

Kato: Sono sakana ryoori wa ikaga deshita ka?

Smith: Totemo oishikatta desu yo. Kono wafuu sarada mo oishikatta desu.

Kato: Sore wa yokatta. Ichido kono resutoran e kite mitakatta n desu ga, nakanaka chansu ga nakatta n desu.

Smith: Soo desu ka. Sono hotate no ryoori wa doo deshita ka?

Kato: Kono hotate no ryoori mo oishikatta desu yo. Ebi ya ika ya muurugai mo haitte ite, ryoo ga ookatta n desu ga, zenbu tabete shimaimashita.

Smith: Demo, watashi mo Kato-san no ryoori o sukoshi itadakimashita kara.

Kato: Wain o moo sukoshi meshiagarimasen ka?

Smith: Jitsu wa kinoo sukoshi nomisugite shimatta n desu. Kinoo, Oda-buchoo ni omenikakatta toki ni, buchoo ga biiruken o kudasatta n desu.

Kato: Soo desu ka. Jaa, dezaato to koohii demo chuumonshimasen ka?

Smith: Ee, tsumetai dezaato ga tabetai desu ne.

Kato: Etto, moo ichido menyuu o mite mimashoo. Keeki shika nai desu ne.

Smith: Uun, aisukuriimu ka shaabetto ga tabetakatta n desu kedo. Sore jaa, watashi wa koohii dake choomonshimasu.

Kato: Jaa, watashi wa chokoreeto keeki to koocha ni shimasu.

---

*Kato: How was that fish dish?*

*Smith: It was really delicious. This Japanese-style salad was also delicious.*

*Kato: That's good. I wanted to try and come to this restaurant once, but I didn't have a chance (until now).*

Smith: I see. How was that scallop dish?

Kato: The scallop dish was also good. Shrimp, cuttlefish, and mussels were also in the dish, among other things; and it was a big dish, but I finished it all.

Smith: I also had a little bit of your (Mr. Kato's) dish, so . . .

Kato: Wouldn't you like to have a little more wine?

Smith: Actually, I had a little too much to drink yesterday. When I saw Division Manager Oda, he/she gave me a beer gift certificate.

Kato: I see. Then, why don't we order dessert and coffee or something like that?

Smith: Yes, I'd like (lit., to eat) a cold dessert.

Kato: Well, let's take a look at the menu again. There are only cakes.

Smith: Well, I wanted to eat ice cream or sorbet, but . . . So, I will order only coffee.

Kato: Then, I will have a chocolate cake and tea.

## NUTS & BOLTS 2
### ONLY: DAKE AND SHIKA + NEGATIVE

Let's learn how to say *only X*. There are two different expressions you can use as described in the following chart.

---

**X dake**
*only X*
**X shika** + negative
*only X, nothing/no one but X*

---

It is important to know that **dake** and **shika** replace particles **ga**, **wa**, and **o**, but do not replace other particles such as **e, ni, de,** and **to**. Now, let's see how these expressions are used.

**Yasai dake tabemasu.**

*I eat only vegetables.*

**Yasai shika tabemasen.**
*I eat nothing but vegetables.*

**Gonin dake paatii ni kimashita.**
*Only five people came to the party.*

**Gonin shika paatii ni kimasen deshita.**
*No one else but five people came to the party.*

**Getsuyoobi to Suiyoobi to Kin'yoobi ni dake hatarakimasu.**
*I work only on Mondays, Wednesdays, and Fridays.*

**Getsuyoobi to Suiyoobi to Kin'yoobi ni shika hatarakimasen.**
*I work on no other days but on Mondays, Wednesdays, and Fridays.*

**Kinoo Mari-san to dake hanashimashita.**
*Yesterday, I only talked with Mari.*

**Kinoo Mari-san to shika hanashimasen deshita.**
*Yesterday, I talked with no one but Mari.*

Even though the two expressions can usually be used inter-changeably, there is a slight difference in the meaning. In most cases, when **X shika** + negative is used there is an implication that the speaker thinks the amount is not sufficient, whereas in the case of **dake** a speaker is just stating the fact, and there is no such implication. For instance, the sentence **Gonin shika paatii ni kimasen deshita** (*No one else but five people came to the party*) implies that the speaker thinks having only five people at a party is not sufficient. On the other hand, the sentence **Gonin dake paatii ni kimashita** (*Only five people came to the party*) is just stating the fact that five people came to the party.

## PRACTICE 2
Rephrase the following sentences using the construction **shika** + negative.

1. Miitingu ni Tanaka-san dake kimashita.

2. Supootsu wa tenisu dake shimasu.

3. Ani wa eego dake hanashimasu.

4. Nihon e itta toki, kyooto e dake ikimashita.

5. Kyoo wa keezai no benkyoo dake shimashita.

6. Buchoo ni dake ome ni kakarimashita.

7. Konshuu Ken-san to dake tenisu o shimashita.

8. Ima ni dake terebi ga arimasu.

## Cool links

Take a look at the following website:
http://www.japaneserestaurantinfo.com.
Even though it introduces Japanese restaurants in Los Angeles, you can enjoy it for other purposes as well. It describes some representative Japanese dishes like **shabu-shabu** and **tempura** in the section *Know More about Japanese Food*. You can also learn about Japanese food culture, such as the Japanese tea ceremony, in the *Special Column* section. Have fun!

## ANSWERS

**PRACTICE 1: 1.** Issho ni ongaku o kikimasen ka? **2.** Donna ongaku o kikimashoo ka? **3.** Nihon no ongaku o kikimashoo. **4.** Kissaten de hanashimasen ka? **5.** Dono kissaten e ikimashoo ka? **6.** Daigaku no tonari no kissaten e ikimashoo. **7.** Issho ni osushi o sukurimasen ka? **8.** Itsu tsukurimashoo ka? **9.** Nichiyoobi ni osushi o tsukurimashoo. **10.** Atarashii terebi o kaimasen ka? **11.** Doko de kaimashoo ka? **12.** Depaato de terebi o kaimashoo.

**PRACTICE 2: 1.** Miitingu ni Tanaka-san shika kimasen deshita. **2.** Supootsu wa tenisu shika shimasen. **3.** Ani wa eego shika hanashimasen. **4.** Nihon e itta toki, kyooto e shika ikimasen deshita. **5.** Kyoo wa keezai no benkyoo shika shimasen deshita. **6.** Buchoo ni shika ome ni kakarimasen deshita. **7.** Konshuu Kenji-san to shika tenisu o shimasen deshita. **8.** Ima ni shika terebi ga arimasen.

# UNIT 9
### *Sports and leisure*

In Unit 9, you will learn how to talk about your favorite sports and hobbies. Also, some key expressions you can use when asking other people questions about their favorite sports and hobbies will be introduced.

——————— Lesson 33 (words) ———————

## WORD LIST 1

| | |
|---|---|
| supootsu | *sports* |
| undoo | *exercise(s)* |
| tenisu | *tennis* |
| gorufu | *golf* |
| yakyuu | *baseball* |
| sakkaa | *soccer* |
| basukettobooru | *basketball* |
| bareebooru | *valleyball* |
| suiee | *swimming* |
| juudoo | *judo* |
| kendoo | *kendo* |
| tenisu kooto | *tennis court* |
| kurabu | *club* |
| shiai | *game* |
| kondo | *next time, this time, shortly* |
| daisuki | *like a lot* |
| joozu | *skillful* |
| heta | *unskillful* |
| tokui | *to be good at* |
| nigate | *to be bad at* |

| yappari | *after all, as expected* |
|---|---|
| **undooshimasu** | *to exercise* |
| **oyogimasu** | *to swim* |
| **naraimasu** | *to take lessons* |
| **yarimasu** | *to do* |

## NOTE 1

**Yarimasu** (*to do*) is less polite than **shimasu** (*to do*). As discussed in Lesson 29, **yarimasu** can be used in the sense of *to give*, but only when the indirect object refers to animals and plants. The use of **yarimasu** in the sense of *to do* is not so limited, and **yarimasu** and **shimasu** are often used interchangeably.

## NUTS & BOLTS 1

### QUESTION WORDS + KA AND MO

Let's learn how to say *something, someone, somewhere, nothing, nobody,* and *nowhere*.

| **nani ka** | *something* | **nani mo** + negative | *nothing* |
|---|---|---|---|
| **dare ka** | *someone* | **dare mo** + negative | *no one, nobody* |
| **doko ka** | *somewhere* | **doko mo** + negative | *nowhere* |

Let's look at how these expressions are used. Notice that the particles **ka** and **mo** replace particles **ga, wa,** and **o**.

A: **Nani ka tokugi** (*special skills*) **ga arimasu ka?**
*Do you have any special skills?*

B: **Iie, nani mo arimasen.**
*No, I don't have any.*

A: **Nani ka tabetai desu ka?**
*Do you want to eat anything?*

B: **Iie, nani mo tabetaku arimasen.**

*No, I don't want to eat anything.*

A: **Kinoo dare ka kimashita ka?**

*Did anyone come yesterday?*

B: **Iie, dare mo kimasen deshita.**

*No, no one came.*

Particles **ka** and **mo** do not replace any other particles but **ga, wa,** and **o.** Pay special attention to the position of particles in affirmative and negative sentences.

A: **Shuumatsu doko ka e ikimashita ka?**

*Did you go anywhere on the weekend/weekends?*

B: **Iie, doko e mo ikimasen deshita.**

*No, I didn't go anywhere.*

A: **Kinoo dare ka ni aimashita ka?**

*Did you meet anyone yesterday?*

B: **Iie, dare ni mo aimasen deshita.**

*No, I didn't meet anyone.*

A: **Ima dare ka to hanashitai desu ka?**

*Do you want to talk with someone now?*

B: **Iie, dare to mo hanashitaku arimasen.**

*No, I don't want to talk with anyone.*

As you can see, the particles **e, ni,** and **to** follow **ka** in affirmative sentences (e.g., **Dare ka to hanashimashita ka?**) but come between the question word and the particle **mo** in negative sentences (e.g., **Dare to mo hanashimasen deshita**).

## PRACTICE 1

Fill in the blanks with the appropriate expressions.

1. _____ eega ga mitai desu ka? *Do you want to see any movies?*

2. _____ mitaku arimasen. *I don't want to see any.*

3. Kinoo _____ ikimashita ka? *Did you go anywhere yesterday?*

4. Iie, _____ ikimasen deshita. *No, I didn't go anywhere.*

5. Ashita _____ aimasu ka? *Will you see anyone tomorrow?*

6. Iie, _____ aimasen. *No, I won't see anyone.*

## WORD LIST 2

| | |
|---|---|
| **shumi** | *hobby* |
| **tokugi** | *special ability, special skill* |
| **e** | *painting, drawing* |
| **dokusho** | *reading books* |
| **eega kanshoo** | *seeing movies (lit., movie appreciation)* |
| **shashin** | *photography* |
| **gakki** | *musical instrument* |
| **piano** | *piano* |
| **baiorin** | *violin* |
| **chero** | *cello* |
| **huruuto** | *flute* |
| **kurarinetto** | *clarinet* |
| **konsaato** | *concert* |
| **mochimasu/motsu** | *to have, to hold* |
| **ensooshimasu/ensoosuru** | *to perform* |
| **hikimasu/hiku** | *to play (piano)* |
| **hukimasu/huku** | *to play (a wind instruments)* |
| **tatakimasu/tataku** | *to play (a percussion instrument)* |
| **hoshii desu** | *to want* |

NOTE 2

Note that **hoshii** is an **i**-adjective, conjugated like other **i**-adjectives.

## NUTS & BOLTS 2
### CREATING NOUNS OUT OF VERBS: NOMINALIZER KOTO

It is possible to create nouns out of verbs in Japanese by adding the nominalizers **koto** and **no** to them. These Japanese nouns usually correspond to English nouns ending in *-ing*, e.g., *knitting*. **Koto** and **no** follow the plain form of verbs as described in the following chart.

plain form of verbs + **koto** or **no**

In most cases **koto** and **no** are interchangeable, but there are also some differences between the two. **No** is preferred when talking about personal matters, such as when talking about what you like doing or what you are good at. So, **no** is more colloquial, and **koto** sounds a little more bookish. Now, let's look at some sentences containing these nominalizers.

**Taberu no to neru no ga suki desu.**
*I like eating and sleeping.*

**Benkyoosuru no wa amari suki ja arimasen.**
*I don't like studying so much.*

**Piano o hiku no ga joozu desu.**
*I'm good at playing the piano.*

**Nihongo o hanasu no wa kantan desu.**
*Speaking Japanese is easy.*

**E o kaku no ga nigate desu.**
*I'm poor at (and dislike) painting.*

**Hon o yomu koto wa ii koto desu.**
*Reading books is a good thing.*

**Hito ni atte hanasu koto wa taisetsu desu.**
*Meeting and talking to people is important.*

**Shumi wa ryoorisuru koto desu.**
*My hobby is cooking.*

**No** cannot appear before the copula, **desu** and **da**. So, you can use only **koto** in the following sentences.

**Shumi wa eega o miru koto desu.**
*My hobby is to watch movies.*

**Tokugi wa kurarinetto o fuku koto desu.**
*My special skill is playing the clarinet.*

## PRACTICE 2
Translate into English.

1. Kanji (*Chinese characters*) o kaku no wa muzukashii desu.

2. Undoosuru koto wa ii koto desu.

3. Shumi wa baiorin o hiku koto desu.

4. Tomodachi to dekakeru no wa tanoshii (*fun, enjoyable*) desu.

5. Eega o miru no ga suki desu.

6. Tokugi wa huruuto o fuku koto desu.

7. Sukina tabemono (*food*) shika tabenai no wa yoku arimasen.

8. Sakkaa o suru no ga nigate desu.

### *Culture note*
Sumo is considered to be the Japanese national sport, even though there aren't so many people who actually practice the sport. Still, many people, especially people in the older generation, enjoy watching sumo competitions on TV. There are also women's sumo competitions—for instance, at the college level—but women

are prohibited from being professional sumo wrestlers. Recently the number of foreign professional sumo wrestlers has been increasing, whereas the number of young Japanese men who want to practice the sport on that level is decreasing. Baseball, on the other hand, is a sport that is popular in Japan with a much wider audience. Recently more and more famous Japanese players have left for the U.S.A. to join Major League Baseball teams, and some of the major league games are broadcast in Japan. After the Japanese professional soccer league (the J League) was established in 1992, soccer became very popular, too, and people became especially involved during the World Cup.

## ANSWERS

**PRACTICE 1: 1.** Nanika; **2.** Nanimo; **3.** doko ka e/doko ka ni; **4.** doko e mo/doko ni mo; **5.** dare ka ni/dare ka to; **6.** dare ni mo/dare to mo

**PRACTICE 2: 1.** *Writing kanji is difficult.* **2.** *Doing exercises/ Exercising is a good thing.* **3.** *My hobby is playing the violin.* **4.** *It's enjoyable to go out with friends.* **5.** *I like seeing movies.* **6.** *My special skill is to play the flute.* **7.** *It's not good to eat only food you like.* **8.** *I'm poor at playing soccer.*

---
## Lesson 34 (phrases)
---

### PHRASE LIST 1

| | |
|---|---|
| **donna supootsu** | *what kind of sports* |
| **juudoo no kurabu** | *judo club* |
| **yakyuu to sakkaa** | *baseball and soccer* |
| **juudoo ka kendoo** | *judo or kendo* |
| **gakusee no toki** | *when I was a student* |
| **shiai ga aru toki** | *when there's a game* |
| **ie no chikaku no tenisu kooto** | *tennis court near my house* |
| **heejitsu tsukatte iru kooto** | *the tennis court I'm using on weekdays* |
| **nijikan gurai** | *for about two hours* |

| | |
|---|---|
| toku ni | *especially* |
| nando ka | *several times* |
| tenisu ga joozu desu | *am/are/is good at tennis* |
| tenisu ga heta desu | *am/are/is bad at tennis* |
| suugaku ga tokui desu | *am/are/is good at (and like) mathematics* |
| suugaku ga nigate desu | *am/are/is poor at (and dislike) mathematics* |
| basukettobooru o yatte imasu | *am/are/is playing basketball* |
| kurabu ni haitte imasu | *belong/belongs to a club* |
| nanika supootsu o shimasu | *play/plays some sports* |
| nanimo supootsu o shimasen | *play/plays no sports* |
| zenzen supootsu o shimasen | *don't/doesn't play sports at all* |
| Maa maa desu. | *So-so.* |

NOTE 1

While **joozu desu** and **tokui desu** both translate as *to be good at*, **joozu desu** is used when describing one's skills and cannot be used when referring to certain academic subjects, like mathematics, physics, or history. **Tokui desu** can be used when talking about playing sports, playing instruments, or having good skills in other areas, including in academic subjects. The same distinction exists between **heta desu** and **nigate desu**.

## NUTS & BOLTS 1
### POTENTIAL FORM OF VERBS: *CAN DO* AND *TO BE ABLE TO DO*
The potential form of verbs is used to express the meaning of the English *can/to be able to* + verb. Let's first see how the potential form of Class I and Class II verbs is formed.

---

### Class I (**u**-verbs)
Drop final -**u** from the dictionary form of a verb and attach **-eru**.

### Class II (**ru**-verbs)
Drop final -**ru** from the dictionary form of a verb and attach **-rareru**.

---

Now, let's look at the conjugation of the potential form of some verbs.

| Class I (u-verbs) | | | | |
|---|---|---|---|---|
| Dictionary form | Potential form of verbs (plain form) | | | |
| | Non-past affirmative | Non-past negative | Past affirmative | Past negative |
| kaku (*to write*) | kakeru | kakenai | kaketa | kakenakatta |
| yomu (*to read*) | yomeru | yomenai | yometa | yomenakatta |
| kiku (*to listen*) | kikeru | kikenai | kiketa | kikenakatta |
| tsukau (*to use*) | tsukaeru | tsukaenai | tsukaeta | tsukaenakatta |
| iku (*to go*) | ikeru | ikenai | iketa | ikenakatta |

| Class II (ru-verbs) | | | | |
|---|---|---|---|---|
| Dictionary form | Potential form of verbs (plain form) | | | |
| | Non-past affirmative | Non-past negative | Past affirmative | Past negative |
| taberu (*to eat*) | taberareru | taberarenai | taberareta | taberarenakatta |
| miru (*to see*) | mirareru | mirarenai | mirareta | mirarenakatta |
| okiru (*to get up*) | okirareru | okirarenai | okirareta | okirarenakatta |
| neru (*to sleep*) | nerareru | nerarenai | nerareta | nerarenakatta |
| oshieru (*to teach*) | oshierareru | oshierarenai | oshierareta | oshierarenakatta |

And here are the conjugations of the two Class III verbs **suru** (*to do*) and **kuru** (*to come*).

| Class III | | | | |
|---|---|---|---|---|
| Dictionary form | Potential form of verbs (plain form) | | | |
| | Non-past affirmative | Non-past negative | Past affirmative | Past negative |
| **suru** (*to do*) | **dekiru** | **dekinai** | **dekita** | **dekinakatta** |
| **kuru** (*to come*) | **korareru** | **korarenai** | **korareta** | **korarenakatta** |

Now, let's look at how the potential form of verbs are used in sentences. Note that the logical direct object of potential form of verbs is marked by the particle **ga** instead of **o**.

A: **Nihongo no hon ga yomemasu ka?**
*Can you read Japanese books?*

B: **Ee, sukoshi yomemasu./Iie, zenzen yomemasen.**
*Yes, I can read a little./No, I cannot read at all.*

A: **Ashita gozen go ji ni okiraremasu ka?**
*Can you get up at 5:00 a.m. tomorrow?*

B: **Tabun okirareru deshoo./Tabun okirarenai deshoo.**
*I probably can get up./Probably, I cannot get up.*

A: **Osashimi ga taberaremasu ka?**
*Can you eat sliced raw fish?*

B: **Iie, taberaremasen. Demo, osushi wa taberaremasu.**
*No, I cannot eat it. But I can eat sushi.*

A: **Nanigo ga hanasemasu ka?**
*What languages can you speak?*

B: **Eego to Supeingo ga hanasemasu.**

*I can speak English and Spanish.*

A: **Suugaku no shukudai ga dekimashita ka?**

*Were you able to do the mathematics homework?*

B: **Hai, dekimashita./Iie, muzukashisugimashita kara, dekimasen deshita.**

*Yes, I was able to do it./No, it was too difficult, so I couldn't do it.*

A: **Nichiyoobi ni kaisha ni koraremasu ka?**

*Can you come to the office (lit., company) on Sunday?*

B: **Hai, korareru to omoimasu./Iie, korarenai to omoimasu.**

*Yes, I think I can come./No, I think I cannot come.*

There is another expression which corresponds to the English *can/to be able to*; it is used in the following structure.

> dictionary form of a verb + **koto ga dekiru**

**Koto** is the nominalizer that was introduced in Lesson 33, and **dekiru** is the potential form of **suru** (*to do*). Let's look at how this expression is used.

**Kawada-san wa Doitsugo to Furansugo o hanasu koto ga dekimasu.**

*Mr./Ms. Kawada is able to speak German and French.*

**Kinoo sono konpyuutaa o tsukau koto ga dekimasen deshita.**

*I was unable to use that computer yesterday.*

**Tomodachi ni ken (*ticket*) o moratta node, yakyuu no shiai o miru koto ga dekimashita.**

*I got a ticket from my friend, so I was able to see a baseball game.*

**Asatte wa kaisha ni kuru koto ga dekinai to omoimasu.**

*I think I am not able to come to the office the day after tomorrow.*

**Nani ka gakki o ensoosuru koto ga dekimasu ka?**
*Can you play any musical instruments?*

## PRACTICE 1
Complete the sentences using the appropriate form of the verbs given in parentheses.

1. Paachii ni _____ ka? (iku) *Can you go to the party?*

2. Nakata-san to _____. (hanasu) *I couldn't talk with Mr. Nakata.*

3. Ashita gakkoo ni _____. (kuru) *I cannot come to school tomorrow.*

4. Miitingu ni _____ ka? (deru)? *Can you attend the meeting?*

5. Yuumeena e ga _____. (miru) *I couldn't see the famous painting.*

6. Nanika supootsu ga _____ ka? (suru) *Can you play any sports?*

## PRACTICE 2
Translate into English.

1. Ane wa piano to baiorin o hiku koto ga dekimasu.

2. Chichi wa ryoorisuru koto ga dekimasen.

3. Kyoo sensee ni au koto ga dekimasen deshita.

4. Ototoi seminaa ni deru koto ga dekimasen deshita.

5. Kore wa taisetsuna mono desu kara, dare ni mo ageru koto ga dekimasen.

## PHRASE LIST 2
| | |
|---|---|
| **baiorin to chero to piano** | *the violin, the cello, and the piano* |
| **Ginza no resutoran** | *a restaurant in Ginza* |
| **kondo no Doyoobi** | *next Saturday* |
| **e o kaku koto to dokusho** | *painting and reading books* |
| **shashin o toru no** | *taking photos* |

| | |
|---|---|
| Megan-san ga kaita e | *the painting that Megan painted* |
| ima tsukatte iru baiorin | *the violin I am using now* |
| atarashii no | *new one* |
| atarashii no ga hoshii | *want/wants a new one* |
| sore kara | *and then* |
| jitsu wa | *actually* |
| ima made ni | *up to now* |
| konsaato de | *at a concert* |
| isshuukan ni nisatsu gurai | *about two books a week* |
| nanika gakki ga ensoodekimasu | *can play some musical instruments* |
| nanimo gakki ga ensoodekimasen | *can play no musical instruments* |
| naratte imasu | *to be taking lessons on* |
| kamera o motte dekakemasu | *go/goes out with a camera* |
| nakanaka joozu ni fukemasen | *cannot play (a wind instrument) well* |
| Sugoi desu ne. | *That's amazing.* |

## NUTS & BOLTS 2
### TO WANT + OBJECT OR PERSON: GA HOSHII
You learned how to express the wish to engage in an activity, in Lessons 19 and 31. Now, let's learn how to say you'd like to get something or someone, like an object or a person.

> **X ga hoshii (desu).**
> *I want X.*

Just like **tai** (*to want to do something*), the conjugation of **hoshii** (*to want someone or something*) is the same as that of **i**-adjectives.

| | Non-past affirmative | Non-past negative | Past affirmative | Past negative |
|---|---|---|---|---|
| Plain form | hoshii | hoshiku nai | hoshikatta | hoshiku nakatta |
| Polite form | hoshii desu | hoshiku nai desu<br>hoshiku nakatta desu | hoshiku arimasen | hoshikatta desu<br>hoshiku arimasen deshita |

Let's look at how this expression can be used. Please note that the direct object of **hoshii** is marked by **ga**.

A: **Ima nani ka hoshii desu ka?**
*Do you want anything now?*

B: **Ee, jitsu wa atarashii kuruma ga hoshii n desu.**
*Yes, actually I want a new car.*

B: **Iie, nani mo hoshiku nai desu/hoshiku arimasen.**
*No, I don't want anything.*

A: **Kyonen no tanjoobi (*birthday*) ni nani ga hoshikatta desu ka?**
*What did you want for your birthday last year?*

B: **Kamera ga hoshikatta desu.**
*I wanted a camera.*

B: **Toku ni nani mo hoshiku nakatta desu./Toku ni nani mo hoshiku arimasen deshita.**
*I didn't want anything in particular.*

Note that you can use **hoshii** only when the subject is either a speaker or an addressee. If the subject is the third person, you have to use **hoshigatte iru**.

the third person + **ga/wa X o hoshigatte iru/imasu.**

**Hoshigatte iru/imasu** expresses someone's current desire; the direct object of **hoshigatte iru/imasu** is marked by the direct object marker **o**.

**Ani wa atarashii kuruma o hoshigatte imasu.**
*My older brother wants a new car.*

**Tsuyoshi-san wa gaarufurendo o hoshigatte imasu.**
*Tsuyoshi wants a girlfriend.*

**Lopez-san wa Nihongo no jisho o hoshigatte imasu.**
*Mr./Ms. Lopez wants a Japanese dictionary.*

When expressing someone's long-term, habitual desire, **hoshigaru** is used.

**Imooto wa itsumo watashi no mono o hoshigarimasu.**
*My younger sister always wants my belongings.*

At this stage, it is important for you to master the expression **hoshii** (*I/you want*). As for **hoshigatte iru** and **hoshigaru**, it is sufficient if you can recognize them.

## PRACTICE 3
Translate into English.

1. Atarashii konpyuutaa ga hoshii desu ga, takai desu kara kaemasen.

2. Sono terebi wa ookisugimasu kara, hoshiku arimasen.

3. Chuugokugo o benkyooshite imasu kara, Chuugokujin no tomodachi ga hoshii desu.

4. Kono kaban wa furui desu kara, atarashii no ga hoshii desu.

5. Otooto wa atarashii kurarinetto o hoshigatte imasu.

## ANSWERS

**PRACTICE 1: 1.** ikemasu ka; **2.** hanasemasen deshita; **3.** koraremasen; **4.** deraremasu; **5.** miraremasen deshita; **6.** dekimasu

**PRACTICE 2: 1.** *My older sister is able to play the piano and the violin.* **2.** *My father is unable to cook.* **3.** *I wasn't able to see my teacher today.* **4.** *I was unable to attend the seminar the day before yesterday.* **5.** *This is an important thing, so I am unable to give it to anyone.*

**PRACTICE 3: 1.** *I want a new computer, but I cannot buy it because it's expensive.* **2.** *That television is too big, so I don't want it.* **3.** *I'm studying Chinese, so I want Chinese friends.* **4.** *This bag is old, so I want a new one.* **5.** *My younger brother wants a new clarinet.*

––––––––– Lesson 35 (sentences) –––––––––

## SENTENCE GROUP 1

| | |
|---|---|
| **Donna supootsu ga suki desu ka?** | *What kind of sports do you like?* |
| **Nanika supootsu o shimasu ka?** | *Do you play any sports?* |

| | |
|---|---|
| Gakusee no toki wa, basukettobooru o yatte imashita. | When I was a student, I played basketball. |
| Gakusee no toki wa, juudoo no kurabu ni haitte imashita. | When I was a student, I belonged to a judo club. |
| Toku ni nani mo undoo o shite imasen. | I am not playing any sports in particular. |
| Zenzen tenisu o shimasen ka? | Don't you play tennis at all? |
| Yoku ie no chikaku no kooto e itte, nijikan gurai tenisu o shimasu. | I often go to the tennis court near my house and play tennis for about two hours. |
| Tenisu ga joozu na n deshoo ne? | You are probably good at tennis, aren't you? |
| Nando ka tenisu o shita koto ga arimasu kedo, heta na n desu. | I have played tennis several times, but I'm not good at it. |
| Yakyuu to sakkaa o miru no ga daisuki desu. | I like watching baseball and soccer very much. |
| Shiai ga aru toki wa, itsumo terebi de mite imasu. | When there is a game, I am always watching it on TV. |
| Yakyuu to sakkaa to dochira no hoo ga suki desu ka? | Which do you like better, baseball or soccer? |
| Yakyuu no hoo ga suki desu. | I like baseball better. |
| Juudoo ka kendoo o naraitai n desu kedo, ima wa jikan ga nai shi . . . | I want to take judo or kendo lessons, but I don't have time now, so . . . |
| Moshi narau n dattara, kendo yori juudoo no hoo ga ii to omoimasu. | If you take lessons, I think judo is better than kendo. |
| Kondo issho ni tenisu o shimasen ka? | Why don't we play tennis together sometime? |
| Boku mo amari joozu ni dekimasen kara, daijoobu desu yo. | I cannot play it so well either, so it's okay. |

Heejitsu tsukatteiru kooto ga    *There's a tennis court near the office that*
kaisha no chikaku ni arimasu.    *I'm using on weekdays.*

Kondo jikan ga aru toki ni    *Let's go there next time when we have*
soko e ikimashoo.    *time.*

## NUTS & BOLTS 1
### COMPARATIVES

You can compare two items A and B using the structure below.

---

**A wa B yori X.**
*A is more X than B.*

---

In this structure, X can be an adjective or the combination of an adverb and a verb, like **takusan tabemasu** (*eat a lot*). Now, let's look at how this structure can be used in sentences.

**Amerika wa nihon yori ookii desu.**
*The U.S.A. is bigger than Japan.*

**Kono apaato wa ano apaato yori benri desu.**
*This apartment is more convenient than that apartment.*

**Mariko-san wa Takeshi-san yori takusan benkyooshimasu.**
*Mariko studies more than Takeshi.*

When asking and answering questions comparing two items, the following structures are used.

---

**A to B to dochira no hoo ga X ka?**
*Which is more X, A or B?*

**A/B no hoo ga (B/A yori) X.**
*A/B is more X than B/A.*

---

Let's see how these expressions can be used. Please note that **B yori** (*than B*) is often dropped when answering questions.

A: Koohii to koocha to dochira no hoo ga suki desu ka?
*Which do you like better, coffee or tea?*

B: Koocha no hooga koohii yori suki desu.
*I like tea more than coffee.*

A: Yoshiko-san to Ichiroo-san to dochira no hoo ga takusan tabemasu ka?
*Who eats more, Yoshiko or Ichiro?*

B: Yoshiko-san no hoo ga takusan taberu to omoimasu.
*I think Yoshiko eats more.*

A: Sushi to piza to dochira no hoo ga oishii to omoimasu ka?
*Which do you think is more delicious, sushi or pizza?*

B: Sushi no hoo ga oishii to omoimasu.
*I think sushi is more delicious.*

## PRACTICE 1
Using the words inside parentheses, form Japanese sentences that match English sentences. Make sure you use the structure **A wa B yori X**.

1. *The U.S. is bigger than England.* (Amerika, Igirisu, ookii desu)

2. *This park is more quiet than that park.* (ano kooen, shizuka desu, kono kooen)

3. *This book is more interesting than that book.* (omoshiroi desu, ano hon, kono hon)

4. *Kenji exercises more (lit., does more exercises) than Akira.* (Akira, takusan, Kenji, undooshimasu)

5. *I think the subway is more convenient than the bus.* (basu, chikatetsu, to, omoimasu, benri da)

## PRACTICE 2

Make questions and answers using the words provided in parentheses. Make sure you use the structures **A to B to dochira no hoo ga X desu ka?** and **A/B no hoo ga (B/A yori) X**.

1. (heejitsu, suki desu, shuumatsu)

   Q. *Which do you like better, weedends or weekdays?*

   A. *I like weekends better than weekdays.*

2. (yoku, nihoncha, nomimasu, koocha)

   Q. *Which do you drink more often, Japanese tea or black tea?*

   A. *I drink black tea more often.*

3. (ookii desu, Kankoku, Chuugoku)

   Q. *Which is bigger, China or Korea?*

   A. *China is bigger than Korea.*

4. (omoimasu, niku ryoori, oishii, sakana ryoori, to)

   Q. *Which do you think is more delicious, fish-based cuisine or meat-based cuisine?*

   A. *I think fish-based cuisine is more delicious.*

5. (takusan, biiru, nomemasu, wain)

   Q. *Which can you drink more of, beer or wine?*

   A. *I can drink more beer.*

## SENTENCE GROUP 2

| | |
|---|---|
| **Nani ka shumi ga arimasu ka?** | *Do you have any hobbies?* |
| **Nani mo shumi ga arimasen.** | *I have no hobbies.* |
| **Shumi wa e o kaku koto desu.** | *My hobby is painting.* |
| **E o kaku no ga suki desu.** | *I like painting.* |
| **Shashin o toru no ga suki desu.** | *I like taking pictures.* |

| | |
|---|---|
| Hon o yomu no mo suki desu. | *I like reading books, too.* |
| Isshuukan ni nisatsu gurai hon o yomimasu. | *I read about two books a week.* |
| Megan-san ga kaita e o mite mitai desu. | *I want to try seeing the paintings that Megan made.* |
| Shuumatsu yoku kamera o motte dekakemasu. | *On weekends, I often go out and take a camera with me.* |
| Nani ka gakki ga ensoodekimasu ka? | *Can you play any musical instruments?* |
| Nani mo gakki ga ensoodekimasen. | *I cannot play any musical instruments.* |
| Baiorin to chero to piano ga hikemasu. | *I can play the violin, the cello and the piano.* |
| Furuuto o naratte imasu kedo, nakanaka joozu ni fukemasen. | *I am taking flute lessons, but I cannot play it well.* |
| Baiorin to chero to piano no naka de dore ga ichiban tokui desu ka? | *Which are you best at, the violin, the cello or the piano?* |
| Moo nijuunen gurai naratte imasu kara, baiorin ga ichiban tokui desu. | *Since I have been taking lessons for twenty years already, I am best at the violin.* |
| Ima tsukatte iru baiorin wa furui node, atarashii no ga hoshii desu. | *The violin I am using now is old, so I want a new one.* |
| Totemo takai desu kara, kaemasen. | *Since it's very expensive, I cannot buy it.* |
| Ima made ni konsaato de ensooshita koto ga arimasu ka? | *Have you ever performed at a concert?* |
| Kondo no Doyoobi ni Ginza no resutoran de ensoosuru n desu kedo, irasshaimasen ka? | *I will perform at a restaurant in Ginza this Saturday, so why don't you come?* |

## NUTS & BOLTS 2
### THE SUPERLATIVE

You can compare three or more items using the structures described below.

---

**A to B to C no naka de A ga ichiban X desu.**
*A is the most X among A, B, and C.*

**D no naka de A ga ichiban X desu.**
*Among D, A is the most X.*

---

Let's see now how these structures can be used.

**Piano to baiorin to furuuto no naka de piano ga ichiban joozu desu.**
*Among the piano, the violin, and the flute, I am the best at the piano.*

**Gakki no naka de piano ga ichiban joozu desu.**
*Among musical instruments, I'm the best at the piano.*

**Mari-san to Ken-san to Ryooko-san no naka de Ken-san ga ichiban wakai (*young*) desu.**
*Among Mari, Ken, and Ryooko, Ken is the youngest.*

**Kono kurasu no gakusee no naka de Ken-san ga ichiban wakai desu.**
*Among the students in this class, Ken is the youngest.*

You can ask and answer the questions comparing three or more items using the structures below.

---

**A to B to C no naka de dore/dare/doko/itsu/etc. ga ichiban X desu ka?**
*Which/Who/Where/When/etc. is the most X, A, B, or C?*

**D no naka de nani/dare/doko/itsu/etc. ga ichiban X desu ka?**
*What/Who/Where/When/etc. is the most X among D?*

---

Note that **dore** is usually used when listing the items to be compared like **tenisu to gorufu to yakyuu no naka de** (*between tennis, golf, and baseball*), and **nani** is usually used when the items are not listed, like **supootsu no naka de** (*among sports*). Let's see how these structures can be used.

A: Ocha to koocha to koohii no naka de dore ga ichiban suki desu ka?
*Which do you like best, Japanese tea, black tea, or coffee?*

B: Koohii ga ichiban suki desu.
*I like coffee best.*

A: Nomimono no naka de nani ga ichiban suki desu ka?
*Among beverages, what do you like best?*

B: Tomato juusu ga ichiban suki desu.
*I like tomato juice best.*

A: Doyoobi to Nichiyoobi to Getsuyoobi no naka de nan-yoobi ga ichiban isogashii desu ka?
*Which day of the week are you busiest, Saturday, Sunday, or Monday?*

B: Getsuyoobi ga ichiban isogashii desu.
*I am busiest on Monday.*

A: Isshuukan no naka de nan-yoobi ga ichiban isogashii desu ka?
*On what day of the week are you busiest?*

B: Kin'yoobi ga ichiban isogashii desu.
*I'm busiest on Friday.*

## PRACTICE 3
Translate into Japanese using the expressions in parentheses. You need to provide the appropriate particles in order to make complete sentences.

1. *Which do you like best, tennis, golf, or jogging?* (suki desu, tenisu, jogingu, ichiban, gorufu, dore, ka, naka)

2. *I am best at the violin, among the musical instruments.* (baiorin, naka, ichiban, gakki, tokui desu)

3. *Which country is the biggest, Japan, China or Korea?* (ookii desu, Nihon, dono kuni, Kankoku, Chuugoku, ichiban, ka, naka)

4. *Who works the most among the employees* (shain)? (takusan, shain, dare, naka, ichiban, ka, hatarakimasu)

5. *December is the busiest month of the year (lit., in a year).* (ichinen, juunigatsu, isogashii desu, naka, ichiban)

## *Discovery activities*

Ask your Japanese friends, classmates, or colleagues what their hobbies are in Japanese. You can also ask them about their favorite sports and whether or not they have some other special skills, like painting or playing instruments. You can extend the conversation by asking if there is something they are particularly good or bad at. These topics are easy to talk about, and people will most likely ask you the same questions in return. If there aren't any Japanese speakers around you, ask the same questions to your family, friends, or colleagues in English. Write down the information you collected, and then try saying it in Japanese.

## ANSWERS
**PRACTICE 1: 1.** Amerika wa Igirisu yori ookii desu. **2.** Kono kooen wa ano kooen yori shizuka desu. **3.** Kono hon wa ano hon yori omoshiroi desu. **4.** Kenji-san wa Akira-san yori takusan undooshimasu. **5.** Chikatetsu wa basu yori benri da to omoimasu.

**PRACTICE 2: 1.** Q. Shuumatsu to heejitsu to dochira no hoo ga suki desu ka? A. Shuumatsu no hoo ga heejitsu yori suki desu. **2.** Q. Nihoncha to koocha to dochira no hoo ga yoku nomimasu ka? A. Koocha no hoo ga yoku nomimasu. **3.** Q. Chuugoku to Kankoku to dochira no hoo ga ookii desu ka? A. Chuugoku no hoo ga Kankoku yori ookii desu.

**4. Q.** Sakana ryoori to niku ryoori to dochira no hoo ga oishii to omoimasu ka? **A.** Sakana ryoori no hoo ga oishii to omoimasu. **5.** Biiru to wain to dochira no hoo ga takusan nomemasu ka? **A.** Biiru no hoo ga takusan nomemasu.

**PRACTICE 3: 1.** Tenisu to gorufu to jogingu no naka de dore ga ichiban suki desu ka? **2.** Gakki no naka de baiorin ga ichiban tokui desu. **3.** Nihon to Chuugoku to Kankoku no naka de dono kuni ga ichiban ookii desu ka? **4.** Shain no naka de dare ga ichiban takusan hatarakimasu ka? **5.** Ichinen no naka de juunigatsu ga ichiban isogashii desu.

─────────── **Lesson 36 (conversations)** ───────────

## CONVERSATION 1

Bill and Kenji are talking about sports during a break at work.

Kenji: Bill-san wa donna supootsu ga suki desu ka?

Bill: Daigakusee no toki wa, basukettobooru o yatte imashita. Demo, ima wa tenisu ga suki de, shuumatsu wa yoku ie no chikaku no tenisu kooto e itte, nijikan gurai tenisu o shimasu.

Kenji: Hee, jaa, tenisu ga joozu na n deshoo ne.

Bill: Maa maa desu. Sore kara, yakyuu to sakkaa o miru no ga daisuki de, shiai ga aru toki wa, itsumo terebi de mite imasu.

Kenji: Soo desu ka. Yakyuu to sakkaa to dochira no hoo ga suki desu ka?

Bill: Uun, yappari yakyuu no hoo ga suki desu ne. Kenji-san wa nanika supootsu o shimasu ka?

Kenji: Boku wa gakusee no toki wa juudoo no kurabu ni haitte imashita ga, ima wa toku ni nanimo undoo o shite imasen.

Bill: Soo desu ka. Demo, Juudoo wa ii desu ne. Boku mo juudoo ka kendoo o narai tai n desu kedo, ima wa jikan ga nai shi . . .

Kenji: Moshi narau n dattara, kendoo yori juudoo no hoo ga ii to omoimasu yo.

Bill: Soo desu ne. Boku mo soo omoimasu. Tokoro de, Kenji-san wa zenzen tenisu o shimasen ka?

Kenji: Nando ka shita koto ga arimasu kedo, heta na n desu.

Bill: Kondo issho ni tenisu o shimasen ka?

Kenji: Demo, boku wa heta desu kara . . .

Bill: Boku mo amari joozu ni dekimasen kara, daijoobu desu yo. Boku ga heejitsu tamani tsukatte iru kooto ga kaisha no chikaku ni arimasu kara, soko de shimasen ka?

Kenji: Ee, jaa kondo jikan ga aru toki ni soko e ikimashoo.


Kenji: *What kind of sports do you like, Bill?*

Bill: *I played basketball when I was a college student. But, now I like tennis and often go to the tennis court near my house and play tennis for about two hours on weekends.*

Kenji: *Well, then, you are probably good at tennis, aren't you?*

Bill: *So-so. And, I also like watching baseball and soccer very much, so when there is a game, I am always watching it on TV.*

Kenji: *I see. And which do you like better, baseball or soccer?*

Bill: *Well, I like baseball better, after all. Kenji, do you play any sports?*

Kenji: *I was in the judo club when I was a student, but now I'm not exercising much.*

Bill: *I see. But, judo is good, isn't it? I'd (lit., I) also like to take lessons in judo or kendo, but I don't have time now, so . . .*

Kenji: *If you take lessons, I think judo is better than kendo.*

Bill: *Yes. I think so, too. By the way, Kenji, don't you play tennis at all?*

Kenji: *I have played several times, but I am bad at it.*
Bill: *Why don't we play tennis together sometime?*
Ken: *But, I'm bad at it, so . . .*
Bill: *I cannot play so well either, so it's alright. The tennis court that I use occasionally on weekdays is near the office, so why don't we play there?*
Kenji: *Yes, so next time when we have time, let's go there!*

## NUTS & BOLTS 1

### TALKING ABOUT PAST EXPERIENCES

You can talk about your past experiences using the structure below.

> plain past tense form of a verb (**ta**-form)
> + **koto ga arimasu/aru**

**Nihon e itta koto ga arimasu.**

*I have been to Japan.*

**Kyooto no shashin o totta koto ga arimasu.**

*I have taken pictures of Kyoto.*

**Konsaato de ensooshita koto ga arimasu.**

*I have performed at a concert.*

When answering questions, you can just use **arimasu** or **arimasen** without repeating the verb in the **-ta** form followed by **koto ga**, as shown in the following example.

A: **Kono eega o mita koto ga arimasu ka?**

*Have you seen this movie?*

B: **Ee, arimasu./Iie, arimasen.**

*Yes, I have./No, I haven't.*

The following time expressions are often used with this structure.

| ima made ni, kore made ni | *up to now* |
|---|---|
| ichido | *once* |
| nando mo | *many times* |
| ichido mo + negative | *never* |
| mada + negative | *not yet* |

A: **Ima made ni Porutogarugo o benkyooshita koto ga arimasu ka?**
*Have you ever studied Portuguese before?*

B: **Iie, ichido mo arimasen.**
*No, I have never (studied it).*

A: **Toshokan de hon o karita koto ga arimasu ka?**
*Have you borrowed books at the library?*

B: **Hai, nando mo arimasu.**
*Yes, I have (borrowed them) many times.*

A: **Nihongo de repooto o kaita koto ga arimasu ka?**
*Have you written a report in Japanese?*

B: **Iie, mada arimasen.**
*No, I haven't (written it) yet.*

A: **Kore made ni osushi o tsukutta koto ga arimasu ka?**
*Have you ever made sushi?*

B: **Hai, ichido arimasu.**
*Yes, I have (made it) once.*

## PRACTICE 1
Translate into English.

1. Ima made ni sono hon o yonda koto ga arimasu ka?

2. Ichido mo piano o hiita koto ga arimasen.

3. Ichido daigaku no tenisu kooto de tenisu o shita koto ga arimasu.

4. Mada sumo o mita koto ga arimasen kara, kondo zehi mite mitai desu.

5. Eki no mae no Itaria ryoori no resutoran e nando mo itta koto ga arimasu.

## CONVERSATION 2
Megan and Ayaka are chatting about their interests and hobbies on their way home from work.

Ayaka: Megan-san wa nani ka shumi ga arimasu ka?

Megan: Etto, e o kaku no ga suki desu. Sore kara, hon o yomu no mo suki de, isshuukan ni nisatsu gurai yomu n desu yo.

Ayaka: Hee, e o kaku koto to dokusho desu ka. Ii desu nee. Kondo, Megan-san ga kaita e o mite mitai desu.

Megan: Amari joozu ja arimasen kedo. Ayaka-san wa nani ka shumi ga arimasu ka?

Ayaka: Watashi wa e o kaku koto wa dekinai kedo, shashin o toru no ga suki na n desu.
Shuumatsu wa yoku kamera o motte dekakeru n desu yo.

Megan: Soo desu ka.

Ayaka: Megan-san wa nani ka gakki ga ensoodekimasu ka?

Megan: Watashi wa nani mo gakki ga ensoodekinai n desu. Ima furuuto o naratte imasu kedo,

nakanaka joozu ni fukemasen. Totemo
muzukashii desu. Ayaka-san wa?

Ayaka: Watashi wa baiorin to chero to piano ga
hikemasu.

Megan: Hee, sugoi desu ne. Baiorin to chero to piano
no naka de dore ga ichiban tokui desu ka?

Ayaka: Moo nijuunen gurai naratte imasu kara, baiorin
ga ichiban tokui desu.

Megan: Soo desu ka.

Ayaka: Ima tsukatte iru baiorin wa hurui node,
atarashii no ga hoshii n desu kedo, totemo
takai desu kara kaemasen.

Megan: Ima made ni konsaato de ensooshita koto ga
arimasu ka?

Ayaka: Ee, nando ka arimasu. Jitsu wa kondo no
Doyoobi ni Ginza no resutoran de ensoosuru n
desu kedo, irasshaimasen ka?

Megan: Ee, zehi ikitai desu.

*Ayaka:*   *Megan, do you have any hobbies?*

*Megan:*   *Well, I like painting. Besides, I like reading books, so I
read about two books per week.*

*Ayaka:*   *Painting and reading books, I see. That's good. I'd like
to see (lit., I want to try seeing) the paintings you've
done some day.*

*Megan:*   *I'm not so good at it, but . . . Ayaka, do you have any
hobbies?*

*Ayaka:*   *I can't paint, but I like taking pictures. On weekends, I
often go out with a camera.*

*Megan:*   *I see.*

*Ayaka:*   *Megan, can you play any musical instruments?*

*Megan:*   *I cannot play any instruments. I am taking flute lessons
now, but cannot play it well so easily. It's very difficult.
What about you, Ayaka?*

*Ayaka:*   *I can play the violin, the cello, and the piano.*

*Megan:*   *Wow, that's amazing, isn't it? Which one are you best
at, violin, cello or piano?*

Ayaka: *I've been taking lessons for about twenty years already, so I'm best at the violin.*

Megan: *I see.*

Ayaka: *Since the violin which I am using now is old, I'd like to buy a new one, but it's very expensive, so I cannot buy it.*

Megan: *Have you ever performed at a concert?*

Ayaka: *Yes, I performed several times. Actually, I will perform at a restaurant in Ginza next Saturday, so why don't you come?*

Megan: *Yes, by all means, I'd like to come.*

## NUTS & BOLTS 2
### RELATIVE CLAUSES

Nouns are usually modified using adjectives, but sentences, or relative clauses, can modify nouns as well. For instance, in the sentence *The book that I bought yesterday is interesting*, *that I bought* is a relative clause modifying *the book*.

There are two major differences between the English and the Japanese relative clause constructions: First, unlike in English, in Japanese the relative clause precedes a noun, just like adjectives do. Second, there are no relative pronouns (such as the English *which*, *who*, *that*, or *whose*) in Japanese. The structure of relative clauses is described below; it differs depending on whether it contains a verb, an adjective + noun, or a noun as a predicate.

---

plain form of a verb/i-adjective

**na**-adjective + **na** (non-past)/**datta** (past) + noun

noun + **no** (non-past)/**datta** (past)

---

As for verbs and i-adjectives, the plain form has to be used in relative clauses. The clauses enclosed in parentheses in the following examples are the relative clauses.

**(Kinoo mita) eega wa totemo yokatta desu.**

*The movie (that I saw yesterday) was very good.*

**(Suzuki-san ga yonde iru) hon ga yomitai desu.**

*I want to read the book (that Mr./Ms. Suzuki is reading).*

**(Sakana ryoori ga oishii) resutoran e ikitai desu.**

*I want to go to a restaurant (where fish dishes are delicious).*

**(Ima ga hiroi) apaato o sagashite imasu.**

*I am looking for an apartment (whose living room is spacious).*

As for **na**-adjectives, a **na**-adjective + **na** (non-past) or **na**-adjective + **datta** (past) appears at the end of a relative clause.

**(Piano to baiorin ga tokui na) hito wa dare desu ka?**

*Who is the person (who is good at the piano and violin)?*

**(Asa wa kiree datta) heya ga moo kitanai desu.**

*The room (which was clean in the morning) is already dirty.*

With nouns, a noun + **no** (non-past) or noun + **datta** (past) also appears at the end of a relative clause.

**(Tanjoobi ga Ichigatsu no) hito wa nannin imasu ka?**

*How many people are there (whose birthdays are in January)?*

**(Otoosan ga bengoshi datta) tomodachi ga imasu.**

*I have a friend (whose father was a lawyer).*

## PRACTICE 2
Use the appropriate forms of the verbs, adjectives and copula inside parentheses to complete the sentences.

1. Kore ga (watashi ga ima hoshii desu) kuruma desu. *This is the car that I want now.*

2. (John-san ga torimashita) shashin ga mite mitai desu. *I want to try seeing pictures that John took.*

---

3. (Shuumatsu mo shizuka desu) kooen ga arimasu ka? *Is there a park that is quiet on weekends, too?*

4. (Furuuto ga totemo joozu ni fukemasu) tomodachi ga imasu. *I have a friend who can play the flute very well.*

5. (Asoko de piano o hiite imasu) onna no hito wa Ryooko-san desu. *The woman who is playing the piano there is Ryoko.*

## PRACTICE 3
Translate into English.

1. Tanaka-san to hanashite iru otoko no hito wa Junko-san no oniisan desu.

2. Otoosan ga Nihonjin de okaasan ga Amerikajin no tomodachi ga imasu.

3. Shuumatsu depaato de katta seetaa wa chotto takakatta desu.

4. Daidokoro ga semai apaato wa fuben da to omoimasu.

5. Nichiyoobi kara Doyoobi made itsumo himana hito wa imasu ka?

### *Cool links*
If you're interested in sports, you can find out much interesting information about popular sports in Japan, such as professional sumo, baseball, and soccer, from the following websites in English.
http://www.sumo.or.jp/eng/index.html
http://www.japanball.com/
http://www.j-league.or.jp/eng

## ANSWERS
**PRACTICE 1: 1.** *Have you ever read that book before?* **2.** *I have never played the piano even once.* **3.** *I played tennis at the university tennis court once.* **4.** *I haven't seen a sumo match yet, so I'd like to try and see one sometime, by all means.* **5.** *I have been to the Italian restaurant in front of the station many times.*

**PRACTICE 2: 1.** watashi ga ima hoshii; **2.** John-san ga totta; **3.** shuumatsu mo shizuka na; **4.** furuuto ga totemo joozu ni fukeru; **5.** asoko de piano o hiite iru

**PRACTICE 3: 1.** *The man who is talking with Mr./Ms. Tanaka is Junko's older brother.* **2.** *I have a friend whose father is Japanese and mother is American.* **3.** *The sweater I bought at the department store on the weekend was a little expensive.* **4.** *I think apartments with small kitchens (lit., whose kitchens are small) are inconvenient.* **5.** *Are there people who have always a lot of free time from Sunday to Saturday?*

# UNIT 10
## *Doctors and health*

In Unit 10, you will learn how to talk about your body and health, speak to a doctor and describe your symptoms when you are sick. Also, some key expressions that you can use when visiting a hospital will be introduced.

———————— Lesson 37 (words) ————————

**WORD LIST 1**

| | |
|---|---|
| shinryoojo | *clinic* |
| uketsuke | *front desk* |
| shinsatsushitsu | *consulting room* |
| machiaishitsu | *waiting room* |
| shinsatsu | *medical consultation* |
| shoshin | *the first medical consultation* |
| kanja | *patient* |
| hokenshoo | *health insurance card* |
| yooshi | *form* |
| karada | *body* |
| atama | *head* |
| kao | *face* |
| me | *eye* |
| kuchi | *mouth* |
| hana | *nose* |
| mimi | *ear* |
| ude | *arm* |
| ashi | *leg, foot* |
| mune | *chest* |
| onaka, hara | *belly, abdomen* |
| koshi | *waist, hip* |

| shinzoo | heart |
| noo | brain |
| i | stomach |
| hai | lung |
| choo | intestine |
| ke | hair |
| itai | painful |
| kinyuushimasu | to fill in |
| yobimasu/yobu | to call |
| suwarimasu/suwaru | to sit down |

## NUTS & BOLTS 1
### PRONOUNS

Let's look at Japanese pronouns corresponding to English *I*, *you*, *he*, *she*, and *it*.

| I | you | he | she | it |
|---|-----|-----|------|------|
| watashi | anata | kare | kanojo | sore |

Japanese pronouns are not used as frequently as English pronouns. In particular, the pronoun **anata** (*you*) is seldom used because such direct address is considered impolite in many contexts, e.g., when speaking to a superior. Instead, the use of the addressee's name or title is preferred. Take a look at the following short dialogue between Division Manager Tanaka and his secretary, Ms. Sato.

**Sato: Buchoo wa ashita no kaigi ni ode ni narimasu ka?**

*Division Manager, are you going to attend tomorrow's meeting?*

**Tanaka: Ee, demasu yo. Sato-san mo demasu ne?**

*Yes, I will. Ms. Sato, you will also attend, right?*

**Sato: Hai.**

*Yes.*

Note that pronouns **kare** and **kanojo** can sometimes be used to refer to or mean *boyfriend* and *girlfriend* respectively.

Now, let's look at the plural form of pronouns.

| *we* | *you* | *they (he)* | *they (she)* | *they (it)* |
|------|-------|-------------|--------------|-------------|
| watashitachi | anatatachi | karera | kanojora | sorera |
| | anatagata | | kanojotachi | |

Both **anatatachi** and **anatagata** are the plural forms of **anata**, but **anatagata** is more polite. Also, the plural form of **kare** (*he*) is **karera**, whereas the plural form of **kanojo** (*she*) is either **kanojora** or **kanjotachi**. **Karera** can also refer to a group of people consisting of both men and women.

Japanese pronouns corresponding to the English possessive pronouns *my, your, his, her,* and *its* and object pronouns *me, you, him, her,* and *it* are formed by using the possessive marker **no**, the indirect object marker **ni** and the direct object marker **o**.

| | | | | | |
|---|---|---|---|---|---|
| watashi no | *my* | watashi ni | *(to) me* | watashi o | *me* |
| atana no | *your* | anata ni | *(to) you* | anata o | *me* |
| kare no | *his* | kare ni | *(to) him* | kare o | *him* |
| kanojo no | *her* | kanojo ni | *(to) her* | kanojo o | *her* |
| sono | *its* | sore ni | *(to) it* | sore o | *it* |

Note that the possessive form of **sore** is **sono** and not **sore no**.

## PRACTICE 1

Fill in the blanks with the appropriate pronouns or pronouns + a particle.

1. Kore wa tomodachi no Jim-san no kamera desu. _____ wa shashin o toru no ga shumi de, takusan kamera o motte imasu.

2. Ashita Lisa-san to John-san to Ichiroo-san to Mariko-san to Bill-san to issho ni eega o mimasu. _____ wa watashi no kurasumeeto desu.

3. Meegan-san wa watashi no tomodachi desu. _____ otoosan wa Amerikajin desu ga, okaasan wa Chuugokujin desu.

4. *(showing a picture)* Kore wa otooto no Hiroshi desu. _____ tokugi wa basukettobooru desu.

5. Nancy-san ni kono kaban o moratta node, watashi wa _____ sukaafu o agemashita.

## WORD LIST 2

| | |
|---|---|
| **netsu** | *fever* |
| **kaze** | *cold* |
| **zutsuu** | *headache* |
| **fukutsuu** | *stomachache* |
| **hakike** | *nausea* |
| **memai** | *dizziness* |
| **geri** | *diarrhea* |
| **shokuyoku** | *appetite* |
| **suimin** | *sleep* |
| **arerugii** | *allergy* |
| **ketsuatsu** | *blood pressure* |
| **hinketsu** | *anemia* |
| **gan** | *cancer* |
| **hiroo** | *exhaustion, fatigue* |
| **sutoresu** | *stress* |

| kega | *injury* |
| kensa | *examination* |
| chuusha | *injection, shot* |
| shujutsu | *operation, surgery* |
| kusuri | *medicine* |
| bitaminzai | *vitamin supplement* |
| sanjuuhachi do | *38 degrees* |
| kesa | *this morning* |
| hidoi | *terrible, severe* |
| hayaku | *early, fast* |
| chanto (*colloquial*), **kichinto** | *properly, exactly, accurately* |
| chuushashimasu/chuushasuru | *to give an injection* |
| shujutsushimasu/shujutsusuru | *to operate* |
| nyuuinshimasu/nyuuinsuru | *to be hospitalized* |
| taiinshimasu/taiinsuru | *to leave the hospital, to be released from hospital* |
| akemasu/akeru | *to open* |
| shimemasu/shimeru | *to close* |
| zangyooshimasu/zangyoosuru | *to work overtime* |
| yasumimasu/yasumu | *to take some rest, to be absent, to take a day off* |
| renrakushimasu/renrakusuru | *to contact* |

## NUTS & BOLTS 2
### DO THINGS BEFOREHAND: VERB + -TE OKIMASU

A special structure, shown below, can be used in Japanese to describe actions taken beforehand, in preparation for some coming events.

te-form of a verb + **okimasu/oku**

Let's see how this structure is used.

**Raigetsu Kanada e ikimasu kara, atarashii suutsukeesu o katte okimasu.**

*I will go to Canada next month, so I will buy a new suitcase beforehand.*

**Ashita uchi de paachii o shimasu kara, tabemono to nomimono o takusan katte okimashoo.**

*We will have a party at home tomorrow, so let's buy a lot of food and beverages beforehand.*

**Kyoo tomodachi to dekakemasu kara, kinoo shukudai o shite okimashita.**

*I will go out with my friend(s) today, so I did the homework yesterday in advance.*

**Saikin tama ni memai ga suru node, shucchoo** (*business trip*) **ni iku mae ni ichido kensa o ukete okimasu.**

*Recently I've been feeling dizzy occasionally, so I will go see a doctor (lit., have a medical examination) in advance before I go on a business trip.*

## PRACTICE 2

Using the **te**-form of the verbs in parentheses, complete the sentences using the structure *verb* + -**te okimasu**. Change **okimasu** into an appropriate form as necessary.

1. Haha wa itsumo chichi ga kaeru mae ni bangohan o _____.
   (tsukuru) *My mother always make dinner in advance, before my father comes home.*

2. Nihon ni kuru mae ni Nihongo o _____. (benkyoosuru)
   *I studied Japanese in advance, before I came to Japan.*

3. Miitingu ni deru mae ni issho ni hirugohan o _____! (taberu)
   *Let's eat lunch in advance, before attending the meeting!*

4. Ashita konsaato de baiorin o hikimasu kara, takusan _____.
   (renshuusuru)
   *I will play the violin at a concert tomorrow, so I practiced a lot beforehand.*

---

5. Ano resutoran wa ninki ga aru kara, iku mae ni _____!
(yoyakusuru) *That restaurant is popular, so let's make a reservation in
advance, before we go there.*

## Cool links

As mentioned earlier, it's a good idea to have a Japanese-
English/English-Japanese dictionary handy to look up words and
expand your vocabulary. If you prefer looking up words on the Internet, here the URLs for some of the online dictionaries.

http://www.alc.co.jp

http://dictionary.goo.ne.jp

http://dictionary.pspinc.com/index.htm

http://www.asahi.com/tool/jisho/index.html

## ANSWERS
**PRACTICE 1: 1.** kare; **2.** karera; **3.** kanojo no; **4.** kare no;
**5.** kanojo ni

**PRACTICE 2: 1.** tsukutte okimasu; **2.** benkyooshite okimashita;
**3.** tabete okimashoo; **4.** renshuushite okimashita; **5.** yoyakushite
okimashoo

————————— Lesson 38 (phrases) —————————

## PHRASE LIST 1

| | |
|---|---|
| **kami, kami no ke** | *hair (on the head)* |
| **atama ga itai desu, zutsuu ga shimasu** | *have/has a headache* |
| **onaka ga itai desu** | *have/has a stomachache* |
| **geri o shimasu** | *have/has diarrhea* |
| **hakike ga shimasu** | *feel/feels like vomiting* |
| **memai ga shimasu** | *feel/feels dizzy* |

| | |
|---|---|
| memai ga hidoi desu | *feel/feels extremely dizzy* |
| samuke ga shimasu | *have/has chills* |
| kaoiro ga warui desu | *look/looks pale* |
| isha ni mite moraimasu | *to be checked by a doctor* |
| byooin de mite moraimasu | *to be checked at a hospital* |
| shinsatsu o ukemasu | *consult/consults a physician* |
| Isha ni mite moratta hoo ga ii desu. | *You'd better consult a doctor.* |
| Shinsatsu o uketa koto ga arimasu. | *I have consulted a doctor.* |
| yooshi ni kinyuushimasu | *fill/fills out a form* |
| yooshi o motte kimasu | *bring/brings the form* |
| hajimete desu | *it's the first time* |
| kore de ii desu | *to be okay with this* |
| arerugii ni kansuru | *concerning (my) allergies* |
| arerugii ni kansuru shitsumon | *questions concerning allergies* |
| shitsumon no kotae | *answers to questions* |
| ima nonderiu kusuri | *the medicine that I'm taking now* |
| hoka no kusuri | *other medicine* |

## NUTS & BOLTS 2
### THE TE-FORM OF ADJECTIVES

You have learned the **te**-form of the copula and different verbs in Lessons 8 and 15 respectively. Now, we'll discuss the **te**-form of adjectives. First, let's look at how the **te**-form of **i**-adjectives is formed.

Drop final -**i** and attach **kute**.

Let's follow this rule and produce the **te**-form of **i**-adjectives.

| ookii (*big*) | ookikute | oishii (*delicious*) | oishikute |
| akarui (*bright*) | akarukute | atatakai (*warm*) | atatakakute |
| isogashii (*busy*) | isogashikute | itai (*painful*) | itakute |

Next, let's look at how the **te**-form of **na**-adjectives is formed.

> stem of **na**-adjectives + **de**

Remember that **de** is the **te**-form of the copula **desu/da**. Let's follow this rule and produce the **te**-form of **na**-adjectives.

| yuumee (*famous*) | yuumee de | shizuka (*quiet*) | shizuka de |
| shinsetsu (*kind*) | shinsetsu de | nigiyaka (*lively*) | nigiyaka de |
| kantan (*easy, simple*) | kantan de | kiree (*beautiful, clean*) | kiree de |

The **te**-form of adjectives is used when connecting two or more adjectives. Just like in the case of verbs, the **te**-form of adjectives cannot appear at the end of sentences. Also, the **te**-form of adjectives does not express tense, which is determined by the adjectives appearing at the end of a sentence. Now, let's see how the **te**-form of adjectives is used.

**Kawada-san no ie wa atarashikute kiree desu.**

*Mr./Ms. Kawada's house is new and clean.*

**Roppongi wa nigiyaka de omoshiroi desu.**

*Roppongi is lively and interesting.*

**Sono kooen wa ookikute, kiree de, shizuka desu kara, yoku ikimasu.**
*That park is big, pretty, and quiet, so I often go there.*

**Kinoo no shukudai wa mijikakute kantan de yokatta desu.**
*Yesterday's homework was short, easy, and good.*

The **te**-form of adjectives can also appear in a prenominal position, as shown in the examples below.

**Ueda-san wa shinsetsu de ii hito desu.**
*Mr./Ms. Ueda is a kind and nice person.*

**Yasukute oishii resutoran o shitte imasu ka?**
*Do you know of any restraurants that are cheap and delicious?*

## PRACTICE 1

Choose the appropriate adjectives from the list below, and fill in the blanks with their **te**-form.

mijikai, nagai, chikai, tooi, muzukashii, kantan, shinsetsu, furui, atarashii, chiisai, ookii, kiree

1. Eki ni _____ benrina apaato ni sumitai desu. *I want to live in an apartment that is close to the station and convenient.*

2. Ano sensee wa _____ ii desu. *That teacher is kind and good.*

3. Sono eegakan (movie theater) wa _____ fuben desu. *That movie theater is old, small, and inconvenient.*

4. Kono hon wa _____ tsumaranakatta desu. *This book was long, difficult, and boring.*

5. Mita-san no ie wa _____ ii desu ne. *Mr./Ms. Mita's house is new, clean, and nice, isn't it?*

## PHRASE LIST 2

| | |
|---|---|
| **kaze o hikimasu** | *catch/catches a cold* |
| **netsu ga arimasu** | *have/has a fever* |

| | |
|---|---|
| netsu o hakarimasu | *check/checks your fever* |
| nodo ga itai desu | *have/has a sore throat* |
| shokuyoku ga arimasu | *have/has an appetite* |
| shokuyoku ga arimasen | *don't/doesn't have an appetite* |
| ketsuatsu ga takai desu | *have/has high blood pressure* |
| ketsuatsu ga hikui desu | *have/has low blood pressure* |
| suimin o torimasu | *get/gets some sleep* |
| fuminshoo desu | *suffer/suffers from insomnia* |
| sutoresu ga tamatte imasu | *to be under a lot of stress (lit., stress has accumulated)* |
| kata ga kotte imasu | *have/has stiff shoulders* |
| kega o shimasu | *get/gets injured* |
| hone o orimasu/ kossetsushimasu | *break/breaks a bone* |
| nenzashimasu | *have/has a sprain* |
| yojikan shika nete imasen | *had only four hours of sleep* |
| watashi ga shitteiru isha | *the doctor that I know* |
| kare ni renrakushimasu | *contact/contacts him* |
| kare ni renrakushite okimasu | *contact/contacts him beforehand* |
| hayaku ie ni kaerimasu | *go/goes home early* |
| yasunda hoo ga ii desu | *you'd better get some rest* |
| kaisha o yasumimasu | *take/takes a day off (from work)* |
| Zangyooshinaide kudasai. | *Please don't work overtime.* |

## NUTS & BOLTS 2
### GIVING AND RECEIVING VERBS

You learned the giving and receiving verbs **agemasu**, **moraimasu**, and **kuremasu**, and their polite forms, **sashiagemasu**, **itadaki-masu**, and **kudasaimasu**, in Lesson 29, so you know how to use them as main verbs. These giving and receiving verbs can also attach to the **te**-form of other verbs; in that case, their meaning is doing or receiving the favor of some action.

> **A ga/wa B ni** *verb*-te agemasu/sashiagemasu.
> *A gives B a favor of doing something. (A does something for B.)*
>
> **A ga/wa B ni** *verb*-te moraimasu/itadakimasu.
> *A receives a favor from B of having something done.*
> *(B does something for A.)*
>
> **A ga/wa B ni** *verb*-te kuremasu/kudasaimasu.
> *(B = a speaker or his/her in-group member)*
> *A gives me/my in-group member a favor of doing something.*
> *(A does something for me/my in-group member.)*

In the case of **-te moraimasu** or **itadakimasu**, the giver of a favor can be marked only by **ni**, whereas the giver of some object can be marked by either **ni** or **kara** when **moraimasu** or **itadakimasu** are used as main verbs.

**Watashi wa Hayashi-san ni/kara hon o moraimashita.**

*I received a book from Mr./Ms. Hayashi.*

**Watashi wa Hayashi-san ni hon o kashite moraimashita.**

*I borrowed a book from Mr./Ms. Hayashi. (lit., I received a favor from Mr./Ms. Hayashi of his/her lending a book to me.)*

In the first example, **Hayashi-san**, the giver of the book, can be marked by either **ni** or **kara**, but in the second example, **Hayashi-san**, the giver of a favor of lending a book, can be marked only by **ni**. Now, let's see how the **te**-form of verbs + giving and receiving verbs are used.

**Haha wa imooto ni atarashii seetaa o katte agemashita.**

*My mother bought a new sweater for my younger sister. (lit., My mother gave my younger sister the favor of buying her a new sweater.)*

**Watashi wa buchoo ni repooto o yonde sashiagemashita.**

*I read a report to the division manager. (lit., I gave the division manager the favor of my reading a report to him.)*

**Watashi wa Daisuke-san ni kare ga totta shashin o misete moraimashita.**

*Daisuke showed me the pictures that he took. (lit., I received a favor from Daisuke of him showing me the pictures that he took.)*

**Watashi wa Campos-sensee ni Supeingo o oshiete itadakimashita.**

*Professor Campos taught me Spanish. (lit., I received a favor from Professor Campos of his/her teaching me Spanish.)*

**Ruumumeeto ga heya o soojishite kuremashita.**

*My roommate cleaned our room. (lit., My roommate gave me the favor of his/her cleaning our room.)*

**Sensee wa itsumo watashitachi ni omoshiroi hanashi o shite kudasaimasu.**

*The professor always tells us interesting stories. (lit., The professor always gave us the favor of his/her telling interesting stories.)*

Note that this is a very important construction and is commonly in use in everyday conversation.

## PRACTICE 2
Choose the appropriate combination of the **te**-form of the verb and the giving or receiving verb to fill in the blanks.

katte kuremasu, totte agemasu, tsukutte moraimasu, misete kudasaimasu, oshiete itadakimasu, yonde sashiagemasu

1. Kyoo wa karee ga tabetakatta node, haha ni _____. *Today I wanted to eat curry, so my mother made it for me (lit., I received a favor from my mother of her making it).*

2. Kinoo watashi wa buchoo ni repooto o _____. *Yesterday I read a report for the division manager. (lit., I gave the division manager the favor of my reading a report.)*

3. Ryooshin wa watashi to imooto ni atarashii konpyuutaa o
_____. *My parents bought a new computer for me and my sister. (lit.,
My parents gave me and my younger sister the favor of their buying a
new computer.)*

4. Sensee ni sono kotoba no imi o _____. *My teacher told me the
meaning of that word. (lit., I received a favor from my teacher of his/her
telling me the meaning of that word.)*

5. Shuumatsu kooen de Kayo-san no shashin o _____. *On the
weekend, let's take a picture of Kayo-san at the park. (lit., On the
weekend, let's give Kayo-san the favor of my taking her picture at
the park.)*

6. Itariago no sensee ga rooma no shashin o _____. *The Italian
teacher showed me/us pictures of Rome. (lit., The Italian teacher gave
(me/us) the favor of his/her showing pictures of Rome.)*

---

### Culture note

While Western medicine is mainstream in Japan, Eastern medicine
is still well-accepted and popular there as well. For instance, some
people prefer getting acupuncture when they catch a cold or have
some other medical problem. Also, some people prefer taking
herbal medicines, which they can get over the counter. Taking vitamin supplements has become more common in Japan recently, but
the number of people who take those supplements is still much
lower compared to the U.S., where vitamins are recommended by
many doctors.

---

**ANSWERS**
**PRACTICE 1: 1.** chikakute; **2.** shinsetsu de; **3.** furukute
chiisakute; **4.** nagakute muzukashikute; **5.** atarashikute kiree de

**PRACTICE 2: 1.** tsukutte moraimashita; **2.** irete sashiagemasu;
**3.** katte kuremashita; **4.** oshiete itadakimashita; **5.** totte
agemashoo; **6.** misete kudasaimashita

## SENTENCE GROUP 1

Hokenshoo o omochi desu ka?
*Do you have an insurance card?*

Kore de ii desu ka?
*Is this okay?*

Yoyaku nasai mashita ka?
*Did you make an appointment?*

Yoyaku o shinakute wa ikemasen ka?
*Do I have to make an appointment?*

Yoyakushite inakattara, chotto omachi ni naru kamoshiremasen.
*If you didn't make an appointment, you may have to wait for a little while.*

Kyoo wa doo nasaimashita ka?
*What is wrong (with you) today?*

Atama ga itakute, hakike ga shimasu.
*I have a headache and I feel like vomiting.*

Kesa wa memai mo shimashita.
*This morning I felt dizzy, too.*

Ichido byooin de mite moratta hoo ga ii to omoimashita.
*I thought I'd better get checked at a hospital right away.*

Izen ni kono byooin de shinsatsu o uketa koto ga arimasu ka?
*Have you consulted a doctor at this hospital before?*

Achira ni suwatte kono yooshi ni kinyuushite motte kite kudasai.
*Please sit down over there, fill out this form, and bring it back.*

Arerugii ni kansuru shitsumon no kotae mo kaite itadakemasu ka?
*Could you write the answers to the questions concerning the allergies?*

Ima nondeiru okusuri ga gozaimashitara, sore mo kaite kudasai.
*If you have any medicine that you are currently taking, please write that, too.*

Arerugii wa toku ni nani mo arimasen.
*I don't have any allergies.*

| Bitaminzai o nonde imasu ga, hoka no kusuri wa nani mo nonde imasen. | *I am taking a vitamin supplement, but I'm not taking any other medicine.* |
| Onamae o oyobishimasu kara, achira de omachi kudasai. | *We will call your name, so please wait there.* |

NOTE 1

**Doo shimashita ka?** and its polite form **Doo nasaimashita ka?** can have different translations in different contexts. Possible translations are *What's the matter?*, *What happened?*, and *What's wrong?*

## NUTS & BOLTS 1
### ASKING FOR PERMISSION
You can ask for permission using the following structure.

> **te**-form of a verb + **(mo) ii desu ka?**
> *May I . . . ?*

The particle **mo** is optional, but it is expressed in most cases. By using a different form of **ii desu ka**, you can change the level of politeness.

> **te**-form of a verb + **(mo) ii?** (with a rising intonation)
> **te**-form of a verb + **ii desu ka?**
> **te**-form of a verb + **ii deshoo ka?**
> **te**-form of a verb + **yoroshii desu ka?**
> **te**-form of a verb + **yoroshii deshoo ka?**

The **te**-form of a verb + **(mo) ii** is the least polite and used in informal situations, while the **te**-form of a verb + **(mo) yoroshii deshoo ka** is the most polite among these five expressions. It is also possible to use **kamaimasen ka** instead of **ii desu ka**. It corresponds to the English *Do you mind . . . ?* Now, let's look at how these expressions can be used.

A: **Sumimasen ga, koko ni suwatte mo ii desu ka?**
*Excuse me, but may I sit down here?*

B: **Ee, doozo.**
*Yes, please.*

A: **Sensee, shitsumonshite mo ii deshoo ka?**
*Professor, may I ask a question?*

B: **Ee, doozo.**
*Yes, please.*

A: **Okaasan, kono keeki tabete mo ii?**
*Mom, may I eat this cake?*

B: **Bangohan no ato tabetara doo?**
*What about if you eat it after the dinner?*

A: **Shachoo, kono hon o okarishite mo yoroshii deshoo ka?**
*President, may I borrow this book?*

B: **Ee, doozo.**
*Yes, please.*

A: **Tabako o suttemo kamaimasen ka?**
*Do you mind if I smoke?*

B: **Sumimasen ga, chotto . . .**
*Sorry, but . . .*

## PRACTICE 1
Construct sentences where you ask for permission using the words provided in parentheses.

1. Kachoo, sumimasen ga, kibun ga warui node, _____? (uchi, mo, deshoo, ni, yoroshii, kaette ka)

2. Otoosan, _____? (kuruma, katte, o, ii, atarashii, mo)

3. Kurejitto kaado de _____? (mo, deshoo, ka, haratte, ii)

4. Chotto samui node, mado (*window*) o _____? (ka, shimete, kamaimasen, mo)

5. Kono bijutsukan (*art museum*) no naka de _____? (o, ii, shashin, ka, totte, desu, mo)

6. Sensee, kaze o hiite netsu ga aru node, _____? (yasunde, ka, yoroshii, gogo no seminaa, mo, deshoo, o)

## SENTENCE GROUP 2

| | |
|---|---|
| Koko ni suwatte kudasai. | *Please sit down here.* |
| Zutsuu to hakike to memai desu ka? | *A headache, nausea, and dizziness?* |
| Ima mo memai ga shimasu ka? | *Do you still feel dizzy?* |
| Kesa wa memai ga hidokute, bikkurishimashita. | *This morning I was extremely dizzy, which scared me.* |
| Netsu o hakatte mimashoo. | *Let's check the (your) temperature.* |
| Sanjuuhachi do desu kara, sukoshi netsu mo arimasu. | *It's thirty-eight degrees, so you have a little fever, too.* |
| Kuchi o akete kudasai. | *Please open your mouth.* |
| Nodo ga itaku arimasen ka? | *Do you have a sore throat?* |
| Geri o shite imasen ka? | *Do you have diarrhea?* |
| Onaka wa itakunai shi, geri mo shite imasen. | *I don't have a stomachache, and I don't have diarrhea either.* |
| Ima shigoto ga totemo isogashikute, maiban zangyooshite imasu. | *I am very busy with my work now and am working overtime every night.* |
| Suimin wa chanto totte imasu ka? | *Are you getting enough sleep?* |
| Yojikan gurai shika nete imasen. | *I'm getting only about four hours of sleep.* |
| Tabun hiroo deshoo. | *Perhaps it's exhaustion.* |
| Ichido kensashite moratta hoo ga ii desu. | *You'd better be examined.* |

| Daigakubyooin ni watashi ga shitte iru isha ga imasu kara, kare ni renrakushite okimasu. | *There's a doctor (whom) I know at the university hospital, so I will contact him beforehand.* |
| Kyoo wa zangyooshinaide kudasai. | *Please don't work overtime today.* |
| Hayaku ie ni kaette yasunda hoo ga ii desu. | *You'd better go home early and get some rest.* |

## NUTS & BOLTS 2
### NEGATIVE REQUESTS

You have learned how to make requests in Lesson 19. Now, let's learn how to make negative requests, as in the English *Please don't . . . !* You can make them using the structure below.

> plain non-past negative form of a verb (**nai**-form)
> **+ de + kudasai**

**Kurasu de nenai de kudasai.**
*Please don't sleep during the class.*

**Soko ni hairanai de kudasai.**
*Please don't enter there.*

**Netsu ga attara, ofuro ni hairanai de kudasai.**
*If you have a fever, please don't take a bath.*

**Kono resutoran de tabako o suwanai de kudasai.**
*Please don't smoke in this restaurant.*

**Bijutsukan (*art museum*) no naka de shashin o toranai de kudasai.**
*Please don't take pictures in the art museum.*

**Sono konpyuutaa o tsukawanai de kudasai.**
*Please don't use that computer.*

**Uso o tsukanaide kudasai.**
*Please don't tell a lie.*

**Kudasai** can be dropped when talking to friends and family members.

**Okaasan, watashi no heya ni hairanai de.**
*Mom, please don't enter my room.*

**Dare ni mo iwanai de ne.**
*Please don't tell it to anyone.*

## PRACTICE 2
Make negative requests using the expressions provided in parentheses. You need to change the form of the verbs.

1. Benkyooshite imasu kara, _____ kudasai. (terebi o miru)

2. Nihongo no kurasu de _____ kudasai. (eego o hanasu)

3. _____ kudasai. (miitingu o yasumu)

4. Amari takusan _____ kudasai. (osake o nomu)

5. _____ kudasai ne. (kaze o hiku)

---

### Tip!

Suppose that you have a profession like a teacher, flight attendant, police officer, landlord, or security guard at a museum. Think about some situations where you would ask people, such as students, customers, drivers, or tenants, not to do certain things. Try making those negative requests in Japanese using **-nai de kudasai.** You should try making sentences using the words you already know. If you need to use words that have not been introduced yet, you can look them up in a dictionary.

---

## ANSWERS
**PRACTICE 1:** uchi ni kaette mo yoroshii deshoo ka; **2.** atarashii kuruma o katte mo ii; **3.** haratte mo ii deshoo ka; **4.** shimete mo kamaimasen ka; **5.** shashin o totte mo ii desu ka; **6.** gogo no seminaa o yasunde mo yoroshii deshoo ka

**PRACTICE 2: 1.** terebi o minai de; **2.** eego o hanasanai de;
**3.** miitingu o yasumanai de; **4.** osake o nomanai de; **5.** kaze o
hikanai de

─────────── Lesson 40 (conversations) ───────────

## CONVERSATION 1

Scott does not feel well, so he is visiting the doctor's office close
to his office.

|  |  |
|---|---|
| Uketsuke: | Onamae wa? |
| Scott: | Scott Jones desu. |
| Uketsuke: | Etto, yoyaku nasaimashita ka? |
| Scott: | Iie. Yoyaku o shinakute wa ikemasen ka? |
| Uketsuke: | Yoyakushite inakattara, chotto omachi ni naru kamoshiremasen kedo, yoroshii desu ka? |
| Scott: | Hai, daijoobu desu. |
| Uketsuke: | Kyoo wa doo nasaimashita ka? |
| Scott: | Kinoo kara atama ga itakute, hakike ga suru n desu. Kesa wa memai mo shita node, ichido byooin de mite moratta hoo ga ii to omoimashita. |
| Uketsuke: | Soo desu ka. Izen ni kono byooin de shinsatsu o uketa koto ga arimasu ka? |
| Scott: | Iie, hajimete desu. |
| Uketsuke: | Sore dewa, achira ni suwatte kono yooshi ni kinyuushite motte kite kudasai. |

(Five minutes later.)

|  |  |
|---|---|
| Scott: | Kore de ii desu ka? |
| Uketsuke: | Etto, arerugii ni kansuru shitsumon no katae mo kaite itadakemasu ka? Sore kara, ima nondeiru okusuri ga gozaimashitara, sore mo kaite kudasai. |
| Scott: | Arerugii wa toku ni nani mo arimasen. Sore kara, bitaminzai o nonde imasu ga, hoka no kusuri wa nani mo nonde imasen. |

| Uketsuke: | Wakarimashita. Sore kara, hokenshoo o omochi desu ka? |
| --- | --- |
| Scott: | Hai, kore desu. |
| Uketsuke: | Sore dewa, onamae o oyobishimasu kara, achira de omachi kudasai. |
| Scott: | Hai. |

| Receptionist: | What's your name? |
| --- | --- |
| Scott: | Scott Jones. |
| Receptionist: | Well, did you make an appointment? |
| Scott: | No. Do I have to make an appointment? |
| Receptionist: | If you haven't made an appointment, you may have to wait for a little while. So is that okay with you? |
| Scott: | Yes, it's ok. |
| Receptionist: | What's wrong with you today? |
| Scott: | I have had a headache since yesterday and I also feel like vomiting. I also felt dizzy this morning, so I thought I'd better be examined at a hospital. |
| Receptionist: | I see. Have you ever consulted a doctor at this hospital before? |
| Scott: | No, it's my first time. |
| Receptionist: | Then, please have a seat there, fill out this form, and bring it back here. |

(Five minutes later.)

| Scott: | Is this okay? |
| --- | --- |
| Receptionist: | Well, could you write the answer to the questions concerning allergies, too? And, if there's any medicine that you are currently taking, please write that, too. |
| Scott: | I don't have any allergies. And, I'm taking a vitamin supplement, but I'm not taking any other medicine. |
| Receptionist: | Okay. And, do you have your health insurance card? |
| Scott: | Yes, here it is. |
| Receptionist: | Then, we will call your name, so please wait there. |
| Scott: | Okay. |

## NUTS & BOLTS 1
### EXPRESSING OBLIGATION

Obligation (*to have to*) is expressed using the structure below.

> te-form of plain negative form of a verb + **wa**
> + **ikemasen/ikenai narimasen/naranai**

You may wonder what the **te**-form of the negative form of a verb is. For instance, what are the **te**-forms of **nomanai**, **tabenai**, and **shinai**, the negative forms of the verbs **nomu**, **taberu**, and **suru**? Since the conjugation of **nai** is the same as that of i-adjectives, **nakute** is the **te**-form of **nai**, based on the rule introduced in Lesson 38. Consequently, the **te**-forms of **nomanai**, **tabenai**, and **shinai** are **nomanakute**, **tabenakute**, and **shinakute** respectively. Either **wa ikemasen** or **wa narimasen** follows the **te**-form of the negative forms of verbs. Let's see how this structure is used.

**Ashita keezaigaku no tesuto ga arimasu kara, kyoo benkyooshinakute wa ikemasen.**
*Since I have an economics test tomorrow, I have to study today.*

**Okyakusan ga kuru node, ima o soojishinakute wa narimasen.**
*We have a guest/guests, so we have to clean the living room.*

**Ashita wa asa hayaku okinakute wa narimasen kara, konban hayaku nenakute wa ikemasen.**
*I have to get up early tomorrow morning, so I have to go to bed early tonight.*

**Konban uchi de paatii o suru node, tabemono ya nomimono o katte okanakute wa ikemasen.**
*We will have a party at home tonight, so we have to buy food and beverages, among other things, beforehand.*

Instead of **nakute wa ikemasen/narimasen**, you can also use **nakereba ikemasen/narimasen**. **Nakereba** is the so-called **ba**-form of **nai**. Because the **ba**-form of verbs and adjectives hasn't

been introduced, you should just remember **nakereba** as a unit.
Compare the pairs of sentences below.

**Miitingu ni denakute wa ikemasen.**
**Miitingu ni denakereba ikemasen.**
*I have to attend the meeting.*

**Motto yasai o tabenakute wa narimasen.**
**Motto yasai o tabenakereba narimasen.**
*You have to eat more vegetables.*

**Byooki desu kara, kusuri o nomanakute wa ikemasen.**
**Byooki desu kara, kusuri o nomanakereba ikemasen.**
*I'm sick, so I have to take medicine.*

## PRACTICE 1
Translate into English.

1. Amerika ni ryuugakusuru mae ni Eego o benkyooshinakute wa ikemasen.

2. Bangohan o tabeta ato shukudai o shinakute wa narimasen.

3. Sanji ni tomodachi ni au node, niji han ni uchi o denakereba ikemasen.

4. Kaisha de mensetsu o ukeru toki, suutsu (*suit*) o kinakute wa ikemasen ka?

5. Daigakubyooin de kensa o ukeru toki wa, yoyakushite okanakereba narimasen.

## CONVERSATION 2
Scott has come into the examination room.

Scott: **Shitsureeshimasu.**
Isha: **Hai, jaa koko ni suwatte kudasai. Etto, zutsuu to hakike to memai desu ka?**

Scott: Hai.

Isha: Ima mo memai ga shimasu ka?

Scott: Ima wa daijoobu desu kedo, kesa wa memai ga hidokute, bikkurishimashita.

Isha: Soo desu ka. Chotto netsu o hakatte mimashoo. (After a little while.) Sanjuuhachi do desu kara, sukoshi netsu mo arimasu ne. Kuchi o akete kudasai. Nodo wa itaku arimasen ka?

Scott: Iie.

Isha: Onaka wa doo desu ka? Geri wa shite imasen ka?

Scott: Iie. Onaka wa itaku nai shi, geri mo shite imasen.

Isha: Uun, kaze ja nai desu ne. Oshigoto wa isogashii desu ka?

Scott: Hai, ima totemo isogashikute, maiban zangyooshiteimasu.

Isha: Suimin wa chanto totte imasu ka?

Scott: Saikin wa maiban yojikan gurai shika nete imasen.

Isha: Soo desu ka. Tabun hiroo deshoo. Demo, ichido kensashite moratta hoo ga ii desu ne.

Scott: Kensa desu ka?

Isha: Daigakubyooin ni watashi ga shitte iru isha ga imasu kara, kare ni renrakushite okimasu. Ashita no gogo ni ji goro wa daijoobu desu ka?

Scott: Hai, daijoobu desu. Kyoo wa kaisha ni modotte shigoto o shite mo ii desu ka?

Isha: Kibun ga warukunakattara, shigoto o shite mo ii desu kedo, zangyooshinaide kudasai ne. Hayaku ie ni kaette yasunda hoo ga ii desu yo.

Scott: Hai, soo shimasu.


Scott: *May I come in? (lit., Excuse me.)*

Doctor: *Yes, please sit down here. So, a headache, nausea, and dizziness?*

Scott: *Yes.*

| | |
|---|---|
| Doctor: | *Do you still feel dizzy now?* |
| Scott: | *Now, I'm fine, but I felt extremely dizzy this morning, which scared me.* |
| Doctor: | *I see. Let's check your body temperature.* (After a little while.) *It's thirty-eight degrees, so you have a little fever, too. Please open your mouth. Does your throat hurt?* |
| Scott: | *No.* |
| Doctor: | *How's your stomach? Don't you have diarrhea?* |
| Scott: | *No, I don't have a stomachache and don't have diarrhea either.* |
| Doctor: | *Well, it's not a cold. Are you busy at your work?* |
| Scott: | *Yes, I'm very busy now and working overtime every night.* |
| Doctor: | *Are you getting enough sleep?* |
| Scott: | *Recently, I've been sleeping for only four hours a night.* |
| Doctor: | *I see. Perhaps it's exhaustion. But you'd better be examined.* |
| Scott: | *An examination?* |
| Doctor: | *There's a doctor I know at the university hospital, so I will contact him beforehand. Is around 2:00 p.m. tomorrow okay?* |
| Scott: | *Yes, that's fine. May I go back to the office and do my work today?* |
| Doctor: | *If you don't feel sick, you may work, but please don't work overtime today. You'd better go home early and get some rest.* |
| Scott: | *Okay, I will do so.* |

## NUTS & BOLTS 2
### GIVING ADVICE

When you want to give other people an advice (*You'd better . . .* ), you can use the structure below.

> plain past affirmative form (**ta/da**-form) of a verb
> **+ hoo ga ii desu**

**Motto yasai o tabeta hoo ga ii desu yo.**

*You'd better eat more vegetables.*

**Netsu ga attara, byooin e itta hoo ga ii deshoo.**

*If you have a fever, you'd better go to a hospital.*

**Ano resutoran wa itsumo konde iru kara, yoyakushita hoo ga ii to omoimasu.**

*That restaurant is always crowded, so I think you'd better make a reservation.*

**Wakaranakattara, sensee ni kiita hoo ga ii desu yo.**

*If you don't understand, you'd better ask a teacher.*

**Bitaminzai o nonda hoo ga ii to omoimasu ka?**

*Do you think it's better to take vitamin supplements?*

You can also advise people not to do something (*you'd better not*) using the structure below.

> plain non-past negative form (**nai**-form) of a verb
> **+ hoo ga ii desu**

**Karada ni yoku arimasen kara, amari tabako o suwanai hoo ga ii desu yo.**

*You'd better not smoke so much, because it's not good for your health.*

**Memai ga suru toki wa, dekakenai hoo ga ii to omoimasu.**

*When you feel dizzy, I think that you'd better not go out.*

**Osake o nomisuginai hoo ga ii desu yo.**

*You'd better not drink too much.*

**Geri o shite itara, bangohan wa tabenai hoo ga ii deshoo.**

*If you have diarrhea, it's probably better for you not to eat dinner.*

**Atama ga itakattara, paatii ni ikanai hoo ga ii to omoimasu.**

*If you have a headache, I think it's better for you not to go to the party.*

## PRACTICE 2

Using the words inside parentheses, give advice using V-**ta/da hoo ga ii desu.**

1. *You'd better attend the meeting.* (miitingu ni deru)

2. *You'd better read more books.* (motto hon o yomu)

3. *You'd better talk with the division manager.* (buchoo to hanasu)

4. *You'd better clean the room.* (heya o soojisuru)

5. *You'd better take a rest.* (yasumu)

6. *You'd better take medicine.* (kusuri o nomu)

## PRACTICE 3

Use the words inside parentheses and the structure verb + **-nai hoo ga ii desu** to give advice. You may need to add some words yourself, too.

1. *You'd better not see this movie.* (kono eega o miru)

2. *You'd better not be absent from school.* (gakkoo o yasumu)

3. *You'd better not drink coffee too much.* (koohii o nomisugiru)

4. *You'd better not do exercises today.* (undoosuru)

5. *You'd better not spend (use) so much money.* (okane o tsukau)

6. *You'd better not buy this car.* (kono kuruma o kau)

### *Tip!*

To practice expressing obligation, you may want to start making a to-do list for the next day every evening. If you haven't learned yet the verbs you want to use, you can look them up in a dictionary and then change them into **nakute** or **nakereba** form. If you continue doing this task for a week, there will probably be some sentences you will repeat every day, but that's fine. Practice, and repetion, makes perfect!

**ANSWERS**

**PRACTICE 1: 1.** *You have to study English before going to study abroad in the U.S.A.* **2.** *I have to do homework after eating dinner.* **3.** *I will meet my friend(s) at three o'clock, so I have to leave home at two-thirty.* **4.** *Do I have to wear a suit when I go to interview at a company?* **5.** *When you go for a medical exam at a university hospital, you have to make an appointment in advance.*

**PRACTICE 2: 1.** Miitingu ni deta hoo ga ii desu. **2.** Motto hon o yonda hoo ga ii desu. **3.** Buchoo to hanashita hoo ga ii desu. **4.** Heya o soojishita hoo ga ii desu. **5.** Yasunda hoo ga ii desu. **6.** Kusuri o nonda hoo ga ii desu.

**PRACTICE 3: 1.** Kono eega o minai hoo ga ii desu. **2.** Gakkoo o yasumanai hoo ga ii desu. **3.** Koohii o nomisuginai hoo ga ii desu. **4.** Kyoo (wa) undooshinai hoo ga ii desu. **5.** Okane o amari tsukawanai hoo ga ii desu. **6.** Kono kuruma o kawanai hoo ga ii desu.

# JAPANESE IN ACTION

## E-MAIL
The following is an e-mail message from Ms. Sachiko Mori, an administrative assistant from Tokyo, to the division manager, Mr. Matsuda, currently on a business trip to Osaka.

Sooshinsha: Sachiko Mori
Atesaki: Matsuda Buchoo
Kenmee: Re: Suiyoobi no miitingu
Tenpu: Sukejuuru.doc

Matsuda Buchoo,
Suiyoobi no miitingu no sukejuuru o tenpuitashimasu.
Nanika mondai ga gozaimashitara, renrakushite kudasai.
Sore kara, miitingu de kubaru eigyoo hookokusho wa
sanjuu-bu kopiishite okimashita ga, yoroshii deshoo ka?
Mata, nanika arimashitara, meeru de renrakuitashimasu
node, yoroshiku onegaiitashimasu.

Mori Sachiko

**ADDITIONAL VOCABULARY:**
**tenpusuru** (*to attach*), **eigyoo hookokusho** (*business report*), **kubaru** (*to distribute*), **sanjuu-bu** (*thirty sets*)

## POSTCARD
The following is the front and the back of a postcard Mark Brown sent from Kyoto to his friend Junko Kato in Hiroshima.

7 3 7 0 0 1 1

Hiroshima-shi Kure Hironakachoo 6–6-18
Sakura Manshon 207
Kato Junko sama

Junko-san,

Ogenki desu ka? Boku wa itsuka mae ni nihon ni tsuite,
tookyoo ni mikkakan imashita. Tookyoo wa hito ga
ookute, nigiyaka de, totemo tanoshii tokoro desu ne.
Demo, hoteru mo resutoran mo chotto takasugiru to
omoimashita. Kinoo no ban shinkansen de kyooto ni
kimashita. Kyooto wa furui kireena machi desu ne. Kyoo
wa otera ya jinja e itte takusan shashin o torimashita.
Tookyoo mo yokatta kedo, boku wa kyooto no hoo ga
suki ni narimashita. Asatte hiroshima ni ikimasu. Eki ni
tsuitara, Junko-san no keetai ni denwashimasu. Sore ja,
oaisuru no o tanoshimi ni shite imasu.

Mark

manshon (*condominium*), nihon ni tsuku (*to arrive in Japan*), otera (*temple*), jinja (*shrine*), oaisuru no o tanoshimi ni shite imasu (*to be looking forward to seeing you*)

## TRAVEL AD
The following is an ad for a travel tour to Okinawa.

---

Aoi sora, Aoi umi . . . Okinawa ga anata o matte imasu!

Hikooki, hoteru, shokuji, kankoo, zenbu fukumarete, nihaku mikka de niman gosen en kara. Totemo oyasuku natte imasu!

Sukejuuru
Ichinichi me:
Gogo ichi ji go fun Haneda kuukoo hatsu, Gogo sanji sanjuugo fun Naha kuukoo chaku, Basu de hoteru e, Jiyuujikan
Futsuka me:
Gozen kuji kara kuruujingu, Gogo wa jiyuu jikan
Mikka me:
Gogo sanji han Naha hatsu, Gogo goji gojuppun Haneda chaku
Tenjooin ichimee dookoo. Opushonaru tsuaa mo gozaimasu.

Goyoyaku, otoiawase wa (03) 0333–5511 made.
ABC Ryokoosha http://www.abcryoko.com
Fax (03) 0333–5512

---

sora (*sky*), umi (*ocean*), shokuji (*meal*), kankoo (*sightseeing*), fuku-mareru (*to be included*), ichinichime (*the first day*), Haneda hatsu (*leave Haneda*), Naha chaku (*arrive in Naha*), nihaku mikka (*two-night-three-day stay*), jiyuujikan (*free time*), kuruujingu ([*yacht*] *cruise*), tenjooin ichimee dookoo (*to be accompanied by a tour guide*), **opushonaru tsuaa** (*optional tour*), **otoiawase** (*inquiry*), **ryokoosha** (*travel company*)

## JOB AD

The following is a help-wanted ad posted in the newspaper by a trading company.

---

Booekijimu Kyuubo

Shigoto               eigyoo asisutanto

Shikaku: Pasokon to eego ga dekiru kata

Nenree               fumon

Kyuuyo               nijuuman en ijoo

Taiguu               shookyuu 1, shooyo nen 2, kakushu shakai hoken kanbi, kootsuuhi shikyuu

Kinmuchi: Tookyoo, Akasaka

Oobo: Rirekisho o yuusooshite kudasai. Gojitsu renrakushimasu.

Kabushikigaisha ABC Booeki, Jinjibu (03) 0828–1234 Tantoo Yamamoto

Minato-ku Akasaka 8–8-10 Minato Biru 5F

---

ADDITIONAL VOCABULARY:

**booekijimu** (*trade office work*), **kyuubo** (*immediate opening*), **asisutanto** (*assistant*), **shikaku** (*qualification*), **pasokon** (*personal computer*), **kata** (*person* [polite]), **nenree** (*age*), **fumon** (*pass over a matter, overlook*), **kyuuyo** (*salary*), **ijoo** (*more than*), **taiguu** (*treatment, labor conditions*), **shookyuu** (*salary increase*), **shooyo** (*bonus, reward*), **kakushu** (*various*), **shakaihoken** (*social insurance*), **kanbi** (*fully furnished*), **kootsuuhi shikyuu** (*transportation costs covered*), **kinmuchi** (*place of work*), **oobo** (*application*), **yuusoosuru** (*to mail*), **gojitsu** (*later*), **kabushikigaisha** (*joint-stock cooperation*)

# SUPPLEMENTAL VOCABULARY

## 1: AT SCHOOL

| | |
|---|---|
| *at school* | **gakkoo ni, gakkoo de** |
| *school* | **gakkoo** |
| *university* | **daigaku** |
| *classroom* | **kyooshitsu** |
| *course* | **katei, kamoku, kooza** |
| *teacher* | **sensei, kyooshi** |
| *professor* | **kyooju** |
| *student* | **gakusei, seito** |
| *subject* | **kamoku, gakka** |
| *notebook* | **nooto** |
| *textbook* | **kyookasho** |
| *math* | **suugaku** |
| *history* | **rekishi** |
| *chemistry* | **kagaku** |
| *biology* | **seibutsugaku** |
| *literature* | **bungaku** |
| *language* | **gogaku, gengo** |
| *art* | **geijutsu, bijutsu** |
| *music* | **ongaku** |
| *gym* | **taisoo, taiiku, jimu** |
| *recess* | **kyuukei, yasumi, kyuuka** |
| *test* | **tesuto, shiken** |
| *grade* | **seiseki** |
| *report card* | **tsuuchihyoo** |
| *diploma* | **sotsugyooshoosho, gakuimenjoo** |
| *degree* | **gakui, shoogoo** |
| *difficult/easy* | **muzukashii/yasashii** |
| *to study* | **benkyoosuru** |
| *to learn* | **narau** |
| *to pass* | **ukaru, gookakusuru** |
| *to fail* | **ochiru, rakudaisuru** |

## 2: WEATHER

| | |
|---|---|
| *weather* | tenki |
| *It's raining.* | Ame ga futteiru. |
| *It's snowing.* | Yuki ga futteiru. |
| *It's hailing.* | Arare ga futteiru. |
| *It's windy.* | Kaze ga tsuyoi desu. |
| *It's hot.* | Atsui desu. |
| *It's cold.* | Samui desu. |
| *It's sunny.* | Hareteiru. |
| *It's cloudy.* | Kumotteiru. |
| *It's beautiful.* | Subarashii desu. |
| *storm* | arashi |
| *wind* | kaze |
| *sun* | taiyoo, nikkoo |
| *thunder* | arashi |
| *lightning* | kaminari |
| *hurricane* | taifuu, harikeen |
| *temperature* | ondo |
| *degree* | do |
| *rain* | ame |
| *snow* | yuki |
| *cloud* | kumo |
| *fog* | kiri |
| *smog* | sumoggu |
| *umbrella* | kasa |

## 3: FOOD

| | |
|---|---|
| *food* | tabemono |
| *dinner* | yuushoku, bangohan |
| *lunch* | chuushoku, hirugohan |
| *breakfast* | chooshoku, asagohan |
| *meat* | niku |

| | |
|---|---|
| *chicken* | toriniku, chikin |
| *beef* | gyuuniku, biifu |
| *pork* | butaniku, pooku |
| *fish* | sakana |
| *shrimp* | ebi |
| *lobster* | robusutaa |
| *bread* | pan |
| *egg* | tamago |
| *cheese* | chiizu |
| *rice* | (o)kome |
| *cooked rice* | gohan |
| *vegetable* | yasai |
| *lettuce* | retasu |
| *tomato* | tomato |
| *carrot* | ninjin |
| *cucumber* | kyuuri |
| *pepper* | koshoo |
| *fruit* | kudamono, furuutsu |
| *apple* | ringo |
| *orange* | orenji |
| *banana* | banana |
| *pear* | nashi |
| *grapes* | budoo |
| *drink* | nomimono |
| *water* | mizu |
| *milk* | gyuunyuu, miruku |
| *juice* | juusu |
| *coffee* | koohii |
| *tea* | koocha, ocha |
| *wine* | wain |
| *beer* | biiru |
| *soft drink, soda* | seiryooinryoo, sofutodorinku, sooda |

| | |
|---|---|
| salt | **shio** |
| pepper | **koshoo** |
| sugar | **satoo** |
| honey | **hachimitsu** |
| hot/cold | **atsui/tsumetai** |
| sweet/sour | **amai/suppai** |

## 4: FAMILY AND RELATIONSHIPS

| | |
|---|---|
| family and relationships | **kazoku to shinrui kankei** |
| mother | **okaasan, okaasama** (respect)**, haha** (one's own) |
| father | **otoosan, otoosama** (respect)**, chichi** (one's own) |
| son | **musuko, musukosan** (polite) |
| daughter | **musume, musumesan** (polite)**, ojoosan** (polite) |
| older sister | **oneesan, ane** (one's own) |
| younger sister | **imooto, imootosan** (polite) |
| baby | **akanboo, akachan** |
| older brother | **oniisan, ani** (one's own) |
| younger brother | **otooto, otootosan** (polite) |
| husband | **dannasama** (someone else's)**, goshujin** (someone else's)**, otto** (one's own)**, shujin** (one's own) |
| wife | **okusan** (someone else's)**, tsuma** (one's own)**, kanai** (one's own) |
| aunt | **obasan, oba** (one's own) |
| uncle | **ojisan, oji** (one's own) |
| grandmother | **obaasan, sobo** (one's own) |
| grandfather | **ojiisan, sofu** (one's own) |
| cousin | **itoko** |
| mother-in-law | **giri no okaasan, giri no haha** (one's own) |

| | |
|---|---|
| *father-in-law* | **giri no otoosan, giri no chichi** (one's own) |
| *stepmother* | **keebo, mamahaha** |
| *stepfather* | **keefu, mamachichi** |
| *stepson* | **keeshi, mamako** |
| *stepdaughter* | **keeshi, mamako** |
| *boyfriend* | **kare, kareshi, booifurendo** |
| *girlfriend* | **kanojo, gaarufurendo** |
| *fiancé(e)* | **konyakusha** |
| *friend* | **tomodachi, yuujin** |
| *relative* | **shinrui, shinseki** |
| *to love* | **aisuru** |
| *to know (a person)* | **(X o) shitteiru** |
| *to meet (a person)* | **(X ni) au** |
| *to marry (someone)* | **(X to) kekkonsuru** |
| *to divorce (someone)* | **(X to) rikonsuru** |
| *to get a divorce* | **rikonsuru** |
| *to inherit* | **soozokusuru** |

## 5: TOWN

| | |
|---|---|
| *around town* | **machi no shuuhen** |
| *town* | **machi** |
| *city* | **toshi, shi** |
| *village* | **mura** |
| *car* | **kuruma, jidoosha** |
| *bus* | **basu** |
| *train* | **densha** |
| *taxi* | **takushii** |
| *subway* | **chikatetsu** |
| *traffic* | **kootsuu** |
| *building* | **tatemono, biru** (highrise) |
| *apartment building* | **apaato** |

| | |
|---|---|
| *library* | toshokan |
| *restaurant* | resutoran |
| *store* | mise |
| *street* | michi, toori |
| *park* | kooen |
| *train station* | eki |
| *airport* | kuukoo |
| *airplane* | hikooki |
| *intersection* | koosaten |
| *lamppost* | gaitoobashira |
| *streetlight* | gaitoo |
| *bank* | ginkoo |
| *church* | kyookai |
| *temple* | (o)tera |
| *mosque* | mosuku |
| *sidewalk* | hodoo |
| *bakery* | panya, beekarii |
| *butcher shop* | nikuya |
| *café, coffee shop* | kissaten |
| *drugstore* | yakkyoku, kusuriya |
| *supermarket* | suupaa |
| *market* | ichiba, maaketto |
| *shoe store* | kutsuya |
| *clothing store* | yoohinten, iryoohinten |
| *electronics store* | denkiya |
| *bookstore* | honya, shoten |
| *department store* | depaato |
| *mayor* | shichoo, choochoo |
| *city hall, municipal building* | shiyakusho |
| *to buy* | kau |
| *to go shopping* | kaimono ni iku |
| *near/far* | chikai/tooi |

| | |
|---|---|
| *urban* | **tokai no** |
| *suburban* | **koogai no** |
| *rural* | **inaka no, den'en no, nooson no** |

## 6: THE HUMAN BODY

| | |
|---|---|
| *the human body* | **ningen no karada** |
| *head* | **atama** |
| *face* | **kao** |
| *forehead* | **hitai, odeko** |
| *eye* | **me** |
| *eyebrow* | **mayuge** |
| *eyelashes* | **matsuge** |
| *ear* | **mimi** |
| *nose* | **hana** |
| *mouth* | **kuchi** |
| *tooth* | **ha** |
| *tongue* | **shita, bero** |
| *cheek* | **hoo, hoho, hoppeta** |
| *chin* | **ago** |
| *hair (on head)* | **kami no ke** |
| *hair (on body)* | **ke** |
| *neck* | **kubi** |
| *chest* | **mune** |
| *breast* | **nyuuboo, mune** |
| *shoulders* | **kata** |
| *arm* | **ude** |
| *elbow* | **hiji** |
| *wrist* | **tekubi** |
| *hand* | **te** |
| *stomach, abdomen* | **hara, onaka** |
| *penis* | **penisu** |
| *vagina* | **chitsu** |

| | |
|---|---|
| *leg* | ashi |
| *knee* | hiza |
| *ankle* | kakato |
| *foot* | ashi |
| *finger* | yubi |
| *toe* | ashi no yubi |
| *skin* | hifu, hada |
| *blood* | chi, ketsueki |
| *brain* | noo |
| *heart* | shinzoo |
| *lungs* | hai |
| *bone* | hone |
| *muscle* | kinniku |
| *tendon* | ken |

## 7: TRAVEL AND TOURISM

| | |
|---|---|
| *travel and tourism* | ryokoo to kankoojigyoo |
| *tourist* | ryokoosha |
| *hotel* | hoteru |
| *youth hostel* | yuusuhosuteru |
| *reception desk* | furonto desuku |
| *to check in* | chekkuinsuru |
| *to check out* | chekkuautosuru |
| *reservation* | yoyaku |
| *passport* | pasupooto |
| *tour bus* | kankoobasu |
| *guided tour* | gaidotsuki no tsuaa |
| *camera* | kamera |
| *information center* | annaijo, infomeeshonsentaa |
| *map* | chizu |
| *brochure* | panfuretto |
| *monument* | kinenhi |

| to go sightseeing | kankoo ni iku, kenbutsu ni iku |
| to take a picture | shashin o toru |
| Can you take our picture? | Watashitachi no shashin o totte kudasai masu ka? |

## 8: PEOPLE

| people | hitotachi, hitobito |
| person | hito |
| man | otoko no hito |
| woman | onna no hito |
| adult | otona, seijin |
| child | kodomo |
| boy | otoko no ko, shoonen |
| girl | onna no ko, shoojo |
| teenager | juudai, tiineijaa |
| tall/short | se (sei) ga takai/se (sei) ga hikui |
| old/young | toshi o totta/wakai |
| fat/thin | futotta/yaseta |
| friendly/unfriendly | shinsetsuna, aiso no ii/fushinsetsuna, aiso no warui |
| happy/sad | ureshii/kanashii |
| beautiful/ugly | kirei, utsukushii/minikui, migurushii |
| healthy/sick | kenkoo na/byooki no |
| strong/weak | tsuyoi/yowai |
| famous | yuumei na |
| intelligent | chiteki na, rikoona |
| talented | sainoo no aru |

## 9: SPORTS AND RECREATION

| sports and recreation | supootsu to rikurieeshon |
| soccer, football | sakkaa |
| American football | Amerikan futtobooru, amefuto |

| | |
|---|---|
| *basketball* | **basukettobooru** |
| *baseball* | **yakyuu** |
| *hockey* | **hokkee** |
| *tennis* | **tenisu** |
| *swimming* | **suiei** |
| *judo* | **juudoo** |
| *kendo* | **kendoo** |
| *sumo* | **sumoo** |
| *game* | **shiai** |
| *team* | **chiimu** |
| *stadium* | **kyoogijoo, sutajiamu** |
| *coach* | **koochi** |
| *player* | **senshu** |
| *champion* | **yuushoosha** |
| *ball* | **booru, tama** |
| *to go hiking* | **haikingu suru/ni iku** |
| *to go camping* | **kyanpu suru/ni iku** |
| *to play a sport* | **undoo o suru** |
| *to play a game* | **shiai o suru** |
| *to win* | **katsu** |
| *to lose* | **makeru** |
| *to tie* | **hikiwakeru** |
| *cards* | **kaado, toranpu** |
| *pool, billiards* | **biriyaado** |

## 10: IN THE OFFICE

| | |
|---|---|
| *in the office* | **jimusho ni, jimusho de** |
| *office* | **jimusho, ofisu** |
| *desk* | **tsukue** |
| *computer* | **konpyuuta(a)** |
| *telephone* | **denwa** |
| *fax machine* | **fakkusuki** |

| | |
|---|---|
| bookshelf | hondana |
| file cabinet | fairu kyabinetto |
| file | fairu |
| boss | jooshi |
| colleague | dooryoo |
| employee | juugyooin |
| staff | shokuin |
| company | kaisha |
| business | gyoomu |
| factory | koojoo |
| meeting room | kaigishitsu |
| meeting | kaigi |
| appointment | yakusoku, yoyaku |
| salary | kyuuryoo |
| job | shigoto |
| busy | isogashii |
| to work | hataraku |
| to earn | kasegu |

## 11: NATURE

| | |
|---|---|
| nature | shizen |
| tree | ki |
| flower | hana |
| forest | mori |
| mountain | yama |
| field | nohara, soogen, bokusoochi |
| river | kawa |
| lake | mizuumi |
| ocean | umi |
| sea | umi |
| beach | hamabe, biichi |
| desert | sabaku |

| | |
|---|---|
| rock | iwa |
| sand | suna |
| sky | sora |
| sun | taiyoo |
| moon | tsuki |
| star | hoshi |
| water | mizu |
| land | riku, tochi |
| plant | shokubutsu |
| hill | oka |
| pond | ike |

## 12: IN THE KITCHEN

| | |
|---|---|
| in the kitchen | daidokoro ni, daidokoro de |
| refrigerator | reizooko |
| kitchen sink | daidokoro no nagashi |
| counter | kauntaa |
| stove | konro, renji |
| oven | oobun |
| microwave | denshirenji |
| cupboard | shokkidana, todana |
| drawer | hikidashi |
| plate | sara |
| cup | kappu |
| bowl | booru, donburi, hachi |
| glass | koppu, gurasu |
| spoon | supuun |
| knife | naifu |
| can | kan |
| box | hako |
| bottle | bin |
| carton | kaaton |

| | |
|---|---|
| coffeemaker | koohii meekaa |
| teakettle | yakan |
| blender | mikisaa |
| iron | airon |
| ironing board | airondai |
| broom | hooki |
| dishwasher | saraaraiki |
| washing machine | sentakuki |
| dryer | kansooki, doraiyaa |
| to cook | ryoorisuru |
| to do the dishes | shokki o arau |
| to do the laundry | sentakusuru |
| dishwashing detergent | daidokoroyoo senzai |
| laundry detergent | sentakuyoo senzai |
| bleach | hyoohakuzai |
| clean/dirty | kirei/kitanai |

## 13: ENTERTAINMENT

| | |
|---|---|
| entertainment | goraku |
| movie, film | eiga |
| to go to the movies | eiga ni iku |
| to see a movie | eiga o miru |
| theater | gekijoo |
| to see a play | shibai (engeki) o miru |
| opera | kageki, opera |
| concert | konsaato |
| club | kurabu |
| circus | saakasu |
| ticket | ken, kippu, chiketto |
| museum | hakubutsukan, bijutsukan |
| gallery | garoo, bijutsukan, gyararii |
| painting, picture | e, kaiga |

| | |
|---|---|
| *sculpture* | **chookoku** |
| *television program* | **terebibangumi** |
| *to watch television* | **terebi o miru** |
| *comedy* | **kigeki, komedii** |
| *documentary* | **dokyumentarii** |
| *drama* | **dorama** |
| *book* | **hon** |
| *magazine* | **zasshi** |
| *to read a book* | **hon o yomu** |
| *to read a magazine* | **zasshi o yomu** |
| *to listen to music* | **ongaku o kiku** |
| *song* | **uta** |
| *band* | **bando** |
| *the news* | **nyuusu** |
| *talk show* | **tookushoo** |
| *to flip channels* | **channeru o kaeru** |
| *to have fun* | **tanoshimu** |
| *to be bored* | **taikutsusuru** |
| *funny* | **okashii, omoshiroi** |
| *interesting* | **kyoomibukai, omoshiroi** |
| *exciting* | **kakkitekina, shigekitekina, wakuwakusaseru** |
| *scary* | **osoroshii** |
| *party* | **paatii** |
| *restaurant* | **resutoran** |
| *to go to a party* | **paatii ni iku** |
| *to have a party* | **paatii o suru** |
| *to dance* | **odoru, dansusuru** |

## 14: AT HOME

| | |
|---|---|
| *at home* | **uchi ni, uchi de** |
| *house* | **ie, uchi** |

| | |
|---|---|
| *apartment* | **apaato** |
| *room* | **heya** |
| *living room* | **ima, ribinguruumu** |
| *dining room* | **shokudoo, daininguruumu** |
| *kitchen* | **daidokoro, kicchin** |
| *bedroom* | **shinshitsu** |
| *bathroom* | **yokushitsu** |
| *hall* | **hiroma, hooru** |
| *closet* | **shuunooshitsu, todana, oshiire, monooki** |
| *window* | **mado** |
| *door* | **to, doa** |
| *table* | **teeburu, chabudai** |
| *chair* | **isu** |
| *sofa, couch* | **sofaa, nagaisu** |
| *curtain* | **kaaten** |
| *carpet* | **juutan, kaapetto** |
| *television* | **terebi** |
| *CD player* | **cd pureeyaa** |
| *lamp* | **ranpu** |
| *DVD player* | **dvd pureeyaa** |
| *sound system* | **onkyoo sisutemu** |
| *painting, picture* | **e, kaiga** |
| *shelf* | **tana** |
| *stairs* | **kaidan** |
| *ceiling* | **tenjoo** |
| *wall* | **kabe** |
| *floor* | **yuka** |
| *big/small* | **ookii/chiisai** |
| *new/old* | **atarashii/furui** |
| *wood/wooden* | **ki/mokusei no** |
| *plastic/made from plastic* | **purasuchikku/purasuchikkusei no** |

# 15: COMPUTERS AND THE INTERNET

| | |
|---|---|
| *computers and the internet* | **konpyuuta(a) to intaanetto** |
| *computer* | **konpyuuta(a)** |
| *keyboard* | **kiiboodo** |
| *monitor, screen* | **monitaa, sukuriin, gamen** |
| *mouse* | **mausu** |
| *modem* | **modemu** |
| *memory* | **memorii** |
| *CD-ROM* | **cd romu** |
| *CD-ROM drive* | **cd romu doraibu** |
| *file* | **fairu** |
| *document* | **bunsho, dokyumento** |
| *cable* | **keeburu** |
| *internet* | **intaanetto** |
| *website* | **uebusaito** |
| *webpage* | **uebupeiji** |
| *e-mail* | **denshimeeru, iimeeru** |
| *chatroom* | **chattoruumu** |
| *blog* | **ueburogu** |
| *instant message* | **insutanto messeeji** |
| *attachment* | **tenpu, atacchimento** |
| *to compose a message* | **messeeji no sakusei** |
| *to print* | **insatsu** |
| *printer* | **purintaa** |
| *to send an e-mail* | **denshimeeru iimeeru o sooshinsuru** |
| *to send a file* | **fairu o okuru, fairu o sooshinsuru** |
| *to forward* | **tensoosuru** |
| *to reply* | **henshinsuru** |
| *to delete* | **sakujosuru** |
| *to save a document* | **bunsho o hozonsuru** |
| *to open a file* | **fairu o hiraku** |
| *to close a file* | **fairu o tojiru** |

| | |
|---|---|
| *to attach a file* | **fairu o tenpusuru** |
| *folder* | **foruda** |
| *inbox* | **jushinbako, jushintorei** |
| *sent (items)* | **sooshinzumi (aitemu)** |
| *deleted (items)* | **sakujozumi (aitemu)** |
| *draft* | **shitagaki** |
| *to cut* | **kiritori** |
| *to copy* | **kopii** |
| *to paste* | **haritsuke** |
| *spell-check* | **superuchekku** |
| *address book* | **adoresuchoo** |
| *encoding* | **enkoodo** |
| *tool* | **tsuuru** |
| *help* | **herupu** |
| *sender* | **sooshinsha** |
| *subject* | **kenmei** |
| *date received* | **jushinnichiji** |

## 16: JOBS

| | |
|---|---|
| *jobs* | **shigoto** |
| *policeman/policewoman* | **keikan/fujinkeikan** |
| *lawyer* | **bengoshi** |
| *doctor* | **isha, ishi** |
| *engineer* | **gishi, enjinia** |
| *businessperson* | **jitsugyooka** |
| *salesperson* | **ten'in, gaikooin, seerusuman, seerusuuuman** (women only), **joten'in** (women only), **joseigaikooin** (women only) |
| *teacher* | **sensei, kyooshi** |
| *professor* | **kyooju** |
| *banker* | **ginkooka, ginkooin** |
| *architect* | **kenchikuka** |

| | |
|---|---|
| *veterinarian* | **juui** |
| *dentist* | **haisha, shikai** |
| *stay-at-home parent* | **shufu** |
| *carpenter* | **daiku** |
| *construction worker* | **kensetsusagyooin** |
| *taxi driver* | **takushii no untenshu** |
| *artist* | **geijutsuka** |
| *writer* | **sakka** |
| *plumber* | **haikankoo** |
| *electrician* | **denkigishi, denkikoo** |
| *journalist* | **kisha, jaanarisuto** |
| *actor/actress* | **haiyuu/joyuu** |
| *musician* | **ongakuka** |
| *farmer* | **noojookeieisha, noofu** |
| *secretary, assistant* | **hisho, asisutanto** |
| *unemployed* | **shitsugyoosha** |
| *retired* | **taishokushita, intaishita** |
| *full-time* | **jookin no, sennin no** |
| *part-time* | **hijookin no, paato taimu no** |
| *steady job* | **teishoku** |

## 17: CLOTHING

| | |
|---|---|
| *clothing* | **irui, ifuku** |
| *shirt* | **shatsu** |
| *pants* | **zubon** |
| *jeans* | **jiipan, jiinzu** |
| *T-shirt* | **tiishatsu** |
| *shoe* | **kutsu** |
| *sock* | **kutsushita, sokkusu** |
| *belt* | **beruto** |
| *sneaker, tennis shoe* | **undoogutsu, suniikaa, tenisu shuuzu** |
| *dress* | **doresu, wanpiisu, ifuku** |

| | |
|---|---|
| *skirt* | **sukaato** |
| *blouse* | **burausu** |
| *suit* | **suutsu** |
| *hat* | **booshi** |
| *glove* | **tebukuro** |
| *scarf* | **sukaafu** |
| *winter scarf* | **mafuraa** |
| *jacket* | **uwagi, jaketto** |
| *coat* | **kooto** |
| *earring* | **iyaringu, mimikazari** |
| *bracelet* | **buresuretto, udewa** |
| *necklace* | **nekkuresu, kubikazari** |
| *eyeglasses* | **megane** |
| *sunglasses* | **sangurasu** |
| *watch* | **tokei** |
| *ring* | **yubiwa** |
| *underpants* | **pantsu, zubonshita** |
| *undershirt* | **hadagi, shatsu** |
| *swimming trunks* | **suieipantsu** |
| *bathing suit* | **mizugi** |
| *pajamas* | **pajama, nemaki** |
| *cotton* | **men, kotton** |
| *leather* | **kawa, rezaa** |
| *silk* | **kinu, siruku** |
| *size* | **saizu, ookisa** |
| *to wear* | **kiru** |

## 18: IN THE BATHROOM

| | |
|---|---|
| *in the bathroom* | **yokushitu ni, yokushitsu de** |
| *toilet* | **otearai, tearaijo, toire** |
| *sink* | **senmendai** |
| *bath tub* | **yokusoo** |

| | |
|---|---|
| *shower* | shawaa |
| *mirror* | kagami |
| *medicine cabinet* | kusuribako |
| *towel* | taoru |
| *toilet paper* | toirettopeepaa |
| *shampoo* | shanpuu |
| *soap* | sekken |
| *bath gel* | nyuuyokuyoo jeru |
| *shaving cream* | higesoriyoo kuriimu |
| *razor* | kamisori |
| *to wash oneself* | karada o arau |
| *to take a shower* | shawaa o abiru |
| *to take a bath* | ofuro ni hairu |
| *to shave* | soru |
| *cologne* | koron |
| *perfume* | koosui |
| *deodorant* | deodoranto |
| *bandage* | hootai |
| *powder* | kona, paudaa |

# INTERNET RESOURCES

| | |
|---|---|
| www.yahoo.co.jp | Japanese version of Yahoo. It is a popular search engine. Online shopping, auctions, yellow pages, etc., are available. It also provides current world and domestic news. |
| www.asahi.com | Homepage of a popular Japanese newspaper. |
| www.yomiuri.co.jp | Homepage of a popular Japanese newspaper. |
| www.amazon.co.jp | Homepage of Amazon.com Japan. One can purchase Japanese books, CDs, and DVDs online. |
| http://dictionary.goo.ne.jp | English–Japanese dictionary, Japanese–English dictionary, and Japanese dictionary are available. |
| www.wanogakkou.com | This site introduces Japanese culture and industry. English site is available for culture section. |
| www.metro.tokyo.jp | Official site of Tokyo metropolitan government. English site is available. Provides a variety of information related to Tokyo. |
| www.us.emb-japan.go.jp | Official site of the Embassy of Japan in the U.S.A. Provides a variety of information including traveling and visa information. |
| www.pia.co.jp | Homepage of a popular Japanese information journal. Provides entertainment information, e.g., for movies, concerts, music, theaters, art exhibitions, sports, and restaurants. |
| http://webjapanese.com | This site offers a variety of information for students of Japanese. |

# Summary of Japanese Grammar

## 1. NOUNS

a. Most nouns in a sentence are accompanied by one or two noun-particles (e.g., *wa, ga, o, mo, no, ni, de, kara*) or by some form of the copula *desu* (it is). Nouns are not declined.

| | |
|---|---|
| *Nihon ni wa yama ga takusan arimasu.* | There are many mountains in Japan. |
| *Fujisan wa takai yama desu.* | Mt. Fuji is a high mountain. |

b. There are certain words, usually having to do with time, degree, or quantity, that may or may not appear with a particle. These may have the functions not only of nouns, but also of adverbs, and may be used to modify predicates or entire clauses.

| | |
|---|---|
| *Kinoo ikimashita.* | I went there yesterday. |
| *Kinoo wa ikimasen deshita.* | I didn't go there yesterday. |

Here is a list of some additional examples of such words:

| | |
|---|---|
| *maiasa* | every morning |
| *mainichi* | every day |
| *ima* | present time, now |
| *moto* | former time, previously |
| *sukoshi* | a small amount, a little, some |
| *takusan* | a large amount, a great deal, plentifully, in a large quantity |
| *hotondo* | nearly all, almost completely |
| *mada* | as yet, still |
| *zenzen* | completely (used with a negative predicate) |
| *nakanaka* | quite, considerably |

c. Some nouns frequently take on the special function of relating or tying one part of a sentence to another. When this occurs, they assume a role comparable to that of a preposition, adverb, or conjunction in the English language. When thus used, they are always modified by a clause and are sometimes classified as particles rather than as nouns. The list that follows contains some of the most widely used of these functional nouns:

| Noun | Noun meaning | Functional word meaning |
|------|--------------|-------------------------|
| *aida* | duration, space; interval | during; as long as; while |
| *ato* | site; place behind; time following; condition following | after, subsequent to (usually preceded by the *-ta*–form of a verb and followed by *de*) |
| *baai* | occasion; situation | in the event that, in case; when; should (something) happen |
| *hazu* | notch (of an arrow) | it (something) is "in the cards," it is expected that, it is supposed that (when followed by *desu*); it is not reasonable to expect that, it is hardly possible that (when followed by *wa* or *ga arimasen*) |
| *hodo* | approximate degree | to the extent of; not as . . . as . . . (usually followed by a negative predicate); the more . . . the more . . . (when preceded by a single verb in the present tense or a verb in the provisional form together with the same verb in the present) |
| *A wa B hodo yoku arimasen.* | | A is not as good as B. |
| *Sono sake wa nomeba nomu hodo motto nomitaku narimasu.* | | The more you drink that sake, the more you want to drink. |
| *hoo* | side, direction, alternative direction | the use of this word denotes that a comparison is being made: |
| *Kono hoo ga yasui desu.* | | This is cheaper. |
| *Kusuri o nonda hoo ga ii desu.* | | It would be better (for you) to take some medicine. |

| Noun | Noun meaning | Functional word meaning |
|------|-------------|------------------------|
| *ijoo (wa)* | the above mentioned | now that, since, inasmuch as, because of |
| *kagiri* | limits, bounds; maximum degree | as far as, so long as, as much as, provided that |
| *kekka* | result, outcome, consequence | with the result that, as a result of, because of |
| *kiri* | limit | nothing happened after: |
| *Nippon e itta kiri tayori ga arimasen.* | | There is no news from him since he went to Japan. |
| *koto* | fact; thing (abstract) (makes a noun equivalent out of inflected words; used in many idiomatic expressions): | the act of doing . . . ; the act of having done . . . |
| *Hanasu koto wa dekimasen.* | | Talking is not permitted (possible)./ I can't talk. |
| *Hanashita koto wa arimasen.* | | I've never talked (with him). (The experience of having talked with him does not exist.) |
| *mae* | the front; prior time, former time | before, prior to (usually followed by ni), ago |
| *mama* | will (wish) | as it is (without doing anything further, without taking additional action); as it stands; exactly as; according to |
| *mono* | thing (tangible); person | the thing that; the one who; it's because (when it is used at the end of a sentence, usually by a female speaker— a use similar to *kara* or *node*); that's the thing to do, you should, it is expected that (when preceded by a verb in the present form and followed by *desu*); used to do (when preceded by the -ta form of a verb and followed by *desu*) |

| Noun | Noun meaning | Functional word meaning |
|------|-------------|------------------------|
| *nochi* | the time after | after (used either with or without *ni* following it); subsequent to having done . . . (when it is preceded by the -*ta* form of a verb) |
| *tabi* | occasion, time | every time that |
| *tame* | sake | for the sake of; for the purpose of; because of |
| *toki* | time | (at the time) when |
| *tokoro* | place | just when, in the act of (when followed by *ni* or *de*); even if, no matter who, no matter what (when followed by *de*); to be on the point of (when preceded by the present form of a verb and followed by *desu*); to have just finished doing . . . (when preceded by the -*ta* form of a verb and followed by *desu*) |
| *toori* | the way, avenue | exactly as |
| *tsumori* | idea in mind | intend to, plan to (when preceded by the present tense of a verb and followed by *desu*); (my) notion (recollection) about it is that (something) was the case (when preceded by the -*ta* form of a verb and followed by *desu*) |
| *uchi* | the inside (the within) | while, during the time when |
| *ue* | top, surface, place over | on top of doing, having done (something), upon doing . . . , besides (doing) . . . ; upon finishing, after (doing something; when followed by *de*) |
| *wake* | reason, meaning, logic | that's the background of it, that's the story of it, that's what it is (when followed by *desu*); it is hardly believable that (something) should happen (or should have happened, when followed by *ga arimasen*) |

d. Some nouns are converted into verbs when used with *suru*. The resultant combination means "do the action of (something)." For instance:

| | |
|---|---|
| *shookai* | introduction |
| *shookai suru* | to introduce |
| *ryokoo* | travel |
| *ryokoo suru* | to travel |

e. The pre-*masu* form of a verb can function as a noun:

| | |
|---|---|
| *yomu* | to read |
| *yomi* | reading; pronunciation |
| *tsuru* | to fish |
| *tsuri* | fishing |

f. The stem of an adjective (i.e., the plain present affirmative, minus the final *i*) can function as a noun:

| | | | |
|---|---|---|---|
| *akai* | red | *aka* | the color red |

The stem of an adjective can also function as a noun when sa or mi is added:

| | | | |
|---|---|---|---|
| *akai* | red | *akasa* | redness |
| *fukai* | deep | *fukasa* | depth (as a measure) |
| | | *fukami* | depth (of thought) |

g. Particles[1] used with nouns:

[1] Note that Japanese has many of these so-called "particles," which show the grammatical relationship of one word to another within a sentence. Mastery of these particles is key to rapidly learning Japanese. See "Particles Used with Verbs," section 18 of the Summary of Japanese Grammar.

Following is a list of particles used with nouns, as well as their respective functions:

*ga* marks an emphatic grammatical subject (see *mo*, below).

*wa* marks a sentence topic that may be either the subject or the object of the sentence, or a modifier.

*no* links a noun to another noun. It is most frequently used to indicate the possessive ("of").

*ni* links a noun or noun equivalent (such as the pre-*masu* form of a verb) to a verb, adjective, or copula.

*o* marks the thing acted upon (see *mo*, below).

*mo* can be used instead of *ga* or *o* (see above) but carries the additional meaning of "that thing/person also."

*e* links a noun to a verb and marks the direction toward which an action is performed.

*to* does one of two things: (i) it links nouns together in a complete list (see also *ya*, below) or (ii) it marks the partner with whom the action is being performed.

*ya* links nouns together in an incomplete list (see also *to*, above).

*yori* marks a noun or noun equivalent as the standard against which a comparison is made.

*kara* marks a starting point in time or space.

*made* marks an ending point in time or space.

*de* marks the means by which or the way, place, or manner in which an action is performed.

*bakari* has one of two functions: (i) it can be used in place of (or sometimes together with) *ga* or *o* to carry the additional meaning of "nothing else," or (ii) if it follows a number, it signifies that the number is only approximate.

*dake* can be used in place of or together with *ga* or *o* to carry the additional meaning of "that was the limit."

*hodo* can be used (i) to mark a thing against which a comparison is made and that is about the same in degree or extent as the thing compared, or (ii) to mark a number that is only approximate.

*kurai* (or *gurai*) marks the approximate quantity, quality, or degree of something, and can often be used interchangeably with *hodo* (see above).

*ka* (i) shows that a statement is a question, or (ii) has the meaning of "either . . . or."

## 2. COUNTERS

Counters form a subclass of nouns often used adverbially to mean "to the extent of." There are several types:

a. Unit counters:
(1) Unit counters name specifically that which is being counted. The following unit counters are used with primary numbers—*ichi, ni, san* (one, two, three), etc.—and are suffixed to these numbers. Where an exception to the general rule occurs, it is shown.

| Counter | Meaning | Exceptions |
|---------|---------|------------|
| *-jikan* | hours | *yojikan* = four hours |
| *-ji* | o'clock | *yoji* = four o'clock |
| *-fun (or -pun)* | minutes | See also section 4-b of the Summary of Japanese Grammar for change of sound |
| *-byoo* | seconds | |

| Counter | Meaning | Exceptions |
|---|---|---|
| *-nichi* | days | |
| *-shuukan* | weeks | |
| *-kagetsu* | months | |
| *-gatsu* | name of the month | |
| *-nen* | years | *yonen* = four years |
| *-en* | yen (Japanese currency) | |
| *-sento* | cent (U.S. currency) | |
| *-doru* | dollar (U.S. currency) | |
| *-shiringu* | shillings (British currency) | |
| *-pondo* | pounds (unit of weight or of British currency) | |
| *-meetoru* | meters | |
| *-kiro* | kilometers, kilograms | |
| *-kiroguramu* | kilograms | |
| *-kiromeetoru* | kilometers | |
| *-mairu* | miles | |
| *-inchi* | inches | |
| *-do* | times | |
| *-peeji* | pages; page number | |
| *-gyoo* | lines; line number | |
| *-wari* | one-tenth | |
| *-paasento* | percent | |
| *-kai* | story (of a building) | |

(2) The following unit counters are used with secondary numbers (*hito-, futa-, mi-,* etc.). They are usually used to count amounts less than four.

| | |
|---|---|
| *-ban* | nights |
| *-heya* | room |
| *-ma* | room |

## b. Class counters:

(1) Class counters are used in a general rather than a specific sense. The following class counters are used with primary numerals (*ichi, ni, san* . . . ):

| Counter | Meaning | Exceptions |
|---|---|---|
| *-hiki* (or *-biki,* or *-piki*) | animals, fish, insects | *ippiki, sanbiki, roppiki, juppiki* |
| *-too* | large animals (such as horses, cows) | |
| *-wa* (or *-ba,* or *-pa*) | birds | *sanba, roppa, juppa* |
| *-satsu* | bound volumes (e.g., of books and magazines) | |
| *-mai* | flat, thin things (such as sheets, newspapers, handkerchiefs) | |
| *-hon* (or *-pon,* or *-bon*) | thin, long things (such as pencils, tubes, sticks, matches, cigarettes) | *ippon, sanbon, roppon, juppon* |
| *-ken* (or *-gen*) | houses | *sangen* |
| *-tsuu* | documents, letters, telegrams | |
| *-dai* | vehicles (such as cars, wagons), machines (such as typewriters, sewing machines) | |

| Counter | Meaning | Exceptions |
|---|---|---|
| *-ki* | planes and other aircraft | |
| *-chaku* | suits of clothes | |
| *-soku* (or | pairs of things | *sanzoku* |
| *-zoku)* | things worn on the feet or legs (such as shoes, socks, stockings) | |
| *-ko* | lumps (such as apples, stones, candy) | |
| *-hai* (or *-pai*, or *-bai*) | something in containers (such as water, coffee) | |

(2) The following class counters are used with secondary numerals (*hito-*, *futa-*, *mi-*, etc.):

| | |
|---|---|
| *-fukuro* | bagful (of) |
| *-hako* | boxful (of) |
| *-kumi* | set, group, couple (of people) |
| *-soroi* | set, group |
| *-iro* | kind, variety |
| *-kire* | slices |
| *-tsumami* | pinch |

## 3. PRONOUNS

All of the Japanese words that correspond to English pronouns are nouns. They take the same particles as other nouns and are modified by the same type of words, phrases, and clauses that are used to modify other nouns. Note that in Japanese, there are more varieties of words that correspond to personal pronouns than there are in English.

A list of Japanese equivalents of personal pronouns and instructions for using them follows:

## a. I, we:

| Singular | Plural | Meaning and usage |
|---|---|---|
| *watakushi* | *watakushitachi* | I, we (formal) |
| *watashi* | *watashitachi* | I, we (slightly less formal than *watakushi* and used most widely) |
| *boku* | *bokutachi* | I, we (used by males only: informal) |
| *ore* | *oretachi* | I, we (used by males, but not in refined speech) |

## b. You:

Avoid using any definite word for "you" as long as the sentence meaning is clear without it. If you cannot avoid such a reference, use the name (usually the surname) of the person you are addressing, and add -*san* with the appropriate particle. If you are speaking to a small child, use the child's given name with -*kun* (for male) or -*chan* (for female). If you are speaking to a teacher, doctor, or someone in a similar position, use *sensei* either preceded by or without the surname of the person you are addressing. If you must employ the pronoun instead of the name, use *anata* (you [sing.]), *anatagata* (you [pl.]), *minasan* (you [pl.]), or *minasama* (you [pl., very formal]). Many of the sentence examples in this course contain *anata* or *anatagata*, but these should be replaced in actual conversation by the name of the person to whom you are speaking whenever possible.

## c. He, she, they:[2]

| Singular | Plural | Meaning and Usage |
|---|---|---|
| *ano kata* | *ano katagata* | he, she, they (respectful) |
| *ano hito* | *ano hitotachi* | he, she, they (respectful) |

[2] Note that the appropriate variants of these pronouns are often context-dependent. Please refer to the "Meaning and Usage" column for explanations about where they are likely to appear.

| Singular | Plural | Meaning and Usage |
|---|---|---|
| *ano otoko no kata* | *ano otoko no katagata* | he, they (respectful; used only when it is necessary to indicate specifically "he [that man]" or "they [those men]") |
| *ano otoko no hito* | *ano otoko no hitotachi* | he, they (neutral; same as above) |
| *ano onna no kata* | *ano onna no katagata* | she, they (respectful; used only when there is need to indicate specifically "she [that woman]" or "they [those women]") |
| *ano onna no hito* | *ano onna no hitotachi* | she, they (neutral; same as above) |
| *kare* | *karera* | he, they (these are relatively direct translations and thus tend to be less context dependent than other pronouns, but they are also less common and less accepted in writing) |
| *kanojo* | *kanojora* | she, they |

## d. Possessives:

There are no expressly possessive pronouns in Japanese. To form the possessive, combine a noun (used for the person referred to) with *no* (things of), as in the following examples:

| | |
|---|---|
| *watashi no* | my, mine |
| *anato no* (or the name of the person) plus *no* | your, yours |
| *kare no/kanojo no* | his, hers |
| *watashitachi no* | our, ours |
| *anatagata no* <br> *minasan no* | your, yours (pl.) |
| *karera no* | their, theirs |

## 4. DEMONSTRATIVES

Demonstratives—words such as *kono* (this) or *konna* (this kind of)—precede a noun and modify its meaning. No particle is used to separate the demonstrative and noun. Demonstratives do not change their forms.

| ]*kono* | this |
|---------|------|
| *sono* | that |
| *ano* | that over there |
| *dono* | which? |
| *konna* | this kind of |
| *sonna* | that kind of |
| *anna* | that kind of |
| *donna* | what kind of? |

## 5. *KO-SO-A-DO* WORDS

Some Japanese nouns and demonstratives come in sets of four words that are usually pronounced alike, except for the first syllable. These sets of words are called "*ko-so-a-do* words" because the first syllable is always one of the following four: *ko-*, *so-*, *a-*, or *do-*. Note that the word in such a group that begins with *do* is always a question word.

a. *Ko-so-a-do* nouns:

| *kore* | this one |
|--------|----------|
| *sore* | that one |

| | |
|---|---|
| *are* | that one over there |
| *dore* | which one? |
| *koko* | this place |
| *soko* | that place |
| *asoko*[3] | that place over there |
| *doko* | which place? where? |
| *kochira, kotchi* | this way, this one (of two) |
| *sochira, sotchi* | that way, that one (of two) |
| *achira, atchi* | that way, that one (of two) |
| *dochira, dotchi* | which way, which (of two)? |

[3] An irregular form.

b. *Ko-so-a-do* demonstratives:

| | |
|---|---|
| *kono* | this |
| *sono* | that |
| *ano* | that over there |
| *dono* | which? |
| *konna* | this sort of |
| *sonna* | that sort of (for something not far removed in feeling or time) |
| *anna* | that sort of (for something more remote in feeling or time) |
| *donna* | what sort of? |

## 6. ADJECTIVES

a. *I*-adjectives:

*I*-adjectives can end in *-ai, -ii, -ui,* or *-oi,* but never in *-ei.*

| | |
|---|---|
| *akai* | (is/are) red |
| *utsukushii* | (is/are) beautiful |
| *samui* | (is/are) cold |
| *kuroi* | (is/are) black |

*I*-adjectives are conjugated as follows:

(1) Plain forms:

| PRESENT | *takai* | it is high |
|---|---|---|
| PAST | *takakatta* | it was high |
| TENTATIVE PRESENT | *takai daroo* | it is probably high |
| TENTATIVE PAST | *takakatta daroo* | it was probably high |

(2) Polite forms:

| PRESENT | *akai desu* | it is high |
|---|---|---|
| PAST | *takakatta desu* | it was high |
| TENTATIVE PRESENT | *takai deshoo* | it is probably high |
| TENTATIVE PAST | *takakatta deshoo* | it was probably high |

## (3) Other forms:

| -TE form | *takakute* | it is (was) high, and . . . |
|---|---|---|
| -KU form | *takaku* | it is (was) high, and . . . highly |
| -BA form | *takakereba* | if it is high |
| -TARA form | *takakattara* | if (when) it is (was) high |

## b. *Na*-adjectives:

### (1) Plain forms:

| PRESENT | *shizuka da* | it is quiet |
|---|---|---|
| PAST | *shizuka datta* | it was quiet |
| TENTATIVE PRESENT | *shizuka daroo* | it is probably quiet |
| TENTATIVE PAST | *shizuka datta daroo* | it was probably quiet |

### (2) Polite forms:

| PRESENT | *shizuka desu* | it is quiet |
|---|---|---|
| PAST | *shizuka deshita* | it was quiet |
| TENTATIVE PRESENT | *shizuka deshoo* | it is probably quiet |
| TENTATIVE PAST | *shizuka datta deshoo* | it was probably quiet |

(3) Other forms:

| -TE forms | *shizuka de* | it is (was) quiet and . . . |
|-----------|--------------|------------------------------|
| -NI forms | *shizuka ni* | quietly |
| -TARA forms | *shizuka dattara* | if (when) it is (was) quiet and . . . |

## 7. COMPARISONS

There are several ways to show comparison:

a. Use *no hoo* (the side of) to show what is being compared:

| | |
|---|---|
| *Kyooto no hoo ga suki desu.* | I like Kyoto better. |
| *Tookyoo no hoo ga samui desu.* | Tokyo is colder (in climate). |
| *Kuruma de iku hoo ga ii desu.* | It is better to go by car. |

Notice that when a verb comes before *hoo, no* is omitted.

b. Use *yori* (than) to mark the standard against which a comparison is made:

| | |
|---|---|
| *Kyooto yori samui desu.* | It is colder than Kyoto. |
| *Kore wa sore yori takai desu.* | This is more expensive than that. |

c. Use both *no hoo* and *yori* in the same sentence to show that a comparison is being made:

| | |
|---|---|
| *Tookyoo no hoo ga Kyooto yori samui desu.* | Tokyo is colder than Kyoto. |
| *Yomu hoo ga hanasu yori muzukashii desu.* | Reading is more difficult than speaking. |

d. Use *zutto* (by far the more) either with or without *no hoo* or *yori*:

| | |
|---|---|
| *Sono densha no hoo ga kono densha yori zutto hayai desu.* *Sono densha ga zutto hayai desu.* | That train is much faster (than this train). |
| *Kore wa zutto yasashii desu.* | This is much easier. |

e. Use *motto* (still more) either with or without *no hoo* or *yori*:

| | |
|---|---|
| *Sore wa motto takai desu./* *Sore wa kore yori motto takai desu.* | That is still more expensive (than this one). |
| *Motto yukkuri hana shite kudasai.* | Please speak more slowly. |

f. Use *ichiban* (number one, most of all) or *mottomo* (the most) when comparing more than two things. (*Mottomo* is more formal than *ichiban*.)

| | |
|---|---|
| *Kare ga ichiban se ga takai desu./* *Kare ga mottomo se ga takai desu.* | He is the tallest. |
| *Ichiban ii no o kudasai.* | Give me the best kind, please. |

g. Use *dochira* or *dotchi* (which of the two), or *dore* (which of more than two) when asking a question involving a comparison:

| | |
|---|---|
| *Nagoya to Kyooto de wa dochira no hoo ga chikai desu ka?* | Which is nearer–Nagoya or Kyoto? |
| *Tenisu to gorufu to suiei no naka de dore ga ichiban omoshiroi desu ka?* | Which is the most interesting–tennis, golf, or swimming? |

h. Use *hodo* (to show approximate degree) and a negative predicate when making a comparison between two things that are not quite alike:

| | |
|---|---|
| *Nagoya wa Oosaka hodo tooku arimasen.* | Nagoya is not as far as Osaka. |
| *Tanaka-san wa Yamada-san hodo kanemochi ja ari masen.* | Ms. Tanaka is not as rich as Mr. Yamada. |

i. Also use *hodo* to describe situations resulting in extreme, intense, or severe effects:

| | |
|---|---|
| *Kimochi ga waruku naru hodo*<br>*takusan tabemashita.* | I ate so much that I began to feel sick. |
| *Onaka ga itaku naru hodo*<br>*waraimashita.* | I laughed so much that I began to get a stomachache. |

j. Use *no yoo ni* (in the likeness of, in the manner of) or *kurai* (or *gurai*) (more or less) when making a comparison between two things or situations that are pretty much alike:

| | |
|---|---|
| *Yamada-san wa Eego ga Amerikajin*<br>*no yoo ni yoku dekimasu.* | Mr. Yamada knows English as well as (just like) an American. |
| *Yamada-san wa Eego ga Amerikajin*<br>*gurai dekimasu.* | Mr. Yamada knows English as well as (just like) an American. |

## 8. THE CLASSES AND FORMS OF VERBS
a. Verb classes:
There are three classes of verbs in Japanese:

Class I—consonant verbs: includes all verbs except those in Class II and Class III.

Class II—vowel verbs: includes the majority of verbs that, in their plain present form, terminate in *-eru* or *-iru*.

Class III—irregular verbs: *kuru* (come) and *suru* (do).

The base of a consonant verb is that part left over after the final *-u* has been dropped from the plain present affirmative form (= dictionary form).

The base of a vowel verb is that part that remains after the final *-ru* has been dropped from the plain present form. It always ends in either *-e* or *-i*.

## b. -*masu* forms:

-*masu* forms (= polite present affirmative forms) are formed in the following ways:

Consonant verbs: Drop the final -*u* of the dictionary form and add -*imasu*.

Vowel verbs: Drop the final *ru* of the dictionary form and add -*masu*.

| DICTIONARY FORM | -*MASU* FORM | |
|---|---|---|
| consonant verb | | |
| *kaku* | *kakimasu* | write |
| *yomu* | *yomimasu* | read |
| vowel verb | | |
| *taberu* | *tabemasu* | eat |
| *miru* | *mimasu* | see |

-*masu* forms of some respect verbs are formed irregularly:

| DICTIONARY FORM | -*MASU* FORM | |
|---|---|---|
| *irassharu* | *irasshaimasu* | go, come, be |
| *ossharu* | *osshaimasu* | say |
| *kudasaru* | *kudasaimasu* | give |
| *nasaru* | *nasaimasu* | do |

These respect verbs are consonant verbs. Notice that in their -*masu* forms, *r* is dropped. For example, the -*masu* form of *irassharu* is *irasshaimasu*, not *irassharimasu*.

c. The tenses:
In Japanese, a verb form referred to as a "tense" actually describes the mood of the action or state.

(1) The present tense (or -*u*-ending form) expresses an incomplete action or state and may have several English translations:

| | |
|---|---|
| *hanashimasu* | I speak; I do speak; I will speak |
| *tabemasu* | I eat; I do eat; I will eat |

(2) The past tense (or -*ta* form) expresses a completed action or state. It, too, can have several English translations:

| | |
|---|---|
| *hanashimashita* | I spoke; I have spoken |
| *tabemashita* | I ate; I have eaten |

The plain form of the past tense is formed from the plain present as follows:

(a) For consonant verbs:
(i) When the final syllable in the plain present is -*u*, -*tsu*, or -*ru*, drop it and add -*tta*:

| PRESENT | PAST | |
|---|---|---|
| *kau* | *katta* | I bought |
| *tatsu* | *tatta* | I stood |
| *toru* | *totta* | I took |

(ii) When the final syllable in the plain present is *-mu, -nu,* or *-bu,* drop it and add *-nda:*

| | | |
|---|---|---|
| *nomu* | *nonda* | I drank |
| *shinu* | *shinda* | he died |
| *yobu* | *yonda* | I called |

(iii) When the final syllable is *-ku* or *-gu,* drop it and add *-ita* in place of *-ku* and *-ida* in place of *-gu:*

| | | |
|---|---|---|
| *kaku* | *kaita* | I wrote |
| *isogu* | *isoida* | I hurried |

(iv) When the final syllable is *-su,* drop it and add *-shita:*

| | | |
|---|---|---|
| *hanasu* | *hanashita* | I spoke |
| *kasu* | *kashita* | I lent |

(b) For vowel verbs:
Drop the final syllable *-ru* and add *-ta:*

| | | |
|---|---|---|
| *taberu* | *tabeta* | I ate |
| *miru* | *mita* | I saw |

(c) For irregular verbs:

| | | |
|---|---|---|
| *kuru* | *kita* | I came |
| *suru* | *shita* | I did |

The polite form of the past tense is formed from the polite present (the *-masu* form) by replacing the final syllable *-su* with *-shita.*

| POLITE PRESENT | POLITE PAST | |
|---|---|---|
| *ikimasu* | *ikimashita* | I went |
| *tabemasu* | *tabemashita* | I ate |
| *mimasu* | *mimashita* | I saw |

(3) The tentative (polite: *-mashoo*; plain: *-oo* or *-yoo*) expresses an action or state that is not certain, definite, or completed. It can have several English translations:

| | |
|---|---|
| *Yomimashoo.* | I think I will read./Let's read. |
| *Yomimashoo ka?* | Shall we read? |

The plain tentative is formed from the plain present as follows:

(a) For consonant verbs:
Drop the final *-u* and add *-oo*:

| PRESENT | TENTATIVE | |
|---|---|---|
| *Hanasu.* | *Hanasoo.* | I think I'll speak/talk./Let's speak/talk. |
| *Yomu.* | *Yomoo.* | I think I'll read./Let's read. |

(b) For vowel verbs:
Drop the final *-ru* and add *-yoo*:

| | | |
|---|---|---|
| *Taberu.* | *Tabeyoo.* | I think I'll eat./Let's eat. |
| *Miru.* | *Miyoo.* | I think I'll see it./Let's see it. |

The polite tentative is formed from the polite present by dropping the final *-su* and adding *-shoo*.

| POLITE PRESENT | POLITE TENTATIVE | |
|---|---|---|
| *Hanashimasu.* | *Hanashimashoo.* | I think I'll speak/talk./Let's speak/talk. |
| *Tabemasu.* | *Tabemashoo.* | I think I'll eat./ Let's eat. |

d. *-Te* forms:
(1) The *-te* form is formed exactly like the plain past affirmative (see Section 17-c-[2]) except that the final vowel is *-e.* A *-te* form actually has no tense; the "tense" feeling is determined by the "tense-mood," that is, the ending (*-u, -ta, -yoo*), of the terminal verb.

| | |
|---|---|
| *Kusuriya e itte kusuri o kaimashita.* | I went to a drugstore and bought some medicine. |

Normally, when there is more than one verb in a sentence, the *-te* form is used for all but the last verb. The pre-*masu* form is sometimes used instead of the *-te* form, but this is considered "bookish."

| | |
|---|---|
| *Kusuriya e itte kusuri o katte uchi e kaette sore o nonde sugu nemashita.* | I went to the drugstore and bought some medicine and returned home and took it and went to bed right away. |

(2) The *-te* form is also used:
(a) Adverbially, to modify a verb or adjective:

| | |
|---|---|
| *Isoide ikimashita.* | He went hurriedly. |
| *Naite hanashimashita.* | He spoke in tears. |
| *Yorokonde shigoto o hikiukemashita.* | She took on the job gladly. |

(b) With *kudasai*, to form a request:

*Kesa no shinbun o katte kudasai.*    Please buy me this morning's paper.

(c) With *imasu*, to form the progressive:

*Hanashite imasu.*    I am speaking.
*Tabete imasu.*    I am eating.

(d) To form the "stative," which expresses the state resulting from a completed action, (i) add *arimasu* to the *-te* form, or (ii) add *imasu* to the *-te* form. The latter kind is identical with the progressive in form, but not in function. Usually, *arimasu* is used after the *-te* form of a transitive verb, and *imasu* after the *-te* form of an intransitive verb.

*Te de kaite arimasu.*    It's handwritten. (It is in the state of his having written it by hand.)

*Moo kekkon shite imasu.*    She is married already. (She is in the state of her being married since she got married.)

| PLAIN PRESENT AFFIRMATIVE (DICTIONARY FORM) | | |
|---|---|---|
| Class I Verbs | Class II Verbs | Class III verbs |
| (Consonant verbs) | (Vowel verbs) | (Irregular verbs) |
| *hanasu* | *taberu* | *suru* |
| speak | eat | do |
| will speak | will eat | will do |

## PLAIN PAST AFFIRMATIVE

| | | |
|---|---|---|
| *hanashita* | *tabeta* | *shita* |
| spoke | ate | did |
| have spoken | have eaten | has done |

## POLITE PRESENT AFFIRMATIVE (-*MASU* FORM)

| | | |
|---|---|---|
| *hanashimasu* | *tabemasu* | *shimasu* |
| speak | eat | do |
| will speak | will eat | will do |

## POLITE PAST AFFIRMATIVE

| | | |
|---|---|---|
| *hanashimashita* | *tabemashita* | *shimashita* |
| spoke | ate | did |
| have spoken | have eaten | have done |

## PLAIN PRESENT NEGATIVE

| | | |
|---|---|---|
| *hanasanai* | *tabenai* | *shinai* |
| do not speak | do not eat | do not do |
| will not speak | will not eat | will not do |

## PLAIN PAST NEGATIVE

| *hanasanakatta* | *tabenakatta* | *shinakatta* |
|---|---|---|
| did not speak | did not eat | did not do |
| have not spoken | have not eaten | have not done |

## POLITE PRESENT NEGATIVE

| *hanashimasen* | *tabemasen* | *shimasen* |
|---|---|---|
| do not speak | do not eat | do not do |
| will not speak | will not eat | will not do |

## POLITE PAST NEGATIVE

| *hanashimasen deshita* | *tabemasen deshita* | *shimasen deshita* |
|---|---|---|
| did not speak | did not eat | did not do |
| have not spoken | have not eaten | have not done |

## EXTRA-POLITENESS

| NEUTRAL | RESPECT | HUMBLE |
|---|---|---|
| *hanasu* | *ohanashi ni naru, hana sareru* | *ohanashi suru* |

## PLAIN -*TE* FORM

| *hanashite* | *tabete* | *shite* |
|---|---|---|
| speak and . . . | eat and . . . | do and . . . |
| will speak and . . . | will eat and . . . | will do and . . . |

## POLITE -*TE* FORM (ONLY USED IN MOST FORMAL SITUATIONS)

| *hanashimashite* | *tabemashite* | *shimashite* |
|---|---|---|

Note that in the following groups, the "a" lines show the plain form of the verb, and the "b" lines show the polite form.

## PRESENT PROGRESSIVE AFFIRMATIVE

| *a. hanashite iru* | *tabete iru* | *shite iru* |
|---|---|---|
| *b. hanashite imasu* | *tabete imasu* | *shite imasu* |
| he is speaking | he is eating | he is doing |

## PAST PROGRESSIVE AFFIRMATIVE

| *a. hanashite ita* | *tabete ita* | *shite ita* |
|---|---|---|
| *b. hanashite imashita* | *tabete imashita* | *shite imashita* |
| he was speaking | he was eating | he was doing |

| PRESENT | PROGRESSIVE | NEGATIVE |
| --- | --- | --- |
| *a. hanashite inai* | *tabete inai* | *shite inai* |
| *b. hanashite imasen* | *tabete imasen* | *shite imasen* |
| he is not speaking | he is not eating | he is not doing |

| PAST | PROGRESSIVE | NEGATIVE |
| --- | --- | --- |
| *a. hanashite inakatta* | *tabete inakatta* | *shite inakatta* |
| *b. hanashite imasen deshita* | *tabete imasen deshita* | *shite imasen deshita* |
| he was not speaking | he was not eating | he was not doing |

| PRESENT | STATIVE | AFFIRMATIVE |
| --- | --- | --- |
| *a. Hanashite aru.* | *Tabete aru.* | *Shite aru.* |
| *b. Hanashite arimasu.* | *Tabete arimasu.* | *Shite arimasu.* |
| The matter has already been mentioned to him. (The matter is in the state of my having spoken about it.) | The meal is finished. (The meal is in the state of my having eaten it.) | It's done. (The work is in the state of my having done it.) |

## PAST STATIVE AFFIRMATIVE (Usually translated into English using the past perfect.)

| | | |
|---|---|---|
| *a. Hanashite atta.* | *Tabete atta.* | *Shite atta.* |
| *b. Hanashite ari mashita.* | *Tabete arimashita.* | *Shite arima shita.* |
| The matter had been mentioned to him. | The meal had been eaten. | The work had been done. |

## PRESENT STATIVE NEGATIVE

| | | |
|---|---|---|
| *a. Hanashite nai.* | *Tabete nai.* | *Shite nai.* |
| *b. Hanashite arimasen.* | *Tabete arimasen.* | *Shite arimasen.* |
| The matter has not been mentioned. | The meal is not finished. | It is not done. |

## PAST STATIVE NEGATIVE

| | | |
|---|---|---|
| *a. Hanashite nakatta.* | *Tabete nakatta.* | *Shite nakatta.* |
| *b. Hanashite arimasen deshita.* | *Tabete arimasen deshita.* | *Shite arimasen deshita.* |
| The matter hadn't been mentioned. | The meal hadn't been finished. | It hadn't been done. |

## PROVISIONAL AND CONDITIONAL

| | | |
|---|---|---|
| *hatarakeba* | *tabereba* | *sureba* |
| *hataraitara* | *tabetara* | *shitara* |
| *hataraku to* | *taberu to* | *suru to* |
| *hataraku nara* | *taberu nara* | *suru nara* |
| *hataraite wa* | *tabete wa* | *shite wa* |
| if I work | if I eat | if I do |

# 9. PARTICLES USED WITH VERBS

The following particles that are used with verbs can also be used with adjectives or the copula.

a. *Bakari desu* =
(*Bakari* is sometimes classified as an adverb instead of a particle.)

(1) (Following a *-u* form) does nothing but (something); does only (something)

| | |
|---|---|
| *Sotsugyoo o matsu bakari desu.* | I am just waiting for graduation. (I have no more school work to do.) |

(2) (Following a *-ta* form) has just done (something); did only (something):

| | |
|---|---|
| *Gohan o tabeta bakari desu.* | I have just finished eating. |

b. *Dake* = that is just about all; that is just about the extent of it; only; just:
(*Dake* is sometimes classified as an adverb instead of a particle.)

| | |
|---|---|
| *Mita dake desu.* | I just took a look at it. |
| *Hanashi o suru dake desu.* | I am just going to discuss it. (I won't make any decision yet.) |

c. *Ga* = but; in spite of the fact stated above (when preceded by either the plain or polite forms):

| | |
|---|---|
| *Ikimashita ga aemasen deshita.* | I went (there), but I couldn't see him. |
| *Kaimashita ga mada tsukatte imasen.* | I have bought it, but haven't used it yet. |

d. *Ka* = a spoken question mark:

*Kyoo wa oisogashii desu ka?*     Are you busy today?

e. *Kara* =
(1) (Following a *-te* form) after doing (something); since doing (something):

*Mite kara kimemasu.*     I will decide after taking (having taken) a look at it.

(2) (Following any sentence-ending form—*-u, -ta, -i*) and so, and therefore:

*Omoi desu kara watashi ga*     It's heavy, so I will carry it.
*omochi shimashoo.*

f. *Keredo(mo)* = in spite of the fact stated before; but; however; although:

*Isoida keredo ma ni aimasen*     I hurried, but couldn't make it.
*deshita.*
*Yonda keredomo yoku*     I read it, but I didn't understand
*wakarimasen deshita.*     it well.

The use of *mo* is optional.

g. *Made* = up to the time of (something)'s happening; until; so far as:

*Yamada-san ga kuru made koko*     I will stay here until Mr. Yamada
*ni ori masu.*     gets here.

h. *Na* =
(1) (Following a plain present affirmative form) don't do (something). Note that this is never used in refined speech; instead, *-naide kudasai* is used:

| *Hairu na!* | Don't enter! |
| *Hairanaide kudasai.* | Please don't enter. |

(2) (Following a sentence-ending form) yeah, that's what it is (used only by men in colloquial speech):

| *Ii tenki da na!* | What fine weather! |
| *Genki da na!* | You are in good shape! (You look fine!) |

(3) (Following a verb and used with *ka*) should I? I wonder if I should? (used in colloquial speech):

| *Dekakeyoo ka na?* | Let's see. Shall we go now? |
| *Eiga de mo miyoo ka na.* | I guess I will see a movie or something. |

i. *-Nagara* = (following a pre-*masu* form, showing that two or more actions or states take place or exist concurrently) while; in the course of:

| *Arukinagara hanashi mashoo.* | Let's talk as we walk (to that place). |
| *Hatarakinagara benkyoo shite imasu.* | He is studying while working (he is supporting himself). |

j. *Nari* =
(1) (When used in a parallel sequence) either . . . or . . . ; whether . . . or . . . :

*Denwa o kakeru nari tegami o kaku nari shite minna ni shirasemashita.*
She informed everybody either by phoning or writing a letter.

(2) (When not used in a parallel sequence) as soon as; the moment (something) has taken place:

| *Kao o miru nari naki hajimemashita.* | He burst into tears the moment he saw me. |

k. *Ni* = the purpose of the "going" or "coming" that is expressed (when it follows the pre-*masu* form of a verb):

| | |
|---|---|
| *Kaimono o shi ni iki mashita.* | He went shopping. (He went in order to shop.) |

l. *Node* = (following a sentence-ending form) and so; and therefore:

| | |
|---|---|
| *Totemo tsukareta node sukoshi yasumitai desu.* | I got very tired, so I would like to (take a) rest. |
| *Okane o harawanakatta node okutte kimasen deshita.* | I didn't send the money for it; that's why it didn't come. |

m. *Noni* = despite that; but; although; and yet:

| | |
|---|---|
| *Yonda noni henji ga nai.* | I called her, but there was no answer. |
| *Itta noni awanakatta.* | Although I went there, I didn't see her. |

n. *To* =
(1) (Following a present form) whenever:

| | |
|---|---|
| *Hima da to sanpo shimasu.* | Whenever I am free, I take a walk. |

(2) Acts as an "end quote" when it precedes a verb meaning "say," "hear," "ask," "think," "believe":

| | |
|---|---|
| *Itsu kimasu ka to kikareta.* | I was asked (as to) when I would be coming. |

(3) (When it follows a tentative and is in turn followed by *shita*) to be on the point of doing (something); to try to do (something):

| | |
|---|---|
| *Uchi o deyoo to shita tokoro e tomodachi ga kimashita.* | Just as I was about to go out, a friend of mine came (to visit me). |

o. *-tari . . . -tari suru* =

(1) Sometimes does (something); at other times does (something else):

| | |
|---|---|
| *Nihon to Amerika no aida o ittari kitari shite imasu.* | She travels back and forth between Japan and the United States. |

(2) Does (one thing) and (another):

| | |
|---|---|
| *Hito ga nottari oritari shite imasu.* | Some people are getting on, some are getting off. |

p. Terminal particles:
(1) *Ne* = isn't it? doesn't it?

| | |
|---|---|
| *Erai hito desu ne?* | He is a great man, isn't he? |

(2) *Sa* = sure it is so (used only by men, slang):

| | |
|---|---|
| *Shitte iru sa!* | Of course I know it. |

(3) *Wa, wa yo* = a diminutive used only by women:

| | |
|---|---|
| *Sanji ni denwa o kakeru wa (yo).* | I will phone you at three. |

The use of *yo* is optional.

(4) *Yo* = an exclamatory particle:

| | |
|---|---|
| *Kyoo wa okyakusan ga arimasu yo!* | We are going to have a visitor today! |

(5) *Zo* = an emphatic particle (used only by men, slang):

| | |
|---|---|
| *Naguru zo!* | I'll hit you! |

## 10. NEGATIVES

a. Used with verbs:

(1) Plain negative present—formed from the base of a consonant verb plus the suffix -anai, or the base of a vowel verb plus -nai:

| | |
|---|---|
| *Kaku.* | I write. |
| *Kakanai.* | I don't write. |
| *Taberu.* | I eat. |
| *Tabenai.* | I don't eat. |

Notice that a verb like *kau* (buy) or *warau* (laugh), whose plain present affirmative ends in two vowels, appends an extra *w* before adding -anai:

| | |
|---|---|
| *Kawanai.* | I don't buy (it). |
| *Warawanai.* | She doesn't laugh. |

(2) Plain negative past—formed from the stem of the negative present (the form without the final -*i*) plus -*katta* (like the plain negative past of an adjective):

| | |
|---|---|
| *Kaita.* | I wrote. |
| *Kakanakatta.* | I didn't write. |

(3) Plain negative tentative:

(a) For a consonant verb, use the plain present affirmative plus -*mai*.

(b) For a vowel verb, use the pre-*masu* form plus -*mai*.

(c) For the irregular verbs, use *komai* and *shimai*.

| | |
|---|---|
| *Kakoo.* | I think I'll write it. |
| *Kakumai.* | I don't think I'll write it. |
| *Tabeyoo.* | I think I'll eat. |
| *Tabemai.* | I don't think I'll eat. |

## b. Used with a copula:
### (1) Plain forms:

| | |
|---|---|
| . . . *da* | It is . . . |
| . . . *de aru* | It is (formal, "bookish") . . . |
| . . . *ja nai* } | |
| . . . *dewa nai* | It is not . . . |
| . . . *datta* | It was . . . |
| . . . *ja nakatta* } | |
| . . . *dewa nakatta* | It was not . . . |
| . . . *daroo* | It is probably . . . |
| . . . *ja nai daroo* } | |
| . . . *dewa nai daroo* | It is most probably not . . . |

### (2) Polite forms:

| | |
|---|---|
| . . . *desu* | It is . . . |
| . . . *ja arimasen* | |
| . . . *dewa arimasen* | It is not . . . |
| . . . *deshita* | It was . . . |
| . . . *ja arimasen deshita* | |
| . . . *dewa arimasen deshita* | It wasn't . . . |
| . . . *deshoo* | It is probably . . . |
| . . . *ja nai deshoo* | |
| . . . *dewa nai deshoo* | It is most probably not . . . |

## c. Used with *i*-adjectives:
### (1) Plain forms:

| | |
|---|---|
| *Takai.* | It is expensive. |
| *Takaku nai.* | It is not expensive. |
| *Takakatta.* | It was expensive. |
| *Takaku nakatta.* | It wasn't expensive. |
| *Takai daroo.* | It may be expensive. |
| *Takaku nai daroo.* | It is probably not expensive. |

### (2) Polite forms:

| | |
|---|---|
| *Takai desu.* | It is expensive. |
| *Takaku arimasen.* | It is not expensive. |
| *Takakatta desu.* | It was expensive. |
| *Takaku arimasen deshita.* | |
| *Takaku nakatta desu.* | It was not expensive. |
| *Takai deshoo.* | It is probably expensive. |
| *Takaku nai deshoo.* | It is probably not expensive. |

## d. Other negative expressions (used with negative predicates):

| | |
|---|---|
| *zenzen* | not (at all) |
| *hitotsu mo* | nothing |
| *dare mo* | no one |
| *doko mo* | nowhere |
| *nani mo* | nothing |
| *dochira mo* | neither . . . nor |
| *kesshite* | never |
| *Zenzen wakarimasen deshita.* | I did not understand it at all. |

## 11. WORD ORDER

There are two very important rules to remember for word order in declarative sentences:

a. A predicate word (the copula, verb, or adjective used as a predicate) is placed at the end of the clause or sentence except when a sentence-ending particle such as *ka* (the question mark particle) or *ne* (isn't it? doesn't it?) is used, in which case the predicate word is usually placed immediately before such a particle.

b. A modifier always precedes the word or clause it modifies:
(1) An adjective or adjectival phrase (a noun plus *no*) always precedes the noun it modifies.
(2) A demonstrative always precedes the noun.
(3) An adverb or adverbial phrase always precedes the adjective, adverb, verb, or copula it modifies.
(4) A modifying clause always precedes the noun it modifies.

| | |
|---|---|
| *akai booshi* | a red hat |
| *ano hito* | that person |
| *ano hito no booshi* | that person's hat; her/his hat |
| *ano hito no akai booshi* | that person's red hat |
| *ookina booshi* | a big hat |
| *ano hito no ookina akai booshi* | that person's big red hat |
| *katta booshi* | the hat she bought |
| *kinoo katta booshi* | the hat she bought yesterday |
| *kinoo Matsuya de katta booshi* | the hat she bought at Matsuya yesterday |
| *kanojo ga kinoo no gogo Matsuya de katta booshi* | the hat she bought at Matsuya yesterday afternoon |
| *kanojo ga kinoo no gogo Matsuya de katta ookina akai booshi* | that big red hat she bought at Matsuya yesterday afternoon |
| *kanojo ga kinoo no gogo watakushi to issho ni itte Matsuya de katta ookina akai booshi* | that big red hat she bought yesterday afternoon with me at Matsuya |

## 12. QUESTIONS

The word order for questions is the same as for declarative sentences. The question particle *ka* may or may not be added at the end to show that a question is being asked. For instance:

When *ka* is used, it is not necessary to use the rising intonation. The intonation may remain similar to that of a declarative sentence, even though a question is being asked. When a question is being asked and *ka* is not used, however, the rising intonation must be employed, and the last syllable should be pronounced with a distinct rise in pitch.

| | |
|---|---|
| *Ikimasu.* | I am going. |
| *Ikimasu?* | Are you going? |
| *Ikimasu ka?* | Are you going? |

See the following section for other words that are used in formulating questions.

## 13. QUESTION WORDS

There are several words that are used to form questions. Study the following list to learn what the words are and how they are used.

| QUESTION WORDS | MEANING | NOTES |
|---|---|---|
| *nan, nani* | what thing? what? how many? | For the usage of *nan*, see Lesson 32. The meaning "how many?" applies only when the word is used before a counter. |
| *nannin* | how many people? | |
| *ikutsu* | what number? how many? | The answer must be a number. |
| *iku-* | how many . . . ? | A prefix used only with a counter. |

| | | |
|---|---|---|
| *itsu* | what time? when? | When used adverbially, it may sometimes be used without a particle. |
| *Itsu kimashita ka?* | When did it arrive? | |
| *Itsu hajimar imasu ka?* | When does it begin? | |
| *Itsu ga ii desu ka?* | When would it be good for you? | |
| *dare* | which person? who? | *dare no*: whose? *dare ni*: to whom? *dare kara*: from whom? *dare to*: with whom? |
| *dore* | which thing? which? | Used when there is a choice of more than two. |
| *dochira* | which of these two? which direction? which place (polite)? | Used when there is a choice of only two. |
| *dochira e* | where to? | |
| *dochira kara* | where from? | |
| *dotchi* | see above | A (more informal) variant for the first two meanings of *dochira*. |
| *doko* | which place? where? | |
| *Doko ni arimasu ka?* | Where is it? | |
| *Doko de tabemashita ka?* | Where did you eat? | |
| *Doko kara kimashita ka?* | Where did you come from? | |
| *Doko ga itai desu ka?* | Where does it hurt? | |
| *dono* | which | A demonstrative used when there is a choice of more than two. Use *dochira no* when there is a choice of only two. |

| | | | |
|---|---|---|---|
| *donna* | what sort of? | A demonstrative used when you are interested in the kind or type of thing being discussed. |
| *doo* | how? in what manner? | An adverb. |
| *ikaga doo* | how (polite)? | An adverb; same as (above), but used in refined speech. |

## 14. SOMETHING, EVERYTHING, NOTHING, ANYTHING

Each of the question words appearing in the first column of this table undergoes a change in meaning when it is used together with one of the particles appearing in the other columns. The new meaning is shown for each combination.

| QUESTION WORD | *+ ka* | *+ mo* (used with affirmative predicate) | *+ mo* (used with negative predicate) | *+ de mo* | *+ -te mo* |
|---|---|---|---|---|---|
| *nani, nan* = what | *nani ka* = something or other | *nani mo ka mo* = everything | *nani mo* nothing | *nan de mo* = anything | *nani . . . te mo* = whatsoever, no matter what |
| *dore* = which one | *dore ka* = one or the other; anyone | *dore mo* = all, any | *dore mo* = no one, not anyone, not a one | *dore de mo* = whichever it may be; any at all | *dore . . . te mo* = whichsoever, no matter which |
| *dochira* = which of the two | *dochira ka* = either one | *dochira mo* = both | *dochira mo* = not either one, neither one | *dochira de mo* = whichever it may be, either one | *dochira . . . te mo* = whichever, no matter which |
| *dotchi* = which of the two | *dotchi ka* = either one | *dotchi mo* = both | *dotchi mo* = not either one, neither one | *dotchi de mo* = whichever it may be, either one | *dotchi . . . te mo* = whichever, no matter which |

| | | | | | |
|---|---|---|---|---|---|
| *doko* = which place | *doko ka* = somewhere or other | *doko mo* = everywhere; all places | *doko mo* = not anywhere, nowhere | *doko de mo* = wherever it may be, any place at all | *doko . . . te mo* = wherever, no matter where |
| *dare* = which person | *dare ka* = somebody | *dare mo* = everybody | *dare mo* = not anybody, nobody | *dare de mo* = whoever it may be, anybody at all | *dare . . . te mo* = whoever, no matter who |

*Dotchi* is more informal than *dochira*.

| QUESTION WORD | + *ka* | + *mo* (used with affirmative predicate) | + *mo* (used with negative predicate) | + *de mo* | + *-te mo* |
|---|---|---|---|---|---|
| *itsu* = what time | *itsu ka* = sometime or other | *itsu mo* = always | *itsu mo* = not anytime, never | *itsu de mo* = whenever it may be; anytime at all | *itsu . . . te mo* = whenever, no matter when |
| *doo* = how | *doo ka* = somehow or other; please, by some means or other | *doo mo* = in every way, very | *doo mo* = somehow; not; in no way | *doo de mo* = however it may be; anyway at all | *doo . . . te mo* = however (one does); no matter how |
| *dooshite* = why | *dooshite ka* = omehow or other, for some unknown reason | *dooshite mo* = by all means, under any circumstances | *dooshite mo* = somehow or other . . . not; however one tries . . . not | *dooshite de mo* = by all means; at all costs | – |

| ikutsu = how many | ikutsu ka = some number, several | ikutsu mo = any number | ikutsu mo = not many, no great number, not much to speak of | ikutsu de mo = however many it may be; any number at all | ikutsu . . . te mo = however many (one may); no matter how many |
|---|---|---|---|---|---|
| ikura = how much | ikura ka = some amount | ikura mo = any amount; ever so much | ikura mo = not much; no great amount | ikura de mo = whatever amount it may be | ikura . . . te mo = however much it may be (one may); no matter how much |

## 15. EVEN IF, EVEN THOUGH

### a. Affirmative:
Use -te plus -mo:

| | |
|---|---|
| *Ame ga futte mo ikimasu.* | I'll (still) go, even if it rains. |
| *Takakute mo kaimasu.* | I'll (still) buy it, even if it's expensive. |

### b. Negative:
Use -nakute plus mo:

| | |
|---|---|
| *Ame ga yamanakute mo ikimasu.* | I will go (anyhow), even if it doesn't stop raining. |
| *Yasuku nakute mo kamaimasen.* | I don't care, even if it's not cheap. |

### c. Permission:
Use -te mo ii desu for "you may (you have my permission to)"; use -nakute mo ii desu for "you don't have to (you have my permission not to; even if you don't, it is all right with me)":

| | |
|---|---|
| *Itte mo ii desu.* | You may go. |
| *Ikanakute mo ii desu.* | You don't have to go. |

**d.** No matter how, no matter who, no matter how much:
Use a question word plus *-te mo:*

| | |
|---|---|
| *Donna ni yasukute mo kaitaku arimasen.* | I don't want to buy it, no matter how cheap it is. |
| *Dare ga shite mo kekka wa onaji desu.* | No matter who does it, the result will be the same. |
| *Ikura yonde mo imi ga wakarimasen deshita.* | I couldn't understand it, no matter how many times I read it. |

## 16. HEARSAY

To express the ideas "I hear that . . ." or "They say that . . ." in Japanese:

**a.** For the affirmative:
Use a plain affirmative form of a verb, an *i*-adjective, or the copula plus *soo desu:*

| | |
|---|---|
| *Kyoo wa Yamada-san ga kuru soo desu.* | I hear that Mr. Yamada is coming to visit us today. |
| *Sapporo de wa yuki ga futta soo desu.* | I hear that it snowed in Sapporo. |
| *Takai soo desu.* | I understand (that) it's expensive. |
| *Tanaka-san wa byooki da soo desu.* | I hear Ms. Tanaka is sick. |

**b.** For the negative:
Use a plain negative form of a verb, an *i*-adjective, or the copula plus *soo desu.*

| | |
|---|---|
| *Rajio no tenki yohoo de wa kyoo wa ame wa furanai soo desu.* | According to the weather forecast, it's not going to rain today. |
| *Yamada-san wa konakatta soo desu.* | I hear that Mr. Yamada didn't come. |
| *Takaku nai soo desu.* | I hear (that) it's not expensive. |

| | |
|---|---|
| *Furansugo wa joozu ja nai soo desu.* | I hear she is not good at French. |

## 17. SEEMING
You can express the idea of "it seems" or "it seems to me that . . ." in several ways in Japanese:

a. For the affirmative:
(1) Use a plain affirmative form plus *yoo desu:*

| | |
|---|---|
| *Moo shitte iru yoo desu.* | It seems to me that he already knows it. |
| *Chotto muzukashikatta yoo desu.* | It seems that it was a little difficult. |
| *Minna genki na yoo desu.* | It seems that everybody is fine. |

The copula *da* (present affirmative) becomes *na* before *yoo desu.*

(2) Use a plain affirmative form plus *rashii desu:*

| | |
|---|---|
| *Moo shitte iru rashii desu.* | It seems to me that he already knows it. |
| *Ano hito wa Amerika e kaetta rashii desu.* | It seems that he has gone back to the United States. |

It is more likely, however, that the sentence with *rashii desu* will be interpreted with the meaning of "hearsay" like *soo desu* in Section 25 than with the meaning of "it seems."
(3) Use an *i*-adjective without the final *-i* or a *na*- adjective without the copula plus *-soo desu*:

| | |
|---|---|
| *Kurushisoo desu.* | It seems that he is finding it painful. |
| *Genki soo desu.* | It seems that she is fine. |

b. For the negative:
(1) Use a plain negative form plus *yoo desu:*

| | |
|---|---|
| *Mada shiranai yoo desu.* | It seems that he is unaware of this. |
| *Amari takaku nai yoo desu.* | It seems that it is not very expensive. |

(2) Use a plain negative form plus *rashii desu*:

| | |
|---|---|
| *Mada shiranai rashii desu.* | It seems that he is unaware of this. |
| *Kare wa Nihon e konakatta rashii desu.* | Apparently (it seems that) he didn't come to Japan. |

(3) Use a negative *i*-adjective without the final *-i* or the negative copula without the final *-i* plus *-sasoo desu:*

| | |
|---|---|
| *Kurushiku nasasoo desu.* | He is apparently (it seems that he is) not finding it painful. |
| *Are wa Nakamura-san ja nasasoo desu.* | That does not seem to be Ms. Nakamura. |

## 18. IMMINENCE

To express the idea "it appears that . . . will soon happen":

a. For the affirmative:
Use the pre-*masu* form of the verb plus *-soo desu*:

| | |
|---|---|
| *Ame ga furisoo desu ne.* | It looks like rain, doesn't it? |
| *Yamada-san wa yamesoo desu.* | It looks as if Mr. Yamada is ready to quit. |

b. For the negative:
Use the pre-*masu* form of a verb plus *-soo ja arimasen:*

| | |
|---|---|
| *Ame wa furisoo ja arimasen.* | It doesn't look as though it will rain soon. |
| *Nedan wa yasuku narisoo ja arimasen.* | It doesn't look as though the price is going down. |

# 19. OBLIGATION AND PROHIBITION

To convey the idea of obligation or impulsion (expressed in English by "should," "must," "ought to," "have to"):

a. For the affirmative:
(1) Use the negative -*ba* form of a verb, an *i*-adjective, or the copula, plus *narimasen* or *ikemasen* (if you don't do it, it won't do; if not (something), it won't do).

(2) Use the negative -*te* form plus *wa* plus *narimasen* or *ikemasen*.

Notice the use of a double negative.

| | |
|---|---|
| *Ikanakereba narimasen.* | I should (must, have to, ought to) go. |
| *Ikanakereba ikemasen.* | |
| *Ikanakute wa narimasen.* | |
| *Ikanakute wa ikemasen.* | |
| *Yoku nakereba narimasen.* | It should (must, has to, ought to) be good. |
| *Yoku nakereba ikemasen.* | |
| *Yoku nakute wa narimasen.* | |
| *Yoku nakute wa ikemasen.* | |

b. For the negative:
(1) Use the affirmative -*te* form of a verb plus *wa* plus *narimasen* (if you do (something), it won't do; if it is (something), it won't do):

| | |
|---|---|
| *Itte wa narimasen.* | I should not (must not, ought not) go. |

(2) Use the affirmative -*te* form of a verb, an *i*-adjective, or the copula plus *wa* plus *ikemasen* or *dame desu*:

| | |
|---|---|
| *Koko de asonde wa ikemasen.* | You should not (must not, ought not) play here. |
| *Yasashikute wa dame desu.* | It should not be easy. |

| | |
|---|---|
| *Kono kaban de wa dame desu.* | You should not use this bag. (It should not be this bag.) |

c. *Beki desu* (should), *beki ja arimasen* (should not):
*Beki* is a form remaining from classical Japanese.

(1) For the affirmative, use the plain present of a verb plus *beki desu:*

| | |
|---|---|
| *Iku beki desu.* | I should (must, have to, ought to) go. |
| *Iku beki deshita.* | I should have gone. |

(2) For the negative, use the plain present affirmative of a verb plus *beki ja arimasen:*

| | |
|---|---|
| *Iku beki ja arimasen.* | I should not go. |
| *Iku beki ja arimasen deshita* | I shouldn't have gone. |

(3) For warning or prohibition (seen in public signs only), the plain present affirmative of a verb is used with *bekarazu* (don't):

| | |
|---|---|
| *Hairu bekarazu!* | No admission! |
| *Tooru bekarazu!* | No trespassing! |
| *Sawaru bekarazu!* | Don't touch! |

Bekarazu, which is a derived form of *beki*, is becoming obsolete in public signs. *-Nai de kudasai* (Please do not–) is now preferred.

## 20. PERMISSION
To express the granting of permission, use *-te* plus mo plus *ii desu* (you may, it's all right to):

| | |
|---|---|
| *Kaitakereba katte mo ii desu.* | If you want to buy it, you may (buy it). |
| *Uchi e motte kaette mo ii desu.* | You may take it home if you wish. |
| *Takakute mo ii desu.* | It may be expensive. (Even if it is expensive, it is all right.) |

| | |
|---|---|
| *Kono jisho de mo ii desu.* | This dictionary will do. (It is all right to use this dictionary.) |

## 21. ALTERNATIVES
In statements setting forth a choice of alternatives, use:

a. *-tari . . . -tari shimasu* (the *-ta* form plus *ri* followed by the *-ta* form plus *ri suru*):

| | |
|---|---|
| *Kyoo wa ame ga futtari yandari shite imasu.* | Today it has been raining off and on. |
| *Kare wa chikagoro gakkoo e ittari ikanakattari shimasu.* | He has been irregular recently in (his) attendance at school. |
| *Nichiyoobi no gogo wa shinbun o yondari terebi o mitari shimasu.* | On Sunday afternoons, I spend my time doing such things as reading newspapers and watching television. |
| *Hito ga detari haittari shite imasu.* | People are going in and out. |

b. *-tari shimasu* (a single *-tari* followed by *suru*):

| | |
|---|---|
| *Eiga e ittari shima-shita.* | Among the various things (I did), I went to the movies. I spent my time going to the movies and doing things like that. |
| *Miyagemono o kattari shimashita.* | I bought souvenirs and did (other) things like that. |

## 22. PASSIVE, POTENTIAL, AND RESPECT
A verb made up of its base plus *-areru* or *-rareru* may be any one of the following: (1) passive, (2) potential, or (3) respect. (Use *-areru* with a consonant verb and *-rareru* with a vowel verb.) The exact meaning of such a verb is determined by the context in which it is used.

## a. Passive:

*Watashi wa keikan ni namae o
kikare mashita.*

I was asked my name by a police
officer.

## b. Potential:

*Nihon no eiga wa Amerika de
mo miraremasu.*

Japanese movies can be seen in the
United States, too. (One can see a
Japanese movie in America, too.)

## c. Respect:

*Itoo-sensei wa kinoo Amerika
kara kae- raremashita.*

My teacher, Mr. Ito, came back from the
United States yesterday.

The passive of some Japanese verbs—most particularly the passive
forms of intransitive verbs—means "(something) happened when
it wasn't wanted," or "I underwent (something)," or "I suffered
from the interference of (something)":

*Densha no naka de kodomo ni
nakarete komarimashita.*

We were embarrassed by our child,
who cried continuously while riding
on a train.

*Ame ni furarete sukkari nurete
shimaimashita.*

We were drenched by the rain.

## 23. CAUSATIVE

To form the causative of a verb, add *-aseru* to the base of a consonant verb and *-saseru* to the base of a vowel verb. The causative
forms of the irregular verbs are (for *kuru*) *kosaseru* and (for *suru*)
*saseru*.

Causative verbs may be used to express the thought that:
a. X causes (makes, forces) Y to do (something)
b. X allows (permits, lets) Y to do (something)

Notice that in each instance the element Y is marked by the particle *ni*.

| | |
|---|---|
| *Tanaka-san wa Yamada-san ni denpoo o utasemashita.* | Ms. Tanaka had Mr. Yamada send a telegram. |
| *Kodomo ni kimono o kisasete kudasai.* | Please have the children put on their clothes. |
| *Kyoo wa itsu mo yori ichijikan hayaku kaerasete itadakitai desu.* | I would like to have your permission to go home one hour earlier than usual. (I would like to have you make me go home . . . ) |

A causative can be combined with a passive ending. If the causative ending comes first, the combination means "be made," not "be allowed."

| | |
|---|---|
| *Ikaseraremashita.* | I was made to go. |
| *Tabesaseraremashita.* | I was made to eat it. |

## 24. DESIDERATIVES
The desiderative is the grammatical term for verbal expressions that signify a desire to do something.

a. To say, "I want to do (something)," use the pre-*masu* form plus -*tai*:

| | |
|---|---|
| *Kyoo wa kaimono ni ikitai desu.* | I want to go shopping today. |
| *Ima wa nani mo tabetaku arimasen.* | I don't want to eat anything now. |

b. To express the idea, "one shows that he/she wants to do (something)," add -*tagaru* to the pre-*masu* form:

| | |
|---|---|
| *Kodomo ga soto e ikitagatte imasu.* | The children can't wait to go outside. |

| | |
|---|---|
| *Uchi no kodomo wa sono kusuri o nomitagarimasen.* | Our child doesn't like to take that medicine. (Our child shows that he doesn't like to take that medicine.) |

c. Use the stem (the form without the final *-i*) of an *i*-adjective plus *-garu* to express the meaning that "someone shows outwardly that he/she feels . . ." (usually not the speaker):

| | |
|---|---|
| *Samugarimashita.* | He showed that he felt cold. |
| *Hoshigarimashita.* | He showed that he wanted to have it. |

d. To say, "I want you to do (something) for me," use the *-te* form of a verb plus *itadakitai desu:*

| | |
|---|---|
| *Kono tegami o Eigo ni yakushite itadakitai desu.* | I would like you to translate this letter into English for me. |
| *Kore o katte itadakitai desu.* | I would like you to buy this for me. |

## 25. TO DO (SOMETHING) FOR . . .

a. To say, "Somebody does (something) for me," in the respect form, use *-te kudasaimasu;* in the neutral form, use *-te kuremasu:*

| | |
|---|---|
| *Sono koto wa Yamada san ga shirasete kudasaimashita.* | Mr. Yamada was kind enough to inform me about it. |
| *Shirasete kudasai.* | Please let me know. |
| *Ani ga katte kure mashita.* | My older brother bought it for me. |

(*Kudasai* is a request form of *kudasaimasu.*)

b. Use *-te agemasu* to say "I (or others) do (something) for you (him, her)." In the humble form, use *-te sashiagemasu.* You can use *-te yarimasu* when the recipient of the favor is an animal or plant. When the recipient of the favor is a person who is inferior to the speaker, such as a child, *-te yarimasu* can be used, but it is not always appropriate. For this reason, it is safer not to use *-te yarimasu* when the recipient of the favor is a person.

| | |
|---|---|
| *Sore wa anata ni katte ageta no desu.* | I bought it for you. |
| *Anata ni katte sashiagemashoo.* | I'll buy it for you. |
| *Inu ni katte yarimashita.* | I bought it for our dog. |

c. Use *-te itadakimasu* to say, "I (or others) have you (him, her) do (something)" in the humble form, and *-te moraimasu* in the neutral form:

| | |
|---|---|
| *Yamada-san ni katte itadakimashita.* | I had Mr. Yamada buy it for me. |
| *Tomodachi ni yakushite moraimashita.* | I had a friend of mine translate it for me. |
| *Yamada-san ni yakushite itadaite kudasai.* | Please have it translated by Mr. Yamada. |

## 26. MAY, PERHAPS, PROBABLY

To say, "something may (might) happen," add *kamoshiremasen* after a plain form of a verb, an *i-* adjective, or the copula.

| | |
|---|---|
| *Ame ga furu kamoshiremasen.* | It may rain (but I can't tell for sure). |
| *Shiken wa muzuka shikatta kamoshire masen.* | The test might have been difficult. |
| *Tanaka-san wa tenisu ga joozu kamoshire masen.* | Ms. Tanaka may be good at tennis. |

The copula *da* (present, affirmative) is deleted before *kamoshiremasen*.

## 27. IF AND WHEN
a. The use of *to*:

(1) Use to between two clauses to show that the second clause follows as a natural result of the first clause. The particle to in such a case comes at the end of the "if" or "when" clause:

| *Ame ga furu to anmari hito ga takusan kimasen.* | When it rains, not too many people come. |
| *Kippu ga nai to haire masen.* | If you don't have tickets, you can't get in. (If there isn't a ticket . . . ) |
| *Atarashii to takai desu.* | When it's new, it's expensive. |

(2) Note that the predicate before *to* is always in the present form regardless of the tense of the rest of the sentence:

| *Ie ni kaeru to dare mo imasen deshita.* | When I got home, nobody was there. |

(3) The predicate before *to* usually appears in the plain present form. When *to* is used for "if" or "when," the predicate of the main clause (that is, the one following the clause ending in *to*) must be the *-u* or *-ta* form; it can never end in *-masyoo* or *-te kudasai.*

b. The use of *-tara:*

To introduce a condition or a supposition, add *-ra* to the *-ta* form of a verb, adjective, or copula:

| *Ame ga futtara ikimasen.* | If it rains, I won't go. |
| *Denpoo ga kitara denwa o kakete kudasai.* | If you get a telegram, please phone me. |
| *Anmari samukattara mado o shimete kudasai.* | If it's too cold (for you), please shut the window. |
| *Nihonjin dattara dare de mo ii desu.* | Anybody who is Japanese will do. (If it's Japanese, anybody will do.) |

c. The use of *nara:*
Use *nara* with a plain form of a verb, an *i*-adjective, and the copula to express "if."

| *Byooki nara yasunda hoo ga ii desu.* | If you are sick, you had better rest. |

| | |
|---|---|
| *Shiranai nara oshiete agemasu.* | If you don't know, I'll teach you. |
| *Yasui nara kaimasu.* | If it is inexpensive, I'll buy it. |

(For present affirmative, the copula is deleted.)

d. The use of *-ba*:
The *-ba* form is used only for unconfirmed situations. The *-ba* form is formed in the following ways:

Consonant verb:
Drop the final *-u* of the dictionary form and add *-eba*.

| | |
|---|---|
| *furu* | *fureba* |

Vowel verb:
Drop the final *-ru* of the dictionary form and add *-reba*.

| | |
|---|---|
| *miru* | *mireba* |

Irregular verb:

| | |
|---|---|
| *kuru* | *kureba* |
| *suru* | *sureba* |

*i*-adjective:
Drop the final *-i* of the dictionary form and add *-kereba*.

| | |
|---|---|
| *takai* | *takakereba* |

Negative of a verb, an *i*-adjective, the copula: Drop the final *-i* and add *–kereba*

| | |
|---|---|
| *furanai* | *furanakereba* |
| *takaku nai* | *takaku nakereba* |
| *shizuka ja nai* | *shizuka ja nakereba* |
| *Ame ga fureba ikimasen.* | If it rains, I won't go. |

| *Ame ga furanakereba ikimasu.* | If it doesn't rain, I will go. |
| *Mireba sugu wakari-masu.* | If I take a look at it, I can readily identify it. |
| *Takakereba kaimasen.* | If it's expensive, I won't buy it. |
| *Shizuka ja nakereba ikitaku arimasen.* | If it is not quiet, I do not want to go. |

**e. The use of -te wa:**
This expression for "if" is most often found in an expression denoting "must" (e.g., "if you don't do . . . , it won't do"):

| *Soko e itte wa dame desu.* | You must not go there. If you go there, it will be no good. |
| *Okane ga nakute wa kaemasen.* | If you have no money, you can't buy it. |
| *Yoku benkyoo shinakute wa ikemasen.* | If you don't study hard (you must!), it won't do. |

## 28. WHETHER . . . OR . . . , IF . . . OR . . .
a. The uses of *ka:*

(1) Use *ka . . . ka* in a sentence conveying the meaning "whether . . . or," "if . . . or":

| *Okane ga aru ka nai ka shirimasen.* | I don't know if he has money or not. |
| *Takai ka yasui ka shirimasen.* | I don't know if it is expensive or not. |

For present affirmative, the copula is deleted:

| *Suki ka kirai ka kiite kudasai.* | Please ask her whether she likes it or dislikes it. |

(2) Use *ka doo ka* to express "whether or not," "if or not":

| *Okane ga aru ka doo ka shirimasen.* | I don't know if he has money or not. |
| *Takai ka doo ka shirimasen.* | I don't know if it's expensive or not. |

| | |
|---|---|
| *Iku ka doo ka shirimasen.* | I don't know whether she is going or not. |

(3) Use *ka* in a sentence having the sense of "either . . . or":

| | |
|---|---|
| *Suiyoobi ka Mokuyoobi ni kimasu.* | She will come on Wednesday or else on Thursday. |
| *Yoshida-san ka mata wa Kida-san ni kite moratte kudasai.* | Please have either Mr. Yoshida or Mr. Kida come. |

## 29. INDEFINITE PRONOUNS
Indefinite pronouns appear at the end of a clause and convert that entire clause into a noun equivalent. For example:

a. *No* = the one (the time, the person, the place); the act of:

| | |
|---|---|
| *Kesa hayaku uchi ni denwa o kaketa no wa Tanaka-san de shita.* | The person who phoned us early this morning was Ms. Tanaka. |
| *Kinoo mita no wa Amerika no eiga deshita.* | The one we saw yesterday was an American movie. |
| *Kyooto e itta no wa Shigatsu deshita.* | It was in April that we went to Kyoto. (The time when we went to Kyoto was April.) |
| *Mainichi yoru osoku made hataraku no wa karada ni warui desu.* | Working until late at night every day is bad for your health. |

b. *Koto* = the act of; the experience of:

| | |
|---|---|
| *Hokkaido e itta koto ga arimasu.* | I have been to Hokkaido. (The experience of having gone to Hokkaido exists.) |
| *Nihongo wa hanasu koto wa dekimasu ga yomu koto wa dekimasen.* | I can speak Japanese, but I can't read it. |

## 30. IN ORDER TO

a. To say, "one goes or comes in order to do (something)":

(1) Use the pre-*masu* form plus ni plus a verb of locomotion such as ikimasu or kimasu:

| | |
|---|---|
| *Mi ni ikimasu.* | I am going there to see it. |
| *Gohan o tabe ni ikimashita.* | He went to eat. |
| *Amerika no shinbun o yomi ni kimashita.* | I came to read American newspapers. |

(2) Use a noun describing an action, plus *ni* plus a verb of locomotion:

| | |
|---|---|
| *Kaimono ni ikimashita.* | He went out to shop (for shopping). |
| *Ryokoo ni dekakemashita.* | He set out on a journey. |

b. To indicate, "one does (something) for the purpose of doing (something else)," the predicate verb can be any verb, including a verb of locomotion.

(1) A present-tense verb plus the indefinite pronoun *no* plus *ni* plus a verb:

| | |
|---|---|
| *Kono megane wa hon o yomu no ni tsukaimasu.* | I use these glasses for reading books. |
| *Kono basu wa shita machi e iku no ni benri desu.* | This bus is convenient for going downtown. |

(2) A present-tense verb plus *tame ni* plus a verb:

| | |
|---|---|
| *Kuruma o kau tame ni okane o karimashita.* | I borrowed some money to buy a car. |
| *Tomodachi o miokuru tame ni eki e ikimashita.* | He went to the station to see a friend off. |

## 31. REQUESTS, COMMANDS

There are several ways to express a request, command, or wish in Japanese. You can use:

a. *-te kudasai* = please do (something):

(1) For the affirmative:

| | |
|---|---|
| *Hayaku kite kudasai.* | Please come early./Come early. |
| *Yukkuri hanashite kudasai.* | Please speak slowly. |

(2) For the negative:

| | |
|---|---|
| *Hayaku konaide kudasai.* | Please don't come early. |
| *Yukkuri hanasanaide kudasai.* | Please don't speak slowly. |

b. *O kudasai* = please give me:

| | |
|---|---|
| *Rokujuunien no kitte o kudasai.* | Give me a sixty-two-yen stamp, please. |
| *Mizu o kudasai.* | Please give me some water. |

c. *Ga hoshii desu* = I want to have (preceded by the noun showing the thing desired):

| | |
|---|---|
| *Puroguramu ga hoshii desu.* | I would like a program. |
| *Osake wa hoshiku arimasen.* | I don't want any sake. |

d. *-Te itadakitai (no) desu (ga)*1 = I would like to ask you to: (The use of no and ga is optional in this construction.)

| | |
|---|---|
| *Kore o yonde itadakitai desu.* | I would like to ask you to read this for me (but do you have time or would it interfere, etc.). |
| *Eigo de kaite itadakitai no desu ga.* | Would you mind writing (may I trouble you to write) this in English? |

e. *Yoo ni shite kudasai* = be careful (not) to, try to:

| | |
|---|---|
| *Kono tegami wa hayaku dasu yoo ni shite kudasai.* | Please make every effort to send this mail out early. |
| *Kore wa otosanai yoo ni shite kudasai.* | Please be careful not to drop this. |

f. *-Te choodai* = please do (something):

This request form is used (primarily by women) in an intimate, informal, or relaxed situation.

| | |
|---|---|
| *Katte choodai.* | Please buy it. |
| *Sore o totte choodai.* | Please pick it up. |

g. The plain imperative of a verb:
Each verb has a form called the "plain imperative," which is constructed by adding *-e* to the base of a consonant verb and *-ro* to the base of a vowel verb. The imperative of the irregular verbs is *koi* for *kuru* (come) and *shiro* for *suru* (do).

| | |
|---|---|
| *Ike!* | Go! |
| *Miro!* | Look at it! |

Take note, however, that the plain imperative is used only in "rough" speech, and should not be used in everyday conversation.

## 32. ADVERBIAL EXPRESSIONS
a. Formation of adverbial expressions:

(1) Many adverbs are formed by adding *-ku* to the stems (the plain present affirmative minus *-i*) of adjectives:

| ADJECTIVE | | ADVERB | |
|---|---|---|---|
| *takai* | expensive | *takaku* | expensively |
| *yasui* | cheap | *yasuku* | cheaply |
| *yasashii* | easy | *yasashiku* | easily |
| *karui* | light | *karuku* | lightly |

(2) Some adverbial expressions are formed from *na*-adjectives by using *ni* following the naadjective:

| ADJECTIVAL PHRASE | | ADVERBIAL PHRASE | |
|---|---|---|---|
| *kantan na* | simple | *kantan ni* | simply |
| *benri na* | convenient | *benri ni* | conveniently |
| *tokubetsu na* | special | *tokubetsu ni* | especially |
| *joozu na* | skillful | *joozu ni* | skillfully |

b. Comparison of adverbial expressions:
Adverbial expressions can be compared like adjectives (see Section 16 of the Summary of Japanese Grammar):

| POSITIVE | COMPARATIVE | SUPERLATIVE |
|---|---|---|
| *takaku* = expensively | *motto takaku* = more expensively | *ichiban takaku* = most expensively |

c. Adverbial expressions of place:
Use *ni* when the verb is *arimasu, imasu,* or *sunde imasu.* Use de for most other cases.

| | |
|---|---|
| *koko ni, koko de* | here |
| *soba ni, soba de* | at the side, near |
| *mae ni, mae de* | before, in front |
| *ushiro ni, ushiro de* | behind |
| *ue ni, ue de* | on top, above |
| *shita ni, shita de* | underneath |
| *naka ni, naka de* | inside |
| *soto ni, soto de* | outside |
| *doko ni mo, doko de mo* | everywhere (with an affirmative verb) |
| *doko ni mo, doko de mo* | nowhere (with a negative verb) |
| *tooku ni, tooku de* | far |
| *chikaku ni, chikaku de* | near |
| *doko ni, doko de* | where |
| *soko ni, soko de* | there (nearby) |
| *asoko ni, asoko de* | there (far off) |

## d. Adverbial expressions of time:

| | |
|---|---|
| *kyoo* | today |
| *ashita, asu, myoonichi* | tomorrow |
| *kinoo, sakujitsu* | yesterday |
| *ototoi, issakujitsu* | the day before yesterday |
| *asatte, myoogonichi* | the day after tomorrow |
| *ima* | now |
| *sono toki* | then |
| *mae ni* | before |
| *moto* | once, formerly |
| *hayaku* | early |
| *sugu* | soon, presently |
| *osoku* | late |
| *tokidoki* | sometimes, from time to time |
| *itsu mo* | always |
| *nagai aida* | for a long time |

| | |
|---|---|
| *... tari ... tari shimasu* | now ... now, sometimes ... sometimes |
| *mada* | as yet, still |
| *moo* | already (with an affirmative) |
| *moo* | no longer (with a negative) |

## e. Adverbial expressions of manner:

| | |
|---|---|
| *yoku* | well, frequently, studiously, hard |
| *waruku* | ill, badly |
| *konna ni* | thus, so |
| *onaji yoo ni* | similarly |
| *hantai ni* | otherwise, conversely |
| *issho ni* | together |
| *taihen* | much, very |
| *yorokonde* | willingly |
| *toku ni* | especially |
| *waza to* | on purpose, expressly |

## f. Adverbial expressions of quantity or degree:

| | |
|---|---|
| *takusan* | much, many |
| *juubun (ni)\** | enough |
| *sukoshi* | little |
| *motto* | more |
| *hidoku* | extremely, excessively |
| *amari, anmari* | too, too much, too many |
| *sonna ni* | so much, so many |

\* The use of *ni* is optional.